no justice, no peace
Voices of Protest

By Arnold Staples
with assistance from Rich Lord

no justice, no peace
Voices of Protest

By Arnold Staples
with assistance from Rich Lord

Copyright 2000

All rights reserved. No part of this book may be used or reproduced in any manner whatsoever without written permission of the publisher.

Printed in the United States of America.

For information address Word Association Publishers.

ISBN: 1-891231-16-2
Library of Congress Catalog Card Number: 99-071400

Cover design by Arnold Staples
Cover art by Scott Bratek and Antonio Nesbeth Jr.

Visit Author's Web Site at www.cyclopz.com

Word Association Publishers
205 5th Avenue
Tarentum, Pennsylvania 15084

Acknowledgments

I am deeply grateful to all the people who helped me bring this book to completion. First I want to thank God. He's numero uno. It was the creator who made it possible to reach my goal. Praise the Lord. When God is with you, who can stand against you?

I also want to thank Ronald Hill, Darius Staples, Asia Shabazz, Montel Staples, John Haygood, Dontane Staples, Robert "Russell" Spence, Arnold "Peeper" Staples and Ralph Ianotti.

A very special thanks goes out to my humble assistant Rich "The Man" Lord. Without his expertise and dedication, I could never have seen this project through to its completion. Rich was a God send. Thank you and God bless you, Rich.

And let's not forget my wife of 27 years, Lillian Staples. Lots of love goes out to her for supporting me for the past four and a half years. Thank you, "Kitty Cat."

"God created the heavens and the earth; Man created injustice." -
                                                            Arnold Staples

*The events and the people in this story are true.
Only the names have been changed.*

Chapter 1

Road Rage: The Wrath of Maniac Cop Mimms

"Yo, man, there's five-0," Devon said, as the white and blue Clairton Police cruiser pulled up behind the old Camaro, then quickly passed it and pulled out in front. Together they crept through the frigid darkness and on to the Ravensburg Bridge, just 50 yards from the Clairton police station. "Can you see if that guy is behind us?"

Derek straightened up from his slumped position in the seat beside him and looked back over his shoulder. "No sign, cuz," he said. "But there's another cop car pulling out back there." Derek straightened up, tugged on his braided hair. "Man, I can't figure how the hell that happened back there. I mean, we didn't do anything."

Devon looked in his rearview, saw the second vehicle exit a side street a ways behind him with its red, white, and blue lights flashing, but no sirens. The two cop cars were probably on their way to another call, but that would just have to wait. There was a madman on the loose, and Devon was determined to get them on the case. "I didn't do a thing," he said. He flicked his high beams, tailgated. "First thing I saw was the guy pulling up, trying to pass me. Next thing I know bullets are flying. You remember anything different?"

"Nope." Derek looked into the back seat, and Devon sneaked another peak in the rearview mirror. Little Sonny was still asleep. He could sleep through anything - a movie, a firefight, a high-speed chase. Lucky him.

Devon followed the first cruiser, its lights whirling, bathing the dark bridge in all the colors of a swirling flag. The cop seemed content to escort him across the bridge, as if he had nothing better to do. Well, Devon had a hell of a story to tell them, a tale of random violence, attempted murder, death barely averted in a miracle escape. So half way across the rusty bridge, he braked and slowed to a halt. The car in front stopped a few yards ahead.

Devon eased back into his red vinyl seat, and let relief flow like a torrent of warm water down his body. It was finally over. He'd tell these cops about the maniac who opened fire on his car out on River Road, and engaged him in a high-speed chase all the way up into the hills above Clairton. Then they could haul ass back to McKeesport or Monroeville, calm down, let the danger of the night fade into a bad joke nervously recounted. Meanwhile the cops could comb the neighborhood for the guy. Maybe they'd bring him in, there'd be a big criminal trial, attempted murder, and Devon would get to look his assailant in the face, where until now all he knew of the attacker was a pair of headlights and flashes of fire, and a dark figure sidling up to his car and shoving a revolver right at his head, point blank.

More than likely, though, the guy was halfway across town by now. And even if they did bring somebody in, Devon wasn't sure how he would pick the guy out of a lineup. He didn't see much of him. He couldn't say what make or color the car was, as all he saw was two blinding beams of light. The guy would probably get off scot-free. But hell, Devon thought, at least he's out of our hair.

Devon stayed put in the car and waited for the cop to come to him. He was in no hurry to roll down his window or step out of the Camaro's warm interior. This winter was so long, so brutal, that people joked that it might never end. Devon had heard that it was the coldest winter since the 1890's, and he believed it. He almost felt bad for making the cop up ahead get out of his probably toasty cruiser. But the lone cop stepped out. He was a little white guy with what Devon could only think of as a Disney character's face. He couldn't have weighed more than 120 pounds.

"That's five-0?" Devon asked. "Looks like a midget to me."

"I don't feel so good about this," Derek muttered from the passenger seat. Devon glanced over at him. He looked stiff. "What do we do, cuz?"

"Aww, chill. We aren't the bad guys here." Devon wasn't a great fan of the Mon Valley police, but having done nothing more than flee from a crazed attacker on the road, he thought he had nothing to fear. "Be cool. Don't provoke this guy. We don't want any trouble."

The meager pinkish light from the bridge's two street lamps and the kaleidoscopic whirl of the police lights glinted off the icy blacktop, the graying snow banks along the side of the road, and the service revolver in the cop's outstretched hand. It was pointed, more or less, at Derek, who must have made an inviting target, pressed as he was against that red vinyl seat.

Devon put his hands up above the dash. Derek raised his, too.

They weren't going to play games with a white cop on an abandoned bridge at, what, three in the morning. Nonetheless, this was beginning to make him nervous. Why was it that a young black man had to feel like a criminal any time he encountered the police, whether he'd done anything or not?

Then two shots - Bang! Bang! - shattered the relative calm. The Disney character was shooting in the direction of the Camaro! Suddenly the two cousins were yelling, screaming, "What now?" and "What the hell!?" and "What is he doing?" and "Oh, God, he's shooting at us!" In the back, Sonny stirred, sat up, looked around, rubbed the sleep from his eyes.

"Von, pull off, man, pull off!" Derek shrieked.

"No, man, then they'll kill us for sure."

"Man, why are we being stopped?" Sonny shouted, sitting bolt upright. "Von's got a license. What the hell is going on, Von?"

Long story, thought Devon. He looked over at Derek. "You okay?"

"Man, why is that mother fucker shooting at us? Is he crazy?"

Devon's heart started to beat fast as he looked down the barrel of a .357 Magnum. The little cop took aim again, standing in a marksman's stance.

Just then a dark figure appeared, on the other side of the car, right by Derek's window. It was a black man, not in uniform of any sort, with a shotgun in his hand, and he was pulling open the passenger side door. His face was contorted in savage rage, his eyes red almost to the point of glowing, like a demon's twisted orbs. In that face, Devon saw that he and his cousins were not out of danger, that their misadventure had just begun, and that the three of them might very possibly die tonight.

The door swung open. The black maniac jabbed Derek with the barrel of a shotgun, knocking his head backward like he was a crash test dummy, then took a fistful of his long, braided hair. Said a growling voice thick with alcohol: "Remember me, mother fucker? Remember me?"

* * *

It was an old piece of junk, but Devon wanted it from the moment he saw it. "It's a Camaro, man," he told Little Sonny as they circled it, looked it up and down, took quick peeks at the rusty underbelly. "I mean, you and me could be driving a Camaro. Doesn't that mean anything to you?"

"It's ancient, Von, and beat to hell," Little Sonny said. He stopped circling, stepped back, put his hands on his hips and appraised it with a disgusted frown. "Probably won't get half way home in that thing before it breaks down."

Devon hoped that the owner, a chubby white guy who chewed on a piece of tall grass plucked from the side of the highway, was out of earshot. "Hell, you seemed to like it when you were test-driving it. And that guy says it runs great. Besides, we can fix it up. Tune it up, do a little body work, give it a new paint job. Little Sonny, man, for what we've got to spend, an Audi 5000 ain't in the cards."

Little Sonny circled around the car, gave Devon a playful shove. "Listen to Mr. Goodwrench here. You know how much time and money it's gonna take to keep this old thing running? You've got a lot of experience with cars, huh, cuz?"

Devon scrunched his face in feigned anger, gave Little Sonny a little push back. "Hey, look, we've got the time, and we can save up some money. Meanwhile it runs good enough to get us around. And it's better than that goddamn K Car you had us looking at yesterday."

They looked at each other. This was an experiment in trust for them both. The two were cousins, Little Sonny the older by six years. Though they'd lived just a few miles from each other for all of their lives, the two had only gotten to know each other over the past year. They'd become fast friends, and what with Little Sonny out of trouble now after a few run-ins with the law, the two had decided to go in on a car. Sharing the purchase price would be the easy part. Trusting each other to come through with cash for insurance, repairs, and inspections would be the challenge.

"What the hell," said Little Sonny, grinning. They clasped hands, shook firmly and hard. Devon saw that mischievous spark in his cousin's eye, the outward reflection of that force within Little Sonny which seemed to propel him headlong into the best and worst of decisions. Suddenly both of them looked up and laughed at the sky like men just set free after a long imprisonment. "Let's do it. Let's get us some wheels."

They dug into their pockets and bought that car then and there, straight cash, with the title transferred into Devon's name. The seller chuckled when they parted ways at the notary's office, but the two cousins didn't think too much of that. They had a car. Sure, the odometer had long since turned over, its body was a patchwork of a half dozen shades of black, it's red vinyl interior was held together with gray duct tape, and it couldn't exactly be called a babe magnet. But it was their car, the first car either of them had ever owned, not counting the occasional vehicle temporarily "borrowed" by Sonny back in his wilder days. It was theirs. And it was a Camaro.

Devon's Camaro, really. Sure, Sonny had helped pay for it, and when he was around Devon was always careful to refer to it as "our car." But the title was free and clear and had one name typed neatly on its blue surface: Devon Grey.

All winter they drove that car up and down the Mon Valley's narrow, winding roads. Drove, skidded, slid, and fishtailed, actually. It was the worst winter in memory, and the wide-tired car with a huge engine and too little weight in the back end slid all over the icy streets. But they didn't much care. For Sonny, 25 and on his way to getting his life back together after years of trouble, it was a chance to have a good time without ending up on the wrong side of the law. For Devon, just turned 18, it was an early taste of sweet freedom, having his own wheels. It got him out to his girlfriend's house in West Mifflin, where he could play the days away with his two babies. And it gave him a way to get out of Monroeville, where he and his family had moved the year before, and back into the Valley where he knew people, where he had friends, where he felt in his element.

The Valley: a long, narrow rift in the Allegheny Mountains, carved out over ten million years by big muddy, the Monongahela River. Where the river had sliced away the hillsides, seams of black coal were visible, and not far to the west were some of North America's great iron ranges. The combination of coal, iron, and water for cooling and barge transportation made the Mon Valley a natural for steel production, or so they'd told Devon in school, and by the early twentieth century the area was America's industrial heart. It churned out the steel which supplied the last half of the Industrial Revolution, and equipped the American fighting machine through four wars and an uneasy peace.

At the top of the Valley, just inside the City of Pittsburgh limits, once stood the giant Jones and Laughlin mill, later renamed the LTV Works, where 12,000 men turned iron, coal, limestone, manganese, magnesium, and heat like the surface of the sun into cold steel rods. From there it was a short drive down Route 837 to the empire of U.S. Steel, which stretched from proud Homestead and tough Braddock, through the cities of Duquesne and McKeesport, and finally down to Clairton, where the world's largest coke works baked coal into the rough matte black material which then became the carbon in the industrial giant's steel.

But by the time Devon started cruising the Valley, the big mills were history. Up at the north end the LTV Works was shut down, torn down, and sold for scrap. All that was left was the coke works, still employing 800 men, still breathing its sulfurous breath into the skies of Pittsburgh's Hazelwood, Oakland and South Side neighborhoods. On the south end, U.S. Steel's Clairton Coke Works still baked down the coal for its master, now called USX. Somewhere between the two in Braddock, right across the river from the thriving Kennywood Amusement Park, was the Edgar Thompson Works. ET, as the locals called it, was the only mill left in the area which performed the whole process, turning raw materials into finished steel. Between those three points on the river was mile after mile of gray, lifeless dirt, punctuated here and there by rows of brick smokestacks no longer connected to the long-gone furnaces they'd once served. The corrugated walls and ceilings of the mills had long since been hauled off and sold as scrap, the blast furnaces carried across the sea for sale to steel-hungry China and India. In McKeesport, a town abandoned by half of the people who had called it home in the boom years, the yellow brick warehouses stood empty, their windows victims of vandals' stones. The old roads to the mill sites degenerated into black moonscapes. Bridges which once carried men and machines into and out of the bowels of hell just dropped off into thin air, piers into a sea of memories.

Devon remembered when his father would join the long lines of men marching into the mills, sometimes for the seven to three shift, other times for the three to eleven or the eleven to seven. He'd put in an eight hour day, sometimes stretching to twelve, in the hot, noxious air of the basic oxygen furnace, or on the railroad where he served as a brakeman. His father would come home tired, his feet sometimes so sore he couldn't walk. But he was a happy man, nonetheless. For the Grey family, the mill meant food, a house paid off early, a new car every few years, and security. And like everyone else in the Valley, Devon thought of the mills as something permanent, a rock upon which to depend, like his home, the community, and the United States government.

When one day the mill gates didn't open, Devon's dad ended up one of the lucky ones. He landed a job in maintenance for the Port Authority of Allegheny County, which allowed him to keep the family afloat through the troubled times that would follow. And when Devon and his family returned from vacation one year and found the house they had paid off in ruins, burned top to bottom by an arsonist, that job made it possible for his dad to leave the crumbling confines of McKeesport for the booming suburb of Monroeville. His dad said they weren't safe in McKeesport, and Devon had seen enough to believe him. Still, it was a bittersweet move, taking him away from everything and everyone he knew, immersing him in a strange world of cookie-cutter houses, each just a little different from the one next door, with eighth of an acre lots and easy access to jam-packed Business Route 22, a strip of asphalt lined with malls, office parks, and a McDonald's every mile.

But his cousins Sonny Brown and Derek Goodman still lived down in the Valley, and as his first year in Monroeville drew to a close, Devon found himself spending more and more time with them. Even before he got the car, it wasn't that hard to keep in touch. His dad was always making runs down that way, trying to pick up part of the slack for old man Goodman, who was usually in jail or out doing something which would soon put him there. Devon's dad was always running down there to help Derek's mom out with something. Like the time Derek blew up an apartment while gassing up his new motorbike in the basement, a few feet from the furnace pilot light. Everything the Goodman family owned was burned up, and a battle with the landlord over liability and security deposits followed. It was Devon's dad who stepped in to buy mother and children new clothes and put a little heat on the recalcitrant landlord. Their families were more than kin; they were a mutual support network in this world where no one can make it all alone. That kept them close. So when he got out of work on the evening of March 5, 1994, Devon aimed the Camaro back down Route 48 towards McKeesport, for the apartment home of Derek Goodman.

Poor Derek, he thought. He never meant any harm to anybody, never stepped on to the wrong side of the law, and would just as soon keep to himself and his small circle of friends and family. But nothing seemed to go quite right for Derek. Devon remembered that day back in the Spring of 1992 when Derek's brother, Cory, was shot five times in the chest and left lying dead. It was a blow to the gut which left the family gasping for breath, stumbling along the road of unanswerable questions. No one ever did figure out why Cory was killed, though there were rumors of stolen guns and mistaken identity. When the criminal case against the killers ended in a plea bargain down to involuntary manslaughter, with a few years of jail time as the sentence, it only deepened the sense of loss. Devon remembered the hollow looks in the eyes of the Goodman family, his own family, and the rest of the clan. "Is this all our lives are worth?" everyone seemed to be asking.

And though Derek kept a stiff upper lip, Devon felt that it changed something intangible but very real inside of him. He always seemed to be thinking, mulling over some math problem or philosophical question which he never could quite solve.

It didn't get any easier for Derek. And every Christmas, when he showed up at the family dinner without his father, Devon wondered how he could keep from lashing out, taking vengeance on someone or something, anyone or anything. Somehow Derek kept his cool. The guy was clearly born under a bad sign. But he was family, and a good friend, and Devon would have done anything to be able to lift the cloud which seemed to hang over his cousin's path.

* * *

It was two o'clock in the a.m. by the time House Party II wound to its predictable conclusion. Devon and Derek had pretty much talked through the whole thing, while Little Sonny lay silent on the bed, presumably dozing after a long day of work, topped off with overtime. Often it seemed life was work, exhaustion, and boredom, and then more of the same. It didn't show much resemblance to the nonstop mayhem and hilarity of House Party II. Still, the film left Devon hungry for a little action, a break in the monotony of winter inactivity, or at least a waffle with blueberries and a big pile of whipped cream on top.

"Wake up, wake up, wake up," he repeated, reaching over and hitting the rewind on the VCR and then stretching across the bed to slap Sonny on the knee. "We gotta roll. I'm hungrier than a polar bear. Plus this sittin' on my butt stuff has gotta stop. I got to ramble."

Little Sonny shook his head, rubbed the sleep from his eyes. "You go ramble all you want, chief. Wake me up when spring comes."

"Spring ain't coming this year. This is the new Ice Age. Didn't you hear? It's all from the ozone, or something like that. So you best get used to it."

"Aww, shut up. What'd you wake me up for, now?"

"Food, man. We gotta go get some. Whadda you say, Derek?"

"Where you wanna go?" said Derek, slowly rising from his chair. You could always count on him to be up for going somewhere. Seemed like wherever he was, Derek was perfectly willing to be somewhere else.

"How about Denny's up in West Mifflin?" Devon suggested. It briefly flashed through his mind that his father and mother were involved in a big lawsuit against Denny's, over the restaurant not serving black people or demanding they paid up front or something, but it didn't much bother him. "They've got bumping waffles over there, cuz." Right now, that mattered more than anything else.

"Man, I just want to get my butt home and get my beauty sleep," said Sonny, giving Devon a little kick. "Besides, it's God awful cold out there. What do you wanna go traipsin' all over creation on a night like this for? This is sleepin' weather."

"Sleep, sleep, sleep! That's all you ever want to do." Devon got up off the floor and stood in front of his older cousin, grinning. He liked taking the piss out of Sonny, though inside he admired his cousin, partly for his past misadventures and partly for how he was leaving them behind. "Denny's has got free refills on coffee, so you can get as wired as you please. C'mon, cuz, get off your butt and live a little."

Little Sonny grinned. "Was it you said you worked a double shift today, 16 hours? Or was it that fool?" He gestured over at Derek. "Oh, wait, that was me. But let me get this straight. You two lazy asses are givin' me shit for wanting to catch some zees? Is that right?"

"Yeah, that's right," said Devon. "You gonna do something about it?" He grinned and backed up. Little Sonny just frowned, rose slowly from the bed. "Not like you have to get up early tomorrow or anything."

Sonny scowled at him out of one sleepy eye, hands on his hips. "Okay, punk, let's go."

Derek went upstairs to tell his mother, Marie, that they were going out for a bite. "You don't have to go out," Marie said, as Devon listened from the bottom of the stair. Their parents were forever trying to keep them cooped up at home. "There's plenty of food in the fridge. Besides, the news is saying that it's freezing cold out there, and the roads are going to be a sheet of ice by morning. Why don't you boys just stay in tonight?"

"Aww, don't worry, Mom," Derek answered. "We'll be careful. Besides, we're just running up to Denny's. It won't take but a little while."

Devon heard her sigh as Derek clambered back down the stairs. The three slipped on jackets and headed for the door. Devon thought to ask Derek whether he could borrow a sweater to slip on over his sweatshirt, but he let it go. Hell, he wouldn't be out in the cold much - just en route to and from the car. Inside the car, the heater should kick in pretty quick. And Denny's ought to be warm enough, even if the reception for three young black men in the middle of the night might not be. Having Derek get him a sweater would just slow things down, and now that he had Sonny moving, Devon didn't want to lose the momentum.

Devon hurried to the car and slid into the driver's seat, felt the coldness of the seat penetrate his clothes and skin and go right to the bone. Derek called shotgun, and Sonny took the back seat. It took a few turns of the ignition, but the Camaro's big old engine turned over. Hmm. It was idling rough. He gave it some gas, pumped it lightly a few times. It smoothed out a bit, but still didn't sound quite right.

"I really gotta get this thing tuned up," he said to Derek. "Next warm day. If there ever is one again." He looked in the rearview, caught Sonny's eye.

"Aww, hell, it's just the cold," Sonny said. "Get her going, and she'll be just fine." With that Little Sonny dropped on to the seat, out of view. Devon thought to say something about how Sonny wasn't exactly holding up his end as far as paying for the maintenance and insurance on the car, but he held back. No sense in breaking the peace.

Devon backed it out and headed through McKeesport toward the bridge. As soon as he got a block from Derek's place, he put the heater on full blast. It would take a minute for the engine to warm up enough to provide much heat; but once it got going, the old car would heat up fast. Back in '78, they knew how to make a heater, Devon thought. Back then, they didn't piss around. You wanted heat, you got heat.

Back then, from what his dad said, you left the mill, went down to the local Chevy dealer, and bought one of these babies new, cash up front, no financing required. The day was long and the overtime was good, and a guy who worked seven twelves, as the 84 hour workweek common to steelworkers was called, could make a handsome living. Then there were incentives, shift differentials, and double overtime and a half on holidays. He remembered his father using these terms way back when, before he himself could decipher them, but now he knew what they meant: money, respect, dignity, $40 grand a year just out of high school for a guy willing to bust some ass and put in the time. Some of the young guys would put in a 16 hour day, catch some shuteye in the back of a big Plymouth Fury or Bonneville parked out in the lot, and then come back in for another 16. It wore on the body and tested the soul, but was damn good for the pocket book. Back then this town of McKeesport, and all the towns in the valley, were full of movie theaters, bars, and big American cars - cars like Devon's Camaro, only newer.

But on this night, in this brave new postindustrial world, the streets were lined with houses in various states of disrepair, many with thick waferboard panels over the windows. The "For Sale" signs of the late eighties were long gone. By March 6, 1994, you could hardly give away a house in this town. The theaters were closed, the big cars rusting hulks with overdue inspection stickers in their windshields. The bars, though, were staying afloat.

"Slow down, cuz," said Derek, as they crossed the bridge from McKeesport into Duquesne. Devon snapped out of his reverie, pumped the brake a little. "It's icy out there."

"You ain't kiddin'." He felt the car fishtail a little as it slowed. The bridge was coated with black ice, the most dangerous of winter's hazards. During the day, some of the snow piled on the sides of the roads had melted, creating little rivulets along the sides of the streets and dampening the asphalt. As night fell and the temperature plummeted into the teens, though, the innocent streams of meltwater had frozen into black ice - hard, slick, and completely invisible.

Devon made a left off the bridge and headed down Route 837, here called River Road, towards Clairton. He'd head up into West Mifflin from there. Just take it slow, he thought, there's nobody else on the road. Take it easy. He looked in the rearview and saw no headlights, just Sonny splayed out across the back seat, already zonked. The guy could drop off like a bomb and sleep through anything. But get him awake and riled up, and look out.

The Camaro bumped across the railroad tracks which crossed the road, and entered Dravosburg. Just another burned out mill town, just like all the others up and down this river, Devon thought. Maybe it was good that his family had taken him the hell out of here. Monroeville wasn't paradise, but the Valley was a desolate pit, especially on a dark and frigid night like this.

Suddenly the inside of the car lit up, and Devon checked his rearview mirror. Somebody had come up behind him really fast, like out of nowhere, and was flashing his or her high beams. Shit. It was hard enough to see the icy road without this joker beaming him. Devon sped up a little, but felt the car swerve menacingly. He was heading into a curvy stretch of 837 with a retaining wall and the railroad on the right side, and a steep and sudden drop into the river on the left, and with trees from the nearby woods hanging like clawing old hags over it all. The road here was one narrow lane in each direction and a double yellow line between them. State Route 837; what a fine piece of asphalt.

"What the hell does he want us to do?" Derek asked, as the high beams kept flashing. "He's like right on our bumper."

"Maybe he wants us to pull over or something," Devon guessed. But there was no place to pull over - just the river and the retaining wall. "He must be out of his mind if he thinks I'm gonna stop on this road, this late. What if he's a fuckin' gangbanger?"

"Von, man, you'd better go a little faster," said Derek. "He's gonna run us off the road!"

Devon gave it a little gas. What with the ice and the curves and the dark silhouette of the woods leaning riverward, he didn't really want to lean on the accelerator. But this guy behind him was still flashing his beams and tailgating. There was something terribly wrong about this. He felt his back stiffen up.

"He's trying to pass," said Derek, and Devon checked his rearview and sideview mirrors with quick turns of his head. The guy had pulled into the oncoming lane, and was trying to come up alongside the Camaro, in a no-passing zone.

"Is this guy drunk or something?" Devon yelled. He took another look at the double-yellow line. If he remembered right, it was a no-passing zone from the Duquesne-McKeesport Bridge all the way to St. Claire Street in Clairton. "Passing on this road, with the ice like this?"

"Bet he's a gangbanger," said Derek.

Devon glanced again into the rearview, but he couldn't make out the person in the driver's seat, or even the color or make of the car, with the high beams still flicking on and off and flooding his mirrors with piercing light. "Think he's gonna pull up and cap us?"

Derek shrugged, slouched down in his seat. Devon gave it some more gas and pulled away. This crazy fucker, he thought, is going to play games like this until I hit a patch of ice and spin into a tree. Still, God knows who might be in there, or what their intentions might be. Better not let them pull up alongside. There are a lot of desperate people around these days, Devon thought; desperate and crazy.

He felt his car's wheels spinning a little, sliding a little, losing their traction as he crossed a patch of ice. The lights behind him shimmied from one side to the other, too, as the pursuing car apparently fishtailed and dropped back for a second. But then it kept coming. This was getting dangerous, and he was no closer to ditching the other car. In fact, it was pulling up yet again. He felt the Camaro's engine stutter a little, struggle just a bit. It didn't like the cold, the speed, the icy road.

"Don't stall out on me now," Devon breathed through his teeth. The car was pulling up beside him, almost right next to him now, and whatever the guy was going to do, he was going to do it soon.

"Von, man, just go," shouted Derek. "Go!" Devon pushed the pedal to the metal, felt the rush of gas, then a slight hesitation, and heard the car's eight cylinder engine fire a noisy complaint back through the exhaust system as it lurched forward along the unlit River Road. Damn thing was always backfiring. The other car suddenly fell behind. Shit, I'm moving fast, Devon thought, maybe 70, but he didn't dare check the speedometer. Keep your eyes on the road, he thought, his car screeching around another curve, and everything will be okay.

In a flash, the lights were gone. Had that joker given up, maybe faded away behind a bend somewhere? Devon started to breathe a little easier.

Then something appeared in the rearview, a shadowy shape that was right on his bumper. The guy was back on his ass, tailgating again, this time with lights off, just like the gangbangers when they're out to burn somebody, he thought.

"Why is he tailgating us?" Derek asked.

"He must be drunk or on drugs," said Devon.

Derek turned around. "Von, we're being shot at! Someone in that ride is shooting at us!"

Just then Devon caught a flash out of the corner of his eye, and heard a popping sound. "What's goin' on back there?" he asked Derek. He didn't dare to check the rearview. Just stay on the road, he thought.

Derek turned. Another flash, and a pop, was followed by a tinging sound. "Get us the hell out of here!" he cried.

This was nuts, absolutely crazy, Devon thought. People don't just start shooting at you on the road for not letting them pass. "Derek, man, try to get a look at him."

But Derek had his head down below the dash now. Sonny was apparently still asleep. He was on his own.

Pop! Pop! Crack. Devon careened under a trestle, and into the don't-blink town of Wilson. Derek shouted at him to make a right, make a right! But at the speed he was going, and with a patch of slick ice in the intersection, there was no way he was going to chance it. Instead he slid on down towards Clairton, towards the looming lights of the gigantic coke works. There was no plan but to go, go, go, and pray for help. But there was still no one on the road except the

Camaro and the lunatic just behind. God, he thought, where are the cops when you need them? The car was still right behind him, bearing down and then falling behind, though the shooting had paused. Out of bullets?

Pop-TIIING! Shit. Fucker must've reloaded. Sooner or later this guy was bound to hit a window, a tire, or the back of someone's head. Devon flew down the road, realized he had just missed the turn for West Mifflin. No waffles tonight. He skidded past the Hollywood Club, an old hang out of his, and blew through the first few lights of the City of Clairton. "Where the hell can I go to ditch this guy?" he screamed at Derek.

"Up the hill," Derek said, peering up over the dash. Devon steered hard right, felt his car sliding, skidding, whining. "Up this hill and then make a left."

Devon skidded on to Maple Ave. without signaling, and remembered that Derek had relatives up this way. The car behind, too, made the turn, and the shooting kept up. Going up hill it sounded a little different, more like, "Toop. Tpp. Tpp." Or maybe it was just that the guy was hitting objects closer and closer to the car. Odd how his mind was sharp and focused and crazy with confusion at the same time, Devon thought, even as the lunatic continued unloading rounds, firing blindly, chasing him up the hill.

As Derek shouted directions, he swung a right at the top of the hill, then a quick left, and found himself sliding down a snow-covered expanse. He could hardly see where the street ended and the tiny front yards began, and the cars were blanketed with wind-blown snow. Shit. Still, maybe this was an opportunity to ditch the guy. If only the Camaro can make it through, Devon thought, maybe this guy will get stuck. Maybe this is the ticket.

No! Devon felt his own car drifting rightward, out of control, as he steered wildly but to no effect. He glided sideways down the white surface, until the Camaro came to rest with its front end buried deep in a snow bank.

"Back out, back out!" Derek screamed. No shit, thought Devon. He felt the other car's headlights brush the side of his face as he jammed it into reverse, then drive, reverse, drive. It shifted and stuttered, but remained lodged in the bank.

"Man, he's stopping," shouted Derek. "Turn the wheel and give it some gas."

He couldn't much ask his cousins to get out and push, not under the circumstances. Besides, Little Sonny was, to all appearances, still sound asleep. Devon put it back in reverse, hit the gas, swung the wheel hard this way and that.

"He's opening his door," Derek reported. "Von, man, he's coming. He's gettin' out of the car, man!"

Devon looked over, saw the driver's side door open part way, saw a dark figure beginning to lean out of the car. He wondered would the guy use the door as a shield and pick them off from afar, or just march up and burn them at point blank range. He felt his heart banging against his ribs like they were the bars of a cage, and looked away from the assassin's small vehicle. Drive. Reverse. Turn the wheel hard. "Come on, you bitch!"

"Sonny, somebody's out to kill us," Derek cried.

"Stop playin'," Sonny growled, and shifted slightly.

"Man, he's right there!" Derek shrieked, and cowered down below the dash.

Devon couldn't look. He thought of his two children, Shataya, just over two years old, and Devon Jr., just turned a year. And there was Asiadawn, almost four, who wasn't technically his but who called him "Daddy." He had really looked forward to seeing them grow up. Through the window he heard a growled threat, something like, "I'm gonna kill you motherfuckers!" And he froze, paralyzed by the sudden, shocking realization that for no apparent reason, he was going to die tonight.

But the car suddenly broke free, skidding forward with a wild screech and a cloud of flying ice. The Camaro flew down the street, and in the rearview Devon saw the figure behind scrambling back into the driver's seat, pulling the door closed. This was his big chance to lose the guy for good.

But the Camaro on the packed snow surface had a mind of its own, and before he knew what was happening, the car was whirling, doing a complete 180, and finally racing the other way. He was heading straight down the narrow street at the little car, which seemed about the size of a Sunbird or a Cavalier. Maybe I should ram him, Devon thought. But the guy had a gun, and Devon sure didn't.

As the headlights from the oncoming vehicle blinded Devon, he jerked the wheel to the right, and slid by the pursuer. He swung a hard right, as Derek shouted, "Back the way we came, man. Let's get the hell out of Clairton. Somebody doesn't want us here."

Devon steered the black beast back down the hill towards 837, saw the headlights a ways behind him. The joker was still after them, but at least they were now pointed back towards McKeesport, more familiar, if not exactly friendly, territory.

Blasting by the stop sign, he made the left back on to 837, back towards Wilson. He watched in his rearview, and to his amazement, saw the pursuer make a right on to the state road, back towards the Clairton business district.

"Man, he's givin' up," he said to Derek. "Maybe he did just want us the hell out of his hood."

"I don't know, cuz. He started after us way back, what, in Dravosburg?"

"I'd love to see the fucker busted. Man, he was gonna kill us back up on the hill there. Point blank! If this thing hadn't peeled out when it did, cuz, you'd be wearin' my brains right now."

Devon felt a surge of nervousness, a sudden shivering. Now that the chase was, apparently, over, the tension was catching up with him quick.

"Maybe we should call the cops," Derek said.

"I ain't gettin' out of this car until I'm either at home, or maybe at a police station," said Devon. "That guy's still around here somewhere."

"Well, we could go to the police station. Man, we really should report this maniac."

"Police, huh? You think that's a ... good idea?" Now Devon felt out of breath, like he'd run a mile. His heart was still pounding, and felt like it would never slow down. He checked his rearview. No headlights. "What do you think ... the police will do? Take a report?"

"Maybe they'll pick the joker up. Lock him up."

Devon checked the rearview, hoping for some advice from Sonny. Besides being the oldest of the three, Sonny had by far the most experience with the police - mostly as a suspect. But Sleeping Beauty was still slumbering soundly. Derek told him to turn around, the station was up on St. Claire Street. So Devon did a quick u-turn in the middle of empty 837, and headed back in the direction his pursuer had gone.

It didn't feel like this was over. Until he was safe at home, or at least sitting in the station under the protection of the police, it wouldn't feel like this night of fear and flight was really at an end.

* * *

"You sure the station was down here?" Devon asked Derek, as they approached that decrepit landmark, the Ravensburg Bridge. He hadn't seen anything which looked remotely like a police station yet. But Derek insisted that it was around here somewhere.

"Look." Derek pointed as a blue and white Clairton Police cruiser pulled out of a side street just behind them, lights whirling. "What'd I tell you."

"Thank God, there's five-0," Devon said, as the car, lights whirling but no siren, pulled up alongside his and then passed without signaling. He trailed the cruiser, then noticed another pulling out of a side street back behind him. Didn't it figure. That joker with the piece chased him all over the Valley, and no cop. Now the maniac was probably long gone, and he had more cops than he knew what to do with.

He and Derek talked nervously as they rolled slowly on to the ill-lit bridge that spanned the steep gorge through the center of Clairton. Being a young black male with dreadlocks down to the shoulder blades, Devon wasn't used to seeking the attention of cops. He usually drove slowly, came to a full stop at traffic lights and stop signs, and avoided anybody with a badge whenever possible. He'd seen enough of the Valley's finest back when he and his family had lived in McKeesport. He'd been set-up, slapped down, and framed enough times to know that by and large, the boys in blue around here were no friends of the black man, or even of the citizenry in general. But this time they'd be working for him, he thought. He slowed to a stop.

The car in front stopped a few car lengths ahead, and out stepped the little cop. Devon and Derek held up their hands and waited expectantly. And in a spasm of gunfire, shouts, and instantaneous panic, all hell broke loose.

Little Sonny was up, shouting, "Von's got a license. Von's got a license!" Another car's headlights were shining in through the

Camaro's rear window. And out of nowhere the black face appeared in the passenger side window, the door swung violently open, and the black face of evil on the outside shrieked, "Remember me, motherfucker? Remember me?" and rammed a shotgun like a bayonet into Derek's right eye.

Devon saw the gun strike his cousin twice and saw the maniac's hand yank a handful of hair straight out of Derek's scalp before an arm wrapped around his neck, his own door swung open, and he felt Little Sonny push his seat forward and dart out, dragging him along. Devon protested, but Little Sonny hissed, "They can't shoot us if we're out of the car!"

The two stood, hands high, in the cold light on the bridge. The little cop still had his gun trained on them, moved it slowly from one to the other. Devon heard a struggle on the other side of the car, and out of the corner of his eye he noticed another cop coming up behind him. He didn't dare turn from the little cop with the revolver, but ducked his head down, ready for a blow.

"Get down on the ground, now!" the cop behind yelled.

"Hey, what's goin' on?" Little Sonny demanded.

"Just get down on the ground, hands behind your heads." Devon peered over the car, saw the black guy dragging Derek out of the car by his long, braided hair. "Now!"

He and Sonny dropped to their knees, then lay prostrate on the pavement. Devon looked under the car in time to see Derek's body crash against the curb. He winced. And he watched as the black maniac's foot pulled back and kicked Derek square in the head, pulled back and kicked again, and again. "You motherfucking niggers!" the man screamed, followed by the thunk of boot striking skin and bone. Devon could see Derek's body shudder from the impact. "I'm gonna kill every damn one of you. Every fucking one!" The lunatic kicked and poked with his shotgun, shouted random epithets and cryptic curses. "You young punk motherfuckers want to fuck with me? I'm gonna put all you mother fuckers in body bags. I'm God around here, you niggers, and you'd best not forget that."

What the hell was going on? This guy was kicking the shit out of Derek, for no reason Devon could ascertain, and these cops were just standing by and watching it all, like spectators at a World Wrestling Federation main event. His spirit screamed to get up and rush to his cousin's defense, and his mind told him the cops should do something to stop this insanity. But when he turned his head around, all he saw was the barrel of a gun, and a sick and distant grin on a white, clean-cut cop's face. Devon felt knots drawing tight in his gut, and a tense pain rising from his neck up the back of his head. He felt he would have to leap up, rush at the guy with the shotgun. His body would not stay down.

Then he noticed other headlights pulling up to the scene, and the rotating flashers of two cop cars, apparently coming from the direction of Jefferson Borough. Maybe those guys would have the sense to end this madness.

But instead a trio of Jefferson cops got out of their cars and sauntered over to the Clairton cops, seemingly blind to the beating a few yards away. One asked if everything was all right, if a tow truck had been called, and if anyone got the registration on the vehicle. Someone said that everything was under control, that these were "the niggers who did the shooting," and that Knuckles Towing had been contacted. The vehicle, a voice said, was registered to a Devon Grey, and didn't appear on the stolen list.

Devon listened with rising incredulousness as the cops discussed mundane points of police procedure while the maniac in a leather jacket and boots kicked Derek and jabbed him repeatedly with the shotgun. What could they be thinking? he wondered. He was about to protest, when, abruptly, the kicking stopped.

For a moment all Devon heard was a low groan from Derek's throat. Then he saw the maniac's booted feet beneath the car, coming around, coming his way, and - WHAM! - something crashed WHAM! into the side WHAM! of his head. Everything spun and seemed to drift from reality into some strange netherworld. The boots came hard and fast, to the body and legs and head, in between screams of, "Where's the gun, you nigger?" and "Tell me which one of you has the piece, you punk!" Gun? Piece? Devon tried to fend off the blows with his elbows, with his legs, and squirmed like a severed worm on the cold asphalt. But he feared to take his hands off the back of his head, with that revolver, he was sure, still pointed right at it.

Everything came into focus and the foaming, spitting face of the attacker was right in front of his eyes, biting the cold air, screaming, "Where's the goddamn gun, motherfucker? Was it you who fired it?

Was it you, nigger?" Devon gasped for breath, tried to mouth the words, "no gun," but nothing came out. The face disappeared, and WHAM! the kicking started again. And the shotgun barrel came down, digging hard like a spear into his guts, again and again and again. "I'm gonna put you black motherfuckers in body bags." WHAM! "Didn't anybody tell you that I was God? You niggers done fucked up. You fucking gangbangers are going to pay!"

Finally it was over, and as he writhed on the pavement the attacker moved on to Little Sonny, returning to the same verse and refrain of kicking and incomprehensible shrieking. Within seconds Sonny's grunting turned into shrill screaming, as the boot and then the shotgun thudded against him again and again. Devon heard a low gurgling coming from his own throat. He shifted around, tried to find a position in which it wouldn't hurt anymore, but everything was bruised, twisted, and throbbing like a fever dream. He tried to shake the fog out of his head, focus on where the yelling, and the thudding of leather against body and bone, was coming from. But all he could think of was that sweater, the one he could have borrowed from Derek back at the apartment, the one that would have kept the cold at bay and maybe even shielded him just a little bit from the blows.

Slowly things came into focus, and he noticed that the thudding and screaming had ceased. Instead there was a dull murmur, and the hum of engines. He looked up, and saw that a few feet from him, cars were creeping slowly by, directed by police who waved them on as if in a hurry to get them gone. He watched a red car approach, and strained to get a glimpse of the driver. Maybe by some miracle it would be someone he knew, someone who would help them out of this bizarre mess they were in. But it was just a young white guy who looked him straight in the eye, and drove slowly on. Devon watched longingly as that, the last of the short string of cars, disappeared into the distance. Why didn't anyone stop to help them? he wondered. Who could just drive by three men, beaten and twisted on the ground and surrounded by indifferent cops and a madman with a shotgun?

Then it struck him: He should have gotten the license plate number. Things were only likely to get worse, he realized somewhere in his aching, whirling skull. Memory and observation might be the only weapons available to him. Must remember everything.

But now the cars were gone, and he was again surrounded by

white cops. One held a shotgun, and if Devon remembered right, it was the very gun he'd just been prodded with. And over on the other side of the car, the guy was screaming again, where the fuck is the fucking gun you motherfucking nigger punk faggot bitch gangbanger. Whump! Whump! The boot crashed - Whump! - into his cousin's gut over and over. Then Devon watched as the black guy grabbed Derek's braids and dragged him across the icy asphalt to the edge of the bridge. Derek's legs thrashed around in a futile effort to keep pace, to keep from having his hair ripped from his scalp.

Now the whole scene was visible to Devon, as he looked under the front of the Camaro. For a second he saw Derek's uncomprehending eyes turn his way, imploring, but with a violent yank the contact was broken. At the metal railing at the edge of the bridge, the guy grabbed Derek by the belt loop and the collar of his sweat shirt and lifted him like a sack of cat litter. Then he slammed Derek down, smashing his gut against the railing, and held him there, face forward, his upper body out in the middle of the frozen air with the rocky chasm and the railroad tracks below his face.

"You gonna tell me where the gun is, boy?" the guy yelled, leaning close to Derek's head. Devon saw Derek's head shake. Then the guy pushed him further out over the edge, and further, until Devon couldn't see his cousin's head at all. "You gonna talk, boy, or you gonna die tonight!"

Little Sonny pleaded with the white cops, "If you cops have any decency you'll stop that maniac from throwing him off the bridge! He's gonna kill him, man. Please stop that maniac!"

Devon looked up, saw a shotgun casually pointed his way. One of the white cops chuckled. "Shut up, nigger," he said, casually. "You two just sit tight. You boys are in for a long night." They would be perfectly content, Devon realized, to watch one black man kill three others.

But one of the white Clairton cops walked over to where the maniac held Derek, tapped him on the shoulder, and asked him if he was all right. It seemed a ludicrous question to Devon. The guy was drunk, probably also stoned out of his mind on something, and in the midst of a mad beating spree. It was clear he was not all right. But the question seemed to momentarily bring the maniac back to reality. He yanked Derek back from the brink and threw him to the asphalt.

Derek's body bounced and shook like an old doll, badly abused. The attacker looked down on it with a demonic scorn, grabbed the already tousled and shredded braids, and slammed the limp skull against the curb. Then he rushed around the car, shouting, "You niggers are in trouble now. You no good nigger gangbangers are gonna be in body bags!"

And he was upon them again, screaming obscenities and spitting gobs of thick saliva at them. The maniac turned to the five white cops standing around, all of whom seemed utterly indifferent to the proceedings. "Whadda you say we give these gangbangers a little bit of their own medicine tonight," he said. "These gangbangers gonna get gangbanged tonight, yessiree."

This didn't make any sense, Devon thought. He'd heard about young blacks getting beat for no reason before, sure. But this wasn't some old white guy from Mississippi with a white hood or a crew cut; this was a black man with a fade who sounded straight out of the 'hood.

"We ain't gangbangers," Devon cried, praying he'd understand. "Look at us. We're wearing every color in the damn rainbow, man!" It was true. From his coat to his shirt, to his pants, socks and shoes, Devon had just about every imaginable hue on: blue, red, black, yellow, purple, brown, the colors of half a dozen opposing gangs. But the white cops just shrugged, backed away, muttered to each other things Devon couldn't hear.

Then the torrent of rage was upon him again, screaming, kicking, wracking his body with shocks of heat, cold, pain, anger. WHAM! A boot crashed into his tensed gut. WHACK! The sole of the boot slashed across his face. WHAM! Leather piercing clothing, slicing through skin, banging straight into bone. Then another blow to his gut, now undefended, indefensible. And another. And another. Until they all blurred together. Until time was just a long string of rhythmic, crashing collisions. Until he forgot where they were coming from, who was delivering them, where he was, who he was. Impossible to stop it, slow it, deflect it, but his body tightened up, curled up, turned into a tiny dot of burning pain.

After a time he realized that it was over, that his body and mind were loosening up, unrolling. Still everything throbbed and spun. He tried to grab his aching, blinded face, but something snatched his hands, wrenched them behind his back, and clasped them together with cold steel. He felt his wallet slide out of his back pocket, felt hands patting him down, searching. Damn. He was helpless, robbed, step by step, of his consciousness and his freedom. Then his arms were jerked upwards, and a searing pain shot through his shoulders. Up went his body, pulled from behind, near as he could tell, by the cuffed hands. The world went green for a second, then black, and he tried to keep his balance. His knees turned to jelly beneath him, and he resigned himself to a slumping back down to the pavement, sweet pavement. But something kept him up. He felt he might vomit.

Then something pushed him forward, but he was unable even to step. Stars spun in front of his squinting eyes, real stars, points of light all blue and red and white and twinkling. Like they said in the movies, "you'll be seeing stars." It's true, he thought, you do see stars.

He hung there, kept upright by some irresistible force somewhere behind, for a time he could not measure. Behind him someone yelped in pain, someone cursed, someone screamed. The spinning gradually slowed, and the stars winnowed down to a few glimmering fragments of brilliance. And then something moved him forward, to where, he did not know.

He knew who he was, approximately where he was, that he and his cousins were in danger, and that he was at present in no condition to do anything about it. He tried to piece it together, how it all came to be, but it was all faded, confused, jumbled like a bad dream now. Then he was hurtling forward, faster and faster, just able to stay on his feet, under the control of some hostile power. And then falling, flying, into a deeper darkness, and landing, to his complete surprise, on something comparatively soft. "These niggers are in for a long night," said a ghostly voice somewhere behind him, somewhere out in the cold darkness. A car door slammed shut behind him.

Chapter 2

At God's Mercy

Devon's brain felt like a bleeding wound, his body a sea of aching misery. He tried to make some sense out of where he was, and what was happening, but his thoughts kept going back to his cousins, who, if he remembered right, were in as much danger as he was. Somebody had made a huge mistake, he thought. This was all just a monstrous case of mistaken identity, and he would have to set the record straight. He struggled to get his head together and rise into a sitting position. It was hard with his hands cuffed behind his back, his joints all seemingly on fire, and the slippery back seat of the police cruiser seemingly fighting him every step of the way, but Devon managed to right himself.

He was in a cop car, staring at the thick fence separating the prisoner in back from the lights, radios, note pads, and shotguns up front. He looked around. This was apparently the car of the little cop who resembled Mickey Mouse, the one who had shot his car. Behind it was his Camaro, and he saw the cops running around it, opening and closing doors, shouting to each other and then gathering into little huddles. He didn't see his cousins, though, anywhere. He remembered the maniac holding Derek out over the bridge's metal railing, threatening him, shouting questions which made no sense. He couldn't quite piece together, though, how the confrontation ended. Did the guy drop Derek? He prayed neither of his cousins was down in that rocky gorge now, or splattered on the railroad tracks below. This whole nightmare trip had been his idea. Good God, if they died, their mothers would kill him.

Then the front doors flew open, and a large white cop slid into the drivers' seat. The black guy, who'd kicked him and held Derek over the gorge, plopped down in the passenger's seat, in front of Devon. They pulled shut the doors, and with the windows rolled up, the stink of booze hit Devon instantly. This man stank like a distillery, and yet somehow had the energy to race about like he was hyped up, beating and kicking and cursing with vigor. Devon wondered what the guy was wired on.

After all of that exertion, the guy was still talking a blue streak. "We got 'em. We really got 'em," he kept repeating as the cruiser drove the length of the bridge, u-turned in an intersection and headed back across the gorge. "We got them motherfuckers. We really did." The maniac turned and leered at Devon with bright red eyes sparkling with feverish intensity. "Nobody, but nobody, gets away with shit in my 'hood."

"That's right," the cop said. "This is your 'hood, bud."

These guys were on familiar terms, Devon thought; certainly familiar enough that the cops would just stand by and watch while this crazy man beat and kicked three young men who did nothing worse than getting shot at and looking for help. He wondered who this drunken lunatic was, some kind of goon hired by the cops to terrorize the 'hood, or a big time gangsta who kept the cops in his pocket, or something worse. Why did the cops stand by and watch him beat on three innocent men and hold one over the side of a bridge and do nothing about it? Why did no one stop this maniac and end this nightmare? Maybe the cops wanted them beaten, but had this maniac do it so they could later pin it all on him, Devon thought.

"Hey man, are you in the mood for some beer?" the maniac asked.

The white cop chuckled.

"Let's go out and celebrate with a case of beer."

The white cop kept driving. "Let's get these gangbangers taken care of, big guy," he said.

There was a moment of tense silence. Then without warning the maniac spun on Devon, and launched into a stream of curses. "You no good mother fucker!" he burst out. "I'm going to put you and your boys in body bags, you no good mother fucker! I hate niggers like you, you mother fucker. I should kill you! You're in for a long night, you no good black mother fucker."

On and on he raved, while Devon thanked God for the fence between them, and dreaded their arrival at wherever they were taking him. He didn't know why he was in a police car. He didn't know who this crazy man was, nor why he was intent on inflicting all manner of torture and abuse on him and his cousins. Terrified of what would happen next, Devon sat quietly and began to pray to God for help and forgiveness. This could be his last day on this earth, he thought.

The cop steered the cruiser into the Clairton Municipal Building parking lot, which was no more than 50 yards from the bridge. It was an ill-lit, poorly marked structure, square and brick with lots of narrow windows. The car rolled around back, where a small black and white sign identified the City of Clairton Police Department. The cop pulled the car up next to a snow bank, and hopped out.

"I'll bring him in," said the maniac. The cop nodded and headed into the building, as this crazy man with apparent police protection circled the car and fumbled with the latch of the rear driver's side door. Devon scrunched up on the passenger side of the back seat. What was going to happen now? He hesitated to even imagine. But he knew he did not want to be left alone with this insane man, not for a second.

The door swung open, and the man lunged across the seat, clawing at him with a drunk's heavy brutality, but still with the energy of a crazed crackhead in urgent need of a fix. If only he had his hands free, Devon might have been able to fend the guy off, or just open the driver's side door and make a run for it. But before he could think, the guy grabbed his long dreadlocks, his pride, and yanked hard. "C'mon, nigger," he said in a loud, commanding voice. "I'm going to fix you good, you punk-ass pussy! Your ass is mine."

Devon struggled to get his footing as the man dragged him out of the car by his dreads, yanked him hard and fast so he thought his scalp would tear from his skull. "My hands!" his mind screamed. "Good Lord, give me my hands!" But they were bound in chains and stainless steel clamps behind his back. Pulled along by his dreads and still spinning from the beating on the bridge, Devon staggered along the sidewalk, looking down, until with a wild jerk he was slammed into the municipal building's brick wall. Then he was spinning, falling, crashing into a heap of hard-packed snow.

And then this reeking man was atop him, huge and heavy on Devon's narrow chest, saliva dripping and flying from his mouth as he screamed, "You punk-ass mother fucker, I'm going to kill you for shooting at my girlfriend, take this, and this!" And then he was pounding on Devon's unprotected face, big hands crashed into him once, twice, again, again, each one coming in harder than the first. Must be aware. Must remember. But they kept coming, sending shocks of burning pain back through his head, cracking his neck, smashing him deeper into the hard packed snow. He lost count of the blows, lost track of everything but the voice which screamed, "Give me just one free hand to ward off these blows, one free hand to fight back!"

He tried to scream, but nothing would come. He tried to think, but his mind's eye filled with that drooling face and the words it spat: "No good mother fucker, you're mine! I'm going to kill you and your gangbanger friends. You scared my girl. It's time to die!"

But then he was lifted out of the snow, still clinging to life, to consciousness. The grinning demon creature looked him straight in the face, mouthed some curse. Then he saw a bleary glimmer of yellowish light, felt himself flying forward, stumbling, struggling for control of his feet and hands. He flew and flew and flew yet further, like a dream, until he smashed against something hard and clear, then slid to the ground, his swollen face pressed against glass, mashing against a hard, cold pane and leaving a thick track of blood as he sank down, down, down to the ground, slumping miserably as the light slipped away.

* * *

The light returned slowly, in tentative, throbbing fragments. He was horribly hung over, Devon thought. His head was pounding. For some reason his eyes would not open, he could not see the unyielding surface he was sitting or lying on, whichever was the case. Where the hell was he? And he couldn't remember drinking anything, either. No, they had just watched a movie. He reached up to rub his eyes. Oof. His hands wouldn't come up. Then it came back to him: handcuffs.

It returned in a flash of pain. Shot at. Chased. Stopped by cops. Kicked and beaten with a shotgun. Separated from his cousins. Beaten in the snow. And slammed into a glass door.

That voice sent shivers through his body, and suddenly it was urgent, utterly critical, to get his eyes open, figure out where the next blow would come from. But every time he let his eyes fall open, the shafts of white light bore holes in his head.

Got to survive, he thought. I've got to get through this. And I've got to remember everything.

He pushed one eyelid open, then let the searing pain slam it back shut. He noticed he was breathing through his mouth, and a hard, dry crust covered his lips. He licked his lip. It stung. Something thick, wet, and salty came in on his quivering tongue. His right ear, too, was clogged up with something. It felt like there was a slug in there, something cold and slimy. Blood, it must be; partly frozen blood. He'd been beaten badly, relentlessly, he recalled, all about his head. He wondered if blood in the ear meant brain damage, or that the tiny bones in the inner ear had been shattered. He seemed to be able to hear well, so far. And he could think, could remember who he was. But the scene around him seemed surreal, as if a product of a mind trapped between sleep and waking.

"Don't we get a phone call, sir?" asked a voice to Devon's right. It was Little Sonny.

Devon pushed open his eyes, held them open this time, and assessed the situation. He was cuffed behind the back still, laying on his side on a concrete floor, in a small and crowded room. Nearby on a chair sat Sonny, similarly constrained, and there was an empty chair on his right. The lunatic was pacing the room, ranting about being God, waving around a big, shiny revolver. A Jefferson Borough cop was sitting on a table in one corner of the room, next to a swinging door which was opposite Devon. A tall, red-haired Clairton cop stood on the other side of the door, and as he took stock of the situation, a white woman walked across the hallway just outside and screamed, "Niggers!" On either side of the room were hallways, and Devon could see cell bars down both wings.

"How about our rights?" asked Devon.

"Rights?" mumbled the black demon as he staggered toward a refrigerator. He opened it, revealing it to be fully stocked with beer. "You black mother fuckers don't have any rights!" he shouted while reaching in and pulling out a 12-ounce can of Old Milwaukee. A sinister grin began to spread across the demon's cold, black face as he began chugging the brew as if it were spring water.

"Rights!" he yelled. "You black mother fuckers want rights? Here! Here's your God damned rights!" He pulled back his right arm and rifled the beer can into the air, striking Little Sonny in the head. "There! There's your rights, you no good niggers! I'm God in my 'hood, and you punks should never have come nowhere near my 'hood. Will somebody please tell these stupid assholes that niggers forfeit their rights once they bring their sorry black asses into the City of Prayer? Don't you sorry fuckers know that niggers don't have any rights in this mill town?"

"That's right, bud," a white voice muttered. "No rights."

Suddenly the maniac seemed to notice Devon's tentative movements on the floor, spun, and launched a football-style kick to his face. "Who fired the gun?" he fumed, as Devon crumpled up against the pain. "Are you going to talk, motherfucker?" Then the man bent down and landed two hard blows to Devon's head. The world started whirling again, spinning and aching and reeking of alcoholic breath, and before he knew it, his head was rising and falling, soaring through the air and then crashing to the concrete floor, over and over again. "Nigger, you ain't shit!" the voice declared, and Devon felt blood rushing out of his nose and mouth.

Then in a flash he was up, suspended in mid-air like a hanged man, and then down, crashing into what seemed like a metal chair. Questions flew at him, carried on foul-smelling breath with machine-gun relentlessness. "Who shot at me? Whose gun was it? I want to know and you're going to tell me! And if you don't, then your black ass is going to be in a body bag, and your friends too. Talk, nigger. Where's the gun?" And on and on and on. Devon had to look away from the crazy, glossy, bloodshot eyes of the torturer, but he couldn't close his own eyes, for fear that the next blow would come the moment he did.

Then the voice moved away, and Devon and Little Sonny sat side by side and watched the maniac prance around the room, his chest out and shoulders high like a prize fighter who has just scored his first knockout, and was feeling big and bad and proud of what he's done.

"Boy, do you have anything to say to me?" the black man asked, strutting back in Devon's direction.

Devon couldn't think of anything.

"You ain't got no rights, nigger, in this white supremacy world," the maniac said, drawing his chrome-plated .357 Magnum revolver. He paced back and forth in the room like a crazy man, then stopped dead in front of Devon, legs spread wide and chest pushed out like some kind of parody of Atlas, the Greek god who held up the world. The man had a bemused look on his face, and Devon wondered if he even recognized the irony in his own words.

"I run this part of town. I decide who comes and who goes. These are my boys," he said, gesturing to the white cops gathered behind him, watching the festivities with shit-eating grins. "They protect me and I protect them. We kicked your asses! What are you going to do about it?"

He waved his gun in the air and Devon didn't know whether to laugh or cry.

"You think your family can help you?" the maniac went on, the words fairly exploding from his mouth and booming down the hallways to either side. "Fuck your family, asshole. I don't care who you get! You can get your friends, dog, cat, mom, dad, aunts, uncles, brothers, or anybody you want. I'm God, and nobody fucks with God!" The man's voice then rose to a shrill shriek. "Go ahead and sue! You'll lose! Lose! Lose!"

The self-proclaimed God walked away, shaking his head, and Devon wondered who this crazy black mother fucker could be. Why is he accusing us of firing shots at him, Devon wondered, when we were the ones who were fired on? What the fuck is going on? If he could only get these handcuffs loose, he thought, the tide might turn. He wasn't exactly sure how, but it would turn.

Alone, the maniac couldn't have beat them, cuffed them and held them here, Devon thought. It was the police who were holding them hostage. It wasn't the first time cops had harassed him. Like most young black men, he'd been presumed guilty plenty of times before. But unlike most black families, his hadn't rolled over and played dead in the face of official oppression. Devon, his brother and father had protested in front of police stations, taken the oppressors to court, and beaten their bogus charges.

"All I can say is that you done messed with the wrong family!" Devon blurted out. He instantly recognized that he might well be beaten, even pistol-whipped for his words, but he couldn't hold back. "They're going to get you for what you did to me!"

The bald, white Clairton cop, a twisted sneer on his face, drew a Glock from his holster and stuck it right between Devon's eyes, the barrel pushing hard against the cartilage of his nose. "I can kill you no good mother fuckers and nothing would be done about it. I'm a cop, and I can get away with it." He spoke in a low monotone, the threats voiced with a terrifying calmness. "Just keep running your mouth. Go ahead, nigger, make my day. See, boy, nobody knows you're here, just us. I could kill your black ass, and nobody would ever know. Nobody would even care."

Devon stared at the barrel, rendered double by his crossed eyes. He didn't know what to say, what to do, because the cop was right. They could cap all three cousins right here and now, bring them out to some secret burial ground, and nobody would ever find them, because of course it's cops who search for bodies, and cops aren't about to fink on cops. He felt tears well up in the corners of his eyes, though he didn't really feel like crying. His eyes wanted to cry, it seemed, for Shataya and little Devon and Asiadawn and his girlfriend and his brothers Peeper and Curtis, who he might never see again. Meanwhile his gut yearned to unleash a primal scream of anger, fear and frustration, letting it all out in one searing cry.

But he was one twitch of a finger from having his brains blown out the back of his head, Devon realized. Better stay quiet.

"You're real quiet now, boy, ain't you?" the black man asked. "You're real nice and quiet now. What'd I tell you? I decide who comes and goes."

"Kill the nigger," the woman hissed. "Blow him straight to hell."

But the cop withdrew the revolver, replaced it in its holster. "Maybe later," he said. "I don't want to make a mess on the wall." The cops on the table and in the corner snickered - a little nervously, Devon thought. This cop, this wanna-be tough guy with a badge and a gun, would get his comeuppance when the time was ripe, Devon vowed.

For a minute everyone was quiet, and Devon realized that every muscle in his body was tense as a guitar string. He tried to relax them, but couldn't, and he felt a strange tremor beginning in his chest and spreading quickly throughout his entire body. He couldn't keep it down, even though it was embarrassing to sit there quivering with the cops, the maniac and the strange woman watching him, milling about, talking, grinning stupidly. But it wouldn't stop.

It wasn't the kind of shivering that comes from cold. It was more like the shakes that used to come over him half an hour after a bad argument with his dad, when the bravado had passed and left behind a gripping anxiety. Or the tremors he got a few months back after just dodging what could have been a fatal highway accident. Under stress, he realized, the body and brain first do what they have to do to survive. Only after the crisis has passed do they allow themselves the luxury of sheer terror.

It was cold enough to make a man shiver in here, though; that much was true. It was almost like a refrigerator, and the cops, "God", and the woman all wore jackets. He, too, wore a jacket, but it didn't seem to give him much protection. Again he wished he'd asked Derek for that extra sweater. The delay, he realized, might have allowed that crazed shooter's car to traverse River Road without ever encountering Devon, Little Sonny and Derek. There would have been no high speed chase, no ill-advised effort to get help from the Clairton cops, no beatings and no round indentation of a pistol barrel between his eyebrows. Amazing how a little decision can have so many consequences.

Little Sonny's voice broke his brief daydream. "Officer, could you help me out?" Sonny asked, turning his attention from the black man to a Jefferson Borough cop. "All I'm asking is to call these boys' mothers, tell them they're okay. Can't you help me out on that?"

"Sorry, but you heard the man," he said, pointing a thumb at the maniac. "This is his 'hood."

"That's right you little motherfucker!" the maniac yelled, rushing back in and waving his gun in Little Sonny's face. "So you just stop tryin' to make friends. You ain't got no friends here. All you got is me, and I'm God, and nobody fucks with God."

Devon felt a sickness rise from his gut. The walls seemed to be breathing in and out, and a spike of pain shot up from his neck into the back of his head. He closed his eyes, listened to the strange dialogue in silence. Little Sonny kept asking the Jefferson Borough cop about phone calls, rights, medical attention. The cop referred all questions to the angry "God." Through it all, the guy kept ranting, making random threats, and declaring himself God with obsessive frequency. And the white woman seemed to pop in every minute or so, screaming racial epithets and urging the captors to "fuck those niggers up."

Little Sonny looked over, caught Devon's eyes, winced and looked away. Man, I must look bad, Devon thought. Little Sonny himself didn't look too good, his light complexion marred with big purple splotches, his thick, short hair caked with blood which drew tracks down his face and colored his clothing dark crimson.

"You okay?" Devon asked.

"I'm livin'," Little Sonny said. "Man, you look like the elephant man. How are you?"

"I dunno." Three pair of eyes, reflecting dumb rage, vague distaste, and total disinterest respectively, watched the two converse. If only he could have a moment alone with Sonny, Devon thought, they might hatch a plan to talk - or bust - their way out of here. That wasn't likely to happen, though. "Have you gotten a phone call?" he asked. "Has anybody gotten a phone call?"

"Nope. See, this ain't America here, cuz. This is Clairton, and American type rights don't apply."

"This is my fuckin' 'hood, and what rights I give apply in my 'hood," the maniac broke in, stepping towards them, using the revolver as a pointer. The guy would be downright comical, Devon thought, if he didn't have a piece and police protection.

"Where's Derek?" Devon asked, remembering his cousin's brush with death out by the bridge railing. "They didn't ... drop him?"

"No, man, he's in the other room," Sonny said, gesturing with his chin to the hallway outside the swinging double door. "I think this knucklehead's been beating on him."

"Who the fuck are you callin' a knucklehead?" he yelled, getting right in Little Sonny's face again, and casually waving the gun before Devon's eyes. "What the fuck position do you think you're in to be calling anybody anything, nigger? You know I could blow you and your boy's heads right off, and nobody, but nobody would even give a fuck?"

On and on he went, repeating the same themes like a child's doll which recites a phrase when you pull the cord. I'm God. This is my 'hood. You're in no position to talk. Again Devon didn't know whether to laugh at the ridiculousness of it all, or cry that this obvious idiot held over them the power of life and death.

Finally, Little Sonny looked past the ranting man, over at the Jefferson Borough cop on the table. "Officer, can you call Mike Grimes, down at Dravosburg Police Station?"

At the sound of the name, "God" backed off for a second.

"You know him?" the Jefferson Borough cop asked. "Grimes, that is?"

"Yeah. I don't know if he'd be at the station now, or at home, or

34

at the hospital, where he guards."

"How do you know Grimes?" the cop asked. Grimes, Devon knew, was one of the most respected cops in the Valley, expected to rise to a position of prominence as soon as one opened up. If he remembered right, Grimes used to work in Clairton, so these cops should know him. Grimes was talked about as a candidate any time a public safety director or chief of police job came open in the Valley.

"He's my uncle," Little Sonny said. "He'll straighten this whole mess out."

"Fuck your Uncle Mike! He's a chump," the maniac declared, swaggering back and forth now. "I'll kick his ass, too. You get Grimes. You go ahead. 'Cause this is my 'hood and I decide who comes" - at this he whirled and shoved the gun in Sonny's face - "and who goes."

Then he spun back around, slapped one of the white cops on the shoulder with a big grin on his face. "You're the man," the cop said, with little enthusiasm, and "God" smiled even bigger. This guy was putting on a show for these white cops, Devon realized, showing them in bold strokes that he, a nigger, could beat on niggers, too. That he was one of the rulers, not one of the ruled. That he was one of the guys. It struck Devon that just this sort of behavior had kept the black people divided and in a state of war with themselves for as long as there had been Africans in America. The whites used offers of acceptance, power and money to play black against black in a psychological ploy which many blacks fell for hook, line and sinker. And tonight their little game had gotten him beaten, and might yet get him killed.

Unless he played a little game of divide and conquer himself. "Umm, sir," he said to the Jefferson Borough cop. "Do you think I could get my phone call now? Just to tell my mom I'm all right."

"You had just better listen to him, you punk-ass bitch," he replied, nodding at the black man. Then he yawned.

"Well, sir, might I get a napkin or something to wipe off my face?" And might I get these cuffs off of me for the same purpose, and to defend myself and even strike back? he wondered.

"You don't look so fucking bad," the cop said. "Sit tight."

The man who called himself God smiled. "See, you no-good mother fucking gangbangers, this is my gang, not yours. You're in my territory now, and ain't no one gonna lift a finger for you here." Devon gulped. It seemed the maniac was right - for whatever reason, these cops were going to let him do whatever he wanted.

The bald cop left the room, then came quickly back in with two clipboards in one hand and pens in the other. He smiled now, said soothingly, "Okay, you niggers, just sign these damn papers and everything's gonna be okay. We'll take you bastards back to your cells, let you niggers rest for a while."

He put one clipboard in Devon's lap, the other in Little Sonny's, and stood before them, holding the pens and jangling a ring of keys - maybe the keys to the handcuffs which held them in bondage. "You niggers are going to sign, right?" he asked. "It's just a paper we need, a little formality before we can put you in the cells, where you can lay down, stretch out a little, get some sleep, whatever."

Devon looked at the typewritten sheet, which said something about his rights at the top. He could just make out the shadow of some handwritten scribblings on the other side of the paper. So, that was their game. They wanted him to sign something confirming that he understood his rights, with a confession conveniently and secretly written on the back.

"I'm not writing on nothing," Devon practically spat. "I'm not reading it, I'm not signing it." He felt a rush of pleasure at his own defiance. They had him chained and surrounded, and they had the firepower to blow him full of holes. But they couldn't make him defile his own name by signing it to a false confession.

"You sure, nigger?" the big white cop said, standing over him with his legs spread wide. He appeared a strong man. Devon didn't relish the idea of taking a full blow to the face from him. "It'll be a lot easier if you just sign the damn paper. A lot easier."

He wanted to scream, "Fuck you and your goddamn paper!" But he held his composure. Why give them an excuse? "I'm not signing anything," he said clearly, and turned his head away from the paper, fully expecting a stinging shot to the face.

But it didn't come. The big cop turned to Little Sonny, who also refused to sign. "How about you guys put me in touch with a lawyer and give me my phone call?" he suggested instead. "That's my rights. You get my lawyer in here. Then maybe we'll talk about signing things."

"Nigger, you've got a hell of a lot of nerve asking for anything!"

the maniac burst out, stepping past the cop with his revolver still in hand, loosely gripped like a teacher might hold a pointer, or a piece of chalk. "Down here, you ain't got no damn rights. Until you tell me who fired the gun, you ain't fuckin' gettin' nothing."

Fired the gun? Devon thought. Then he remembered this man's strange rants back on the bridge, his repeated questions about where the gun was, the relentless kicking and striking over the whereabouts of some mythical piece. It occurred to him like a flash of lightning that this whole thing was an incredible miscommunication gone very wrong. He wondered if an explanation of the car ride, the shooter on River Road, and their hunt for police help might clear the whole thing up.

But Little Sonny was leaning forward, as far as his cuffed hands would allow, leaning into the maniac's face, clearly enunciating the words: "I ain't going to tell you nothing." Devon knew that was as it should be. These cops had already allowed the maniac to beat them, threatened them at gun point, and tried to trick them into signing false confessions. There was no sense trying to tell them anything.

The two stared each other in the face, nose to nose, for a long minute. But Little Sonny refused to blink or back away, and "God" backed up. "This is gonna be a long-ass night for you, nigger. You're gonna regret you ever set foot in the City of Prayer."

But Devon felt the momentum shifting. These cops and this black traitor weren't going to get what they wanted - signed confessions to God knows what. They weren't going to get anybody to admit to being the shooter in some trumped up incident. And it didn't seem they had the courage to blow three conscious, handcuffed black men's brains out at point blank. Although that might change. For the time being, though, Devon felt a rush of power. They couldn't move or fight back. But they could refuse these Barney Fifes what they obviously wanted most.

The big cop gathered up the clipboards and disappeared through the double doors and down the hallway. The black man went on pacing, ranting about his 'hood, him being God, how he was going to send three niggers back home in body bags tonight, and how nobody's uncle, aunt, mother, father, cat, dog or great grandfather was going to come into God's turf and do fuck all. Nobody. Again Devon had to wonder about the guy's stamina. He still stank like a dive after a Friday night bar fight. But he dashed about and recited his endless litany of bragging and showed no signs of slowing down. There was something unnatural about it. And then there were those blazing red eyes.

Then the white woman moved aside, and Devon saw a black and battered figure in the double doorway. The clothing was Derek's, but the face and head were like something out of a horror film. His hair was a chaotic mix of braids and tufts with large bald spots where whole sections of hair had obviously been yanked out. His jaw was blown up like he had a football in his mouth. Dark red streams still oozed from two big cuts just above his forehead, where hair and smashed skin and cakes of blood mixed in a lump. From there the blood ran down his face and on to his shirt, nearly saturating it. A lump the size of a mouse stood out above his eye. He wobbled as the little cop, the Mickey Mouse cop who'd shot the car, pushed him into the room. Derek was barely standing, just shuffling along with his hands, also bloodied, cuffed behind him.

"Jesus, what the hell did they do to him?" Devon muttered.

"You ain't lookin' much better," Little Sonny said, his voice low and jagged with anger.

Derek met Little Sonny's eyes, then Devon's, and nodded slightly. He looked frightened and dazed, like a bull in a ring just before the matador makes the kill. The little cop led Derek through the room and down the hallway to Devon's right, where the cells were. He heard the clattering of keys, a short conversation he couldn't quite make out, the sound of keys being turned in a lock. Devon wondered if they would lock him in and then hang him, and claim it was suicide. Like any young black man, Devon had heard plenty of stories about blacks dying in jail cells, on empty highways, or out on bridges late at night, with cops as the only witnesses. The newspapers always said it was suicide. Once in a while, they called it resisting arrest. Either term usually meant, "The nigger mouthed off."

But after a minute or two, the little cop came back, and Devon hadn't heard a gunshot or the sickening tug of the noose. "God" was still pacing and spouting nonsense, but the big cop nodded at the Mickey Mouse cop, and said, "Lock 'em all up."

"This one first?" the little cop asked, pointing at Devon.

"Yeah," the black guy broke in. "Leave this mouthy one with me for a minute." He gestured at Little Sonny with his gun. "I want to have a little private chat with my man." The assembly of cops, from Clairton and Jefferson Borough, and the woman started to file out.

Devon didn't want to leave Little Sonny alone, but he wanted badly to check out Derek, and to make sure he was okay. Although Derek was a year older than he was, Devon often felt a brotherly protectiveness for his troubled cousin. And when the little cop grabbed his arms and jerked him up and out of his chair, Devon couldn't help but feel relief at getting out from under the eyes of all of these cops, and the white woman who seemed to be with the black guy, and yet kept yelling nigger this, nigger that.

Whoa! Suddenly wrenched up out of the chair, Devon felt his head spin, and feared he would stumble, or faint, if the cop didn't keep hold of his arms. Jesus, he felt dizzy. He wondered if it was loss of blood, or all of those blows to the head he took. Suddenly the crusty layers of blood in his nose seemed to break apart, and a stream of the stuff burst down his face and dribbled into his mouth, which was open to breathe. His face, cold and raw, tingled as it flowed down past his chin and dripped on to his shirt and the floor. Ooh! It stung, and all the blood made it hard to breathe. Still the little cop pushed him forward, down the hallway where he'd taken Derek.

Devon turned his head, tried to wipe some of the blood off on his shoulder. It was all he could do with his hands cuffed behind him and the cop holding his arms up so high he felt like something in his shoulder was going to pop. He didn't want to swallow the blood, but it was oozing into his mouth. As the cop drove him forward, past the cell where he saw Derek laying down, he tried to blow some of it off of his smashed lips.

"You aren't trying to spit on me, are you, you nigger?" the little cop growled.

And what if I was, Devon thought? All alone, this Mickey Mouse cop didn't seem so menacing. Devon had been in his share of street fights before, and felt that if the cuffs were off, he could take this little guy on. The other cops had looked to be heading out of that holding room, leaving only Little Sonny and the mysterious maniac. Maybe he could stun Mickey with a punch to the head, get his gun, blow away that fucker who'd beaten him and set Derek and Little Sonny loose. It was a risky proposition, sure. But so was staying here, locked up, unarmed and at the mercy of a bunch of sadists in a police state.

Derek, he noted, was in the second cell from the holding room. The cop led Devon further down the block, to the fourth cell, and stopped him in front of the iron door. Other than the two cousins and the cop, the cell block was empty. Maybe that's why they were getting so much attention. These cops apparently didn't bust many of the drug dealers, gangbangers and small time thieves who ravaged Clairton, and particularly menaced the poor folks in the projects. No. They picked on three unarmed young men intent only on going to Denny's.

With two quick turns of a key, the cop released the cuffs from around Devon's wrists, and his hands fell to his sides. Free again! he thought; free to wipe blood from his face, to feel the lumps on his swollen head and to make a fist. The skin where the cuffs had rubbed was raw, but that was nothing. It wouldn't feel raw hurtling towards the cop's childlike face.

"We'd really like to know whose that gun was and who was the shooter," the cop said in a friendly voice, still behind Devon and jingling the cuffs and keys like bells. "Why don't you talk to me?"

"Talk about what, about how you and that maniac tortured and beat me and my two cousins?" Devon shot back.

The cop's tone of voice changed markedly. "Take off your boots, mother fucking nigger," he ordered. Devon wondered if there was any real chance he could whack this cop, grab his gun, burn a couple of these fuckers, and make an escape of it. At the worst, he thought, he'd be dying for a good cause.

"Take off your damn boots!" the cop barked. He still looked Devon in the face. But he seemed taken aback, insecure.

Devon bent down slowly to unlace his boot. Gotta think fast. If he came up fast with a right uppercut to the jaw- but then WHAM! something struck him in the face, hard, cracking his neck. He wobbled backwards. It was the cop's foot, come up in a sharp, stinging strike. The fucker must know karate or something, Devon thought, as he stood up.

"I told you to take off your damn boots," Mickey Mouse repeated, with a sickening grin.

Devon felt an unquenchable rage rising in his gut. He should just attack, go for broke, throw the little fucker through the cinder block wall, he thought. He could picture the cop's scrawny body striking the wall, then breaking into a thousand pieces, leaving only a pinkish stain on the gray paint.

But the element of surprise was lost, for the moment. So again Devon bent down and took the boot laces in his trembling hands. Again the cop's foot delivered a sharp blow to the face. Devon's head rang like a bell, and he felt all of the clotted, blocked blood breaking loose in his nose, throat, even ears. He reeled backwards, but just kept his balance. He came up dazed, but still raging, nearly blinded with rage.

Slowly, he turned his back on the cop, lifted his leg, and wobbling like a drunken crane unlaced one, then the other boot. He turned back and shoved them into the cop's waiting left arm. I can take him, Devon thought. He can't be more than 120 pounds. A featherweight.

"You go ahead and try something," the cop said, smiling and patting his pistol with his right hand. "You just take your best shot, because you'll only get one. See, nigger, you're in no position to start anything with me. Because I'm a cop, and I can kill you and walk away scot-free."

Devon stared at the arrogant prick for what seemed like minutes. The cop was ready now, would pull his gun and start pumping rounds into Devon at the least provocation. The element of surprise, if it had ever existed, was long gone. To attack now would be suicide. Worse yet, it might start a slaughter of the only witnesses - his cousins, Derek and Little Sonny. This wasn't the time. But the cop was wrong about one thing - he wouldn't get off scot-free. All three torturers, the black collaborator and the two white cops, would pay a price someday, Devon vowed.

"That's a good nigger. Now take off your coat."

Devon took his jacket off, handed it over to the cop.

"Now into the cell, asshole."

Devon turned, took a step, and felt an explosion of stars as something hard crashed into the back of his head. He stumbled forward, caught himself against the metal bed, and listened to a low chuckling and the metallic clang of the lock.

"Oops," the little cop said, strolling away from the locked cell. "My hand slipped." He paused by Derek's cell, just long enough to launch a gob of spit through the bars and say, glibly, "Umm, boy, you didn't see that."

God damn it! Devon screamed inside. A few hours ago he'd been a free man, going for a bite to eat in his own Camaro, able to travel as far as his gas money would carry him. Since then he'd been shot at, beaten, cuffed, kicked and jailed. All for nothing. Had he ever really been free in the first place? At least the blood wasn't seeping into his mouth anymore. He probed around with his tongue. No, apparently the blood on his face was freezing instead. There was no heat in the cell block, it seemed, and the karate kid had taken his jacket.

"Turn the fuckin' heat on!" he yelled down the corridor. There was no answer but his own echo and the chattering of his achy teeth.

"Cuz, you all right?" he asked Derek. He could see his cousin's form, broken up by two sets of parallel bars, stretched out on the primitive rubber mattress on a spare metal bed. It was just like the one in Devon's cell, and every other one. He sat down.

"No, man. I'm bleedin', man." Derek sounded on the edge of tears. He had always been a little reserved, and Devon wondered if he could handle this. "You think they're gonna kill us tonight? I mean, after all they've already done, don't they kinda have to?"

"I dunno, man. Did they give you any phone call?"

"Nope, 'Von."

"Then nobody even knows we're here." Shivering, Devon lay back on the mattress, wishing a little heat would rise off of it, trying to relax his tense, twisted neck and back. "Just don't go to sleep, cuz. If we're asleep, they can do anything to us."

"Right, man. No sleep 'til freedom."

As if he'd be able to sleep anyway, with his face, back, head and ribs alternatively screaming and stinging and throbbing like childbirth. And with his throat afire with a roaring thirst. God damn them! The cops hadn't even given them anything to drink, and now he was locked up. Damned if he was going to ask those cops for anything now, though. He'd sooner die of thirst.

He tried to slow his breathing, calm his pounding heart. But the minute his adrenaline-fired body started to ease up, the maniac started shouting again. Devon couldn't make out the words, but he heard Little Sonny responding to the maniac's louder and louder taunts, heard the slurred shouts of the madman growing shriller and shriller.

"What's goin' on, Derek?" he asked.

"Fucker's laying into Little Sonny, man."

Then something thumped, and it sounded like a piece of furniture was sliding across the floor. The crash of objects against objects, the thud of a human body against a hard cinderblock wall echoed down the cell block. It sounded like more than two men, like a war, like buffalo stampeding down a hall. Then the floor seemed almost to shudder as something hit it, hard.

"He's beatin' on Little Sonny!" Derek shouted.

Devon, now up against the cell bars, remembered the revolver this maniac had been swinging around like a toy, what, a quarter of an hour ago? He recalled the crazed glow of the guy's eyes, the way he showed up at the door of their car with a shotgun in his hand and a cryptic cry of, "Remember me?" The guy was on the edge, and now he was laying into Little Sonny. The least provocation, Devon feared, and he would as likely as not put a slug into Little Sonny. That would give him no choice but to kill them all.

Then the crashing and thudding were replaced with the grunting and gasping sounds of struggle. "Get the fuck off of me!" Little Sonny yelled, followed by the loud bang of, Devon thought, bodies hitting the refrigerator. Devon tried to see into the little room, but couldn't. He pushed against the bars, hoping against hope that the cell door hadn't closed and locked properly. But it held fast.

"Say you a bitch!" the man yelled. Shit, Devon thought, the guy must have Little Sonny in some kind of submission hold. Knowing Little Sonny, he'd sooner die than call himself a bitch, especially for the pleasure of this asshole. And the fucker, with his mysterious police protection, would probably be more than happy to break Sonny's arms for the sheer thrill of it.

"Say you a bitch!" the maniac repeated.

"Fuck ... you," Sonny gasped.

"Say you a bitch! Say you a bitch, boy. Boy, you say you a bitch, or you gonna be my bitch."

The struggle went on. Devon turned his head. He didn't want to know what was going on. He had dragged Sonny out in the cold, but how could he have known this would result? All he could do now was vow that when he got out of here, there would be hell to pay. If he got out of here alive.

"Say you a bitch!"
"Say you a bitch!"
"Say ... you ... a ... bitch!"
"Okay, I'm a bitch! I'm a bitch! I'm a bitch."

The sound of struggle stopped, and Devon saw another cop, he couldn't tell which one, pass from the hallway into the little room. "Yeah, you my ho," the guy said, and from the sound of it, he was probably standing up now. "Maybe I oughtta make you squeal like a pig, too."

He heard the cops talking, then some strange sounds he couldn't identify. Little Sonny was silent, and then the cop told the black guy that he would lock "nigger number three" up. He heard a low groan, footsteps moving away, and then the sound of keys jingling. It seemed the beating was over. All three of them, Devon suspected, were locked up now, and although that made them more vulnerable than ever, it also meant the cops might be through playing with them. The whole affair brought a rush of nausea to him, and an instantaneous weakness in the knees, and Devon stumbled back to sit on the so-called bed.

If Little Sonny hadn't have been cuffed, Devon thought, he could have taken the guy. The three cousins could have taken the whole lot of them if they weren't armed with guns and cuffs and badges. But those badges won't protect them forever, Devon thought. And whoever this devil was who beat on him and Little Sonny, and held Derek over the side of the bridge, well, nothing would protect him. Nothing.

He turned, cocked his head to better hear a sound from down the block. At first it sounded like dice rattling in a cup, and he wondered if the cops were shooting craps, maybe wagering for who would get to kill each of the young black prisoners. But no, it was only Derek's teeth chattering, and it reminded him that he, too, was bitterly cold. Again, the extra sweater haunted him. But there was nothing he could do about it now, and there was no sense complaining to his cousin. Better to just deal with it, to survive it, and to remember all of the details.

He pressed close to the dirty rubber mattress, where probably a thousand other men had lain. Many of them had probably done something to warrant being locked up, at least for a night, be it attempted murder or just public drunkenness. But Devon had done nothing more than flash his high beams at a cop car, and honk his horn for help. It didn't make any sense. "Remember me, motherfucker? Remember me?" What did that mean? And now here he was, in a cell, cold and uncomfortable, battling dizziness and utter exhaustion, but too frightened to let soothing sleep take hold.

* * *

I didn't think too much about where Devon was that night. I knew he'd gone to Derek's, and it wasn't unusual for one cousin to end up sleeping over another one's house. I didn't have any reason to be alarmed until a panicked voice over the telephone announced, "The boys were beaten!" And when Curtis called me into the family room to catch on an item on the noon news, and I heard the names of three black men accused of ambushing, shooting at and beating a black off-duty Clairton police officer, I knew something was horribly wrong. See, one of the names was Devon Grey, who I knew wasn't capable of hurting even a chipmunk. See, Devon Grey is my son.

Chapter 3

Mean Green Machine

I could feel my blood boiling as I stormed out of the crib, down a flight of stairs and on to an aging concrete driveway. Tightly clenched in my hands was my future, an AK-47 assault rifle I had named Mr. Justice. A 30-round banana clip was inserted into Mr. Justice, and draped across my chest was a green military ammo belt. It was time to rain some payback on the perpetrators who'd maliciously assaulted and hospitalized my son and two nephews. It was time to lock and load on some unlucky motherfuckers who had abused their police powers. Vengeance is mine, saith the Lord.

I didn't know at the time what Devon's condition was. All I had to go on was what my sister Marie related to me, some jibber jabber from a constable who said my son had been beaten on the Ravensburg Bridge by the Clairton police, taken to the hospital emergency room with multiple head injuries, and later locked up at the county jail.

That's right: Assaulted by police. Because as we would soon find out, the black maniac in leather jacket and jeans, like the whites who kicked and threatened my son, was a cop.

It was torture knowing so little about what happened to my son and what his condition was. Apparently he hadn't even gotten a phone call. From the news reports and the little we knew from the constable, I had a feeling the young men were beaten out of revenge for some perceived slight.

It wasn't the first time the ones I love had been hurt by vindictive Barnie Fifes, and I knew from experience that protests and lawsuits would do little to bring them down. So this time some unlucky Fife was going to be wasted for putting his blood-soaked hands on my child.

I thanked God he hadn't been killed, but I would have given anything, I would have made a pact with the devil, to be able to go back in time and drive across that bridge just as the first blow was laid on my son. Someone would have been in deep shit then. I would have locked and loaded on those no-good motherfuckers, and killed every one of them without hesitation. They'd have gotten an introduction to Mr. Justice they would never forget. Then I would end my life, not by suicide, but in a blazing fire fight with SWAT. I would have left this world in a ball of fire. County Coroner Joshua Perper would have had a busy night pulling hot metal out of the asses of a few dead Fifes.

As a man and a father, I decided that I, and I alone, had to take care of this problem with the Fifes. I often wondered how they would like it if I assaulted one of their kids with a baseball bat or shot gun. They'd want some kind of justice. If I had brutalized my son, my black ass would be hauled off to jail kicking and screaming. The Fifes would have no mercy on me. They'd charge me with child abuse and maybe recklessly endangering another person or even attempted murder. That is, unless I died "resisting arrest."

I love my son as much as any cop or mayor loves their children. I wondered if those cops even thought about that when they were beating Devon, Little Sonny and Derek - that these young men are somebody's sons, somebody loves them, somebody will be frightened, saddened, and then mad as hell when they find out about this. I doubt they did. They probably assumed that they could brutalize the three black men and get away with it. Maybe some parents don't want to prosecute rouge cops; maybe it's all right with them, but it's not all right with yours truly.

The law wasn't likely to bring the Fifes to justice, so it would be my job to mete out punishment for the beating of my son and nephews. It was time to show the world that black folks are sick and tired of being victims of police brutality. It was time to kick some asses Marine Corps style. It was time to kill, or be killed. I was ready and willing to die.

I would be dead today, or sitting on death row, were it not for Ron Jackson. Mr. Justice and I were standing on the drivers' side of my van when Ron, my brother-in-law, pulled his 4 x 4 into my driveway, blocking me in.

Ron turned the ignition off, jumped out and stood in front of me.

"Hey, man, where are you going with that gun?"

I said nothing, just stood there, trembling.

"My sister called me and said she saw on the news where your son and nephews were arrested in Clairton for shooting at a cop," he said. "That doesn't sound like your son at all. I knew it just didn't jibe," he said. "So I rushed over. What happened?"

"What the news forgot to tell you was that Devon, Derek and

Little Sonny were beaten and hospitalized by the police," I said, still shaking. "They all had to be treated at the hospital before they were taken off to jail. Those no good mother fucker Clairton cops beat my son, and now they're going to pay with their lives. Ron, if I go to jail, I don't care. If I'm killed in a gun battle, I don't care. Someone is going to pay for what they did to my son. I'm sick and tired of this cop bullshit."

He looked me up and down, his eyes stopping on the semiautomatic weapon over my shoulder. "Let's do it the right way, Buster," he said. "Let's go up there and check it out. And if it don't pan out, we can do it your way. With violence, if it comes down to that."

Sometimes I wish I hadn't listened to Ron Jackson. I'd be dead today, sure. But so would a few other people who have made a mess out of a lot of lives, including those of my son, my nephews, and myself. And as for "doing it the right way," that hasn't gotten me or my son or my nephews anything but a sour taste like urine in our mouths. Because that's what the system has to say to the people who are darker than blue, who are without political power: Bend over, touch your toes, and open wide.

Ron alone couldn't have stopped me. Ron's a lieutenant down at the Allegheny County Jail, and a strong man, but no man alive could have stopped me with physical force after those words - "Our kids have been beaten" - reached my ears. But as we were standing in the driveway, Ron urging cautious deliberation and myself a fountain of hellfire words I can't even recall, little Peeper, my youngest son and then eight years old, tugged on my pant leg. "Dad," he said, "if something happens to you, what's going to happen to me?"

"That's a good question," I told my son, named Leon after me but called Peeper thanks to a childhood fascination with playing Peek-a-boo. "That's a really good question."

It was good enough to convince me to put down Mr. Justice and go with Ron. It would soon prompt me to instigate an FBI investigation, a civil suit, a federal grand jury, a media circus and a personal campaign of protest that has not ended to this day. But as I've said, that has gotten me nothing but an unwanted education in how the American criminal justice system protects its own. Peeper is almost old enough to fend for himself, with some help from a little spot of money I have set aside. And my patience with "doing it the right way" has damn near run out.

Not that I'm surprised. I haven't been surprised since 1972, the year I had to deal with housing discrimination just a month before going overseas to help the U.S.A. fight a small country where Muhammad Ali said a black man had no business being. That year I enlisted in the Marines, went to boot camp, and while on leave married my high school sweetheart and the love of my life, Lillian. None of that was really surprising. What woke me up, what opened my eyes, was a little old lady on Grant Street in Duquesne who told me I couldn't rent an apartment from her because my wife and I were black. She didn't hide it in couched terms about insufficient credit history or suddenly change the rental price upon sight of the color of my skin or even promise to call us and then never get around to it. She didn't play the games they play today. She said, "I can't rent you this apartment. See, you and your wife are black."

So I'd noticed. Though, really, I wasn't black, still am not. There's as much of my mother's Italian blood running in my veins as of my father's black plasma. That makes me, as they say, a mulatto. And as my mother raised me and my brother and three sisters on her own, and as I never really knew my father, an argument could be made that I'm more white than black, though I've never heard a white person try to make that particular point. Certainly not that little old landlady, who saw something darker than her own pallid skin and said, "Why don't you look for something down around Second Street?"

Back then, the blacks in Duquesne lived on Second Street and below, and in the Cochrandale Projects at the bottom of the slope. The whites lived up the hill, and Grant Street was definitely up the hill. I knew that was white territory, growing up in Cochrandale as I did and learning, in theory, where the color and class lines were drawn. But I hadn't really thought about it as something that applied to me. Maybe, I briefly thought, the fact that I was a U.S. Marine made a difference, made all of those invisible barriers null and void.

Nope.

It was the kind of epiphany every young black male has at some point early in his manhood, I suspect. Because we grow up largely separate, like I did in the projects where my mother was one of a handful of whites, we grow up largely naïve. Housing is segregated.

Though we may go to the same schools, we are rarely in the same classes. Cafeterias and sports teams split along jagged racial lines. There are black parks and white parks, black clubs and white clubs, black bars and white bars. So we don't get our reality check, as they might call it today, until we go for an apartment, or a job, and run smack into the white world.

That old lady was my first collision with the whitewashed ceiling of my possibilities. At the time, it hurt. I was going overseas, presumably to fight a foreign enemy in a land I knew nothing about, and the people of my own country wouldn't even give me the courtesy of renting an apartment to me for my pregnant wife. But when my head bounced off of the Second Street color line, it didn't break my skull - it just pissed me off. Lillian and I took the matter to the Pennsylvania Department of Human Relations and lodged a complaint. We would've prevailed, too, had the department not put the matter on hold while I was serving in the Far East. Before I returned, the old landlady died.

That was the North, the land of equal rights. The South is, of course, different, and to this day I'm not sure which one is worse. Down there, as I learned while at Parris Island and Camp Lejeune for Marine Boot Camp, and while attending several military schools thereafter, they dispense with the pleasant charade of integration. If they don't want you in a bar, they meet you at the door, and tell you, "This ain't a black bar, boy." If they don't want you in a neighborhood, they meet you on the street and say, "Why don't you just turn around and go back the way you came, boy?" At least that's how it was in 1972. I haven't been back much since.

And I didn't really get more than a little taste of that Southern hospitality even then, being, as I was, fully engaged in the process of turning from a human being into a U.S. Marine. It started with 13 weeks on Parris Island, a hell designed to turn blacks, whites, reds and yellows into greens - as in "I'm mean, I'm green, I'm a killing machine." Even though the Marines resisted integration for a long time, by the time I got there race didn't matter much. You were treated like a dog no matter what the color of your skin. They could do whatever they wanted to you, and there was no place to run, they constantly reminded you. Once you're on Parris Island, no one, not your mother or your father or even your Congressman, can do a damn thing to get you off. It was good practice for being a black man in America.

When I first arrived on Parris Island, and two big black sergeants - so black all I could see in the predawn darkness was their eyes - jumped on the bus I came on and started screaming and cursing us, I wondered what the hell had possessed me to join the Marines. These guys were huge and hard as tempered steel, and I'd never been called "communist puke" or "a turd" before. But by that time it was too late. "I'm going to give you communist pukes ten seconds to get your fuckin' asses off this bus!" they screamed, and the screaming never stopped from there. At times three would be in my face, one right in front and one on each side, shouting all kinds of senseless curses at the top of their lungs. It was one of the craziest scenes I'd ever seen. But you can't just quit the U.S. Marines.

And the Corps knows exactly what it's doing. In boot camp, those drill sergeants turned me into a rock-hard, mean, green killing machine. No more soft-talking, easy going young man. By the time I got out of boot camp, I was gung-ho to kill. We ate, slept, and breathed that word - "kill" - and when it was over I was hot to get to Vietnam and kill some gooks.

I got a little bit lucky, though. Thanks to taking some typing and business courses in high school, they picked me out as someone with more than ground pounder potential. Despite my fever to kill, I was awarded a job title of communication specialist.

So once I'd learned the basics of killing with a rifle, bayonet, knife or bare hand, rather than handing me a machete and a basic Vietnamese phrase book, they shipped me off to a special school for riot control. That school was part of a government plan to use special Marine units to handle the anti-war activity right at home. Thankfully, it never came to that. So when that was over, I was transferred to Iwakuni, Japan, from where they assigned me to a spanking new communications ship, the U.S.S. Blue Ridge. On that ship we cruised the South China Sea, turning our state-of-the-art, top-secret hardware on the enemy on the ground. We were spies, pure and simple, every one with a top secret security clearance. Though I spent time in Japan, Korea, the Philippines, Thailand and even Cambodia, I never set one foot on that piece of troubled real estate called Vietnam.

As a whole, those days weren't so bad. Still, I knew a career as a leatherneck wasn't for me. I wanted to go home and be a husband and a father, make some real money, and take care that my bride, who I'd barely had a chance to be a husband to, was safe and happy. So when the end of my two year tour came around, I said so long to the Corps and headed back to Cochrandale.

You could take me out of the Marines, but it wasn't so easy to take the Marines out of me. Like most men who've experienced boot camp and been in the Marine Corps, I came out hyped up on a constant flow of adrenaline. My mind was stuck in kick-ass mode, I didn't take shit from anyone. I was a killing machine who couldn't stand being told what to do, but had long since gotten out of the habit of making decisions for himself. I've got to say it took me 10 years to recover from two years with the U.S. Marines.

When I got back, I was black. Not green, not mulatto, not a U.S. Marine, but black, in spite of my Italian momma, because that was what the white folks saw when they looked at me. I joined Lillian back in Cochrandale Projects, where I'd been raised, and set about looking for a job. I wasn't really close to anybody in my mother's family, and my dad was long out of our lives, so I didn't have any connections. But in 1974 in the Mon Valley, you didn't need connections. You showed up at the U.S. Steel employment office, you filled out some papers, and you waited until your phone rang. It wasn't too long before I was down in U.S. Steel's Duquesne Works, picking up scrap metal, hooking coils, and driving the big Ross carriers, 12 or 14 feet high and heavier than a tank.

A lot of blacks had it tough in the mill, which was run mostly by Italians and Eastern Europeans who didn't much like each other and certainly couldn't care less about anybody with African blood in their veins. By that time most of the formal barriers were down, but by tradition a lot of the blacks were still kept out of the good jobs and on the casting gang or in the blast furnace. Like most blacks in the mill, I did have to spend some time in the Basic Oxygen Furnace, with the casting gang, staring into the thousand degree metal and feeling my copper mask heat up until it very nearly burned its shape into my face. But I didn't much mind the mill work. I was generally treated fairly, probably on account of the fact that I still had that Marine Corps intensity in my eyes. The few times they did try me, they learned quickly that I wasn't going to take any shit. After a while I bid into a job working as a brakeman on the narrow-gauge railroad, and although my feet hurt at night, it got me out and away from the worst of the noise, heat and pollution.

And then there was payday, when I had to walk sideways because of the weight of all of the money in my pocket. Whew! In 1977, I was part of the two-car American dream, driving a Chevy Monza to work and back, but tooling around in a canary yellow '77 Lincoln Continental Mark on days off, with the moon roof open in the white leather top. I was stylin'.

And I was moving up in the world. After a year back in Cochrandale, I moved my wife out to Camden Hills in mostly-white West Mifflin. Back then, as now, most realtors only showed you certain areas if you were black, and I think Camden was on the list because it was next to the Allegheny County Airport, a corporate jet and biplane facility. Nonetheless, we were glad to have our own place, outside of the projects where things seemed to be on a downward flight path. Our neighbors whined about the noise, but the whir of twin engines sounded a lot like a song of prosperity to us.

Then in 1977, after the births of Devon and Curtis, we found a three bedroom place in McKeesport. Back then McKeesport was a booming mill town and the second city of Allegheny County, behind only mighty Pittsburgh. If I have any regret from back then, it is that I hardly saw my first two sons, what with working 12 hour shifts, often seven days a week down the mill. But I was building a foundation for a better life. I intended to raise my boys in that house, then pass it down to one or another of them when my time on this earth was at an end. Instead, we would be in that house, watching McKeesport crumble beneath us, until 1992, when we would be driven out by a bunch of thugs no better than most Third World death squads. But more on that later.

While I was fathering kids and changing addresses, the Great American Engine of Prosperity rolled on, and there was no sign it would ever run out of gas. The Vietnam War ended, but the market for steel didn't seem to suffer a whit, as the post-war build-down quickly gave way to Ronald Reagan's arms race with the Soviet Union. Most of the guys out on the railroad thought U.S. Steel was some kind of quasi-arm of the federal government, that it would last forever, that the rolling mills would roll on, and on, and on.

But in the early eighties, from my vantage point out on the railroad, I caught a whiff of a trend. The trains weren't bringing in as much in the way of new or replacement parts anymore. But gondola after gondola of equipment rolled out, bound mostly for U.S. Steel's Edgar Thompson Works - known locally as ET - across the river in Braddock. It seemed clear they were pillaging our mill for old ET, but at such a gradual pace that only us crazy coots on the railroad could see it.

I figured the good days were numbered. After all, there was a Republican in the White House again, a guy named Ronald Reagan, who everybody else seemed to think of as some big, cuddly grandfather figure, but who seemed to me to be more of a grim reaper than a grandfather. Under shifty Dick Nixon, I hadn't had it so good; I'd been out there on a boat, then back in the states hunting for a job, then working shifts in the mill with occasional periods on layoff. Things were okay under Ford, who wasn't really much of anything at all. But my glory days were under Jimmy E. Carter, the president who never got any respect. Well, I didn't have any problem with him. At least people were working.

That wouldn't last. One of Reagan's first acts was to bust the air traffic controllers union. A lot of people cheered, even down in the mills, and said those overpaid white-collar whiners deserved whatever they got. But from my vantage point down on the railroad, I saw them as just a bunch of people trying to make a living, union folks on hourly wages, who were trying to get what they were worth. I mean, the CEOs, presidents, and chairmen of the boards of those big airlines weren't living on rice and beans, I was sure of that. The controllers were just trying to get their share of a fat pie, and near as I could tell that wasn't any crime. But they lost. Somebody else got those jobs, and got less money to do them.

Much the same happened to the miners down in West Virginia, and in the hill country south of Pittsburgh. They got laid off, but those jobs went all the way to South America, as near as I could tell. They were coming after us, I realized, targeting anyone and everyone who insisted on an honest dollar for an honest day's work. They wouldn't be happy until we were all working three jobs, each for minimum wage and no benefits. I knew I was wearing a bull's eye as sure as those controllers and those miners were.

Most of the guys figured U.S. Steel would never go down. You always needed steel, right? For cars, houses, buildings, furniture - and why would anyone bring it in from Japan or Germany when you can make it right here? But for me, it all started coming together. Those Japanese who would visit our mills back in the early seventies, taking notes and laughing quietly among themselves, had it all figured out. The mills that Japan and Germany were firing had continuous casters. The Duquesne Works, where I labored, did not. Even a guy like me, who worked the railroad but kept his eyes open and read as much as he could about the future of steel, knew that continuous casters were the future. Like the casters, the rest of the mill was pretty much obsolete, and U.S. Steel wasn't exactly pouring money into the place. They were just barely keeping it running, and were carting off everything that wasn't nailed down. So by 1983 and '84, when a few of the mills up and down the Monongahela River went idle, I figured it wasn't just a "cyclical downturn," as the liars in the boardrooms called it. This time we were all going down, and we were going down for good.

Most of the guys pooh-poohed doubters like me. As long as the molten metal flowed, as long as the checks cleared, they didn't ask questions. A lot of people don't like to believe that shit stinks.

But in early 1985 the cold end of the Duquesne Works, the end next to the soaring roller coasters of Kennywood Park, shut down. The hot end, down by the Duquesne-McKeesport Bridge, where I worked, lasted until the fall, when they shut the whole thing down for good. Like the rest of the Valley, I went on unemployment.

For a while everybody down there just sat around in the bars, drinking away those unemployment checks and talking about how great it would be when the mills re-opened. Then when the Valley folk saw U.S. Steel carting off the metal walls of our fully-integrated mills to be melted down by mini-mills in Alabama and Tennessee, they scratched their heads and wondered what those crazy executives at the top of their rusty Downtown tower were thinking. I mean, they'd have to replace those walls once the mills were fired up again, right? And when they saw the furnaces dissected and shipped in pieces to China and India, they shrugged and watched the water for the barge which would inevitably come around the bend carrying the brand new continuous caster which must, had to!, be destined for the shores of Old Muddy. And when U.S. Steel bought Marathon Oil and sold the land along the river to the Park Corporation, they patiently waited for the next industrial giant to come and employ us. "That's a prime spot for steelmaking!" they exclaimed. "Easy access by barge, nearby coal and iron reserves, a skilled work force - it'll only be a matter of time before LTV or Bethlehem Steel moves in."

Much of what's left of the Valley is still waiting.

Not me. As my unemployment ran down, I pounded the pavement hard in search of a new job. When I think back on it, that wasn't such a bad time. I got to know my kids better, after 12 years of working up to 80 hour weeks. Devon was 10 years old when the plant gates swung shut for the last time, and he was developing into a responsible boy, holding his own in school, and already becoming popular with the ladies. He stayed out of the kind of trouble a lot of the other kids in the Valley were drifting into; vandalism and small-time gang activity for the boys 10 and 12 years old, and full-fledged gangbanging and drug dealing for the teens. You can't much blame them, really. They were only taking their cue from the adults, many of whom had turned to drinking, drugs and gambling to wile away the hours until the captains of industry would come back to town, take them by the hand, and say "Work for me." It wasn't easy for a child growing up in those surroundings to get up the gumption to rise above the mire around them.

But Devon managed to keep his head above water. He never, thank God, got into drugs or heavy drinking. And though he could defend himself in a pinch, Devon did his best to avoid any violence. It was about that time I decided to do something to make the world safer for young men like him, a decision which eventually led to the formation of Kids for Kids, a youth group aimed at curbing drug abuse. Ironically, it would be the success of Kids for Kids which would lead to my troubles with the Mon Valley's finest, the City of McKeesport Police Department, and the whole political elite in that valley of malice and jealousy. More on that later.

In the meantime, I found a job at the Port Authority of Allegheny County, often called PAT, the Pittsburgh area's public transit agency. From an entry-level gig in the body shop, I moved up to a post as a working foreman on the subway system, then did general maintenance work at PAT headquarters on Pittsburgh's North Side, and eventually ended up servicing the shelters at the system's bus stops. It was mostly night work, which I took to right from the start. It didn't pay like the mills did, but it covered the bills, and that was better, as they say, than the alternative.

One alternative was farting around on welfare or disability, which a lot of the people in the valley are still doing. Another was leaving town. The Valley started emptying out, led by whites scared shitless by real estate agents howling about plunging property values and pitching a paradise in the 'burbs with two cars in every asphalt driveway and a shopping mall on every corner. Well, property values did plunge, thanks to the very real estate agents who predicted just that. And thanks to them the color lines, like the one running just above Second Street in Duquesne, broke down. By about 1990, whoever owned that apartment on Grant Street would have probably kissed my feet to get a paying tenant in there. But by then, with Peeper rounding out my collection of sons, I was long past wanting it.

I had my own house, and it was all paid off, but all around me the "For Sale" signs were going up. Many of them stayed up a long time without attracting much interest from buyers, and some ended up either boarded up or rented to Section 8 tenants. That's how I became acquainted with the Adams family. The Adamses moved to the street in 1991, and right away things got strange. The mother, Carol Adams, had men over all the time. Different men, all the time; men who stayed an hour or so and sneaked out the back, or furtively hurried to their cars with their heads down low. Some of them, I knew, were cops, who came mostly in street clothes and paid most of their visits early in the morning when the only person up and around was a crazy coot who worked at Port Authority, drove a big blue van, and often pulled in after a night's work not long after dawn.

That was about the same time Kids for Kids was really gearing up. That endeavor, which would eventually teach me a lot about what's wrong with this world, was the product of a vision. I was in bed - whether awake or asleep, I'm not sure - when a tiny point of light appeared before my eyes, which then expanded into a near-blinding cloud of brilliance. I wasn't sure what to do, so, naturally, I didn't do anything but try to shield my eyes, and at the same time try to kind of see what the shape of this light was, and try to figure out if this was God or the devil or some kind of bad fever dream. Then the light said to me - or maybe communicated to me is the better description: "Go to Duquesne, and help the children there." And then it was gone. I woke Lillian, who had stayed asleep next to me through the whole thing, and asked her what she thought of it. She said I would have to assume that it was God's voice, though she said I was a pretty unlikely guy to receive a divine vision.

I got up, went to the bathroom, and as I sat on the pot, it occurred to me: drugs! I had been raised in Cochrandale, in Duquesne, and now that rundown old housing project was a viper's pit of junkies and pushers, and the young, particularly, were being sucked in to that culture of despair. One way I could give something back to the community in which I was born and raised would be to do my part to fight the scourge of drugs among Cochrandale's youth. And that night, sitting on the toilet, I vowed to go in there and keep 40 kids off drugs.

So the following week I went down to Cochrandale, where I hadn't spent much time in years, and looked around. It was worse than I'd expected. Hell, back when I was growing up, there were alcoholics and reefer smokers and the occasional smack addict, too. But mostly that started among the older teens, some of whom would develop the sense to pull out of it before it could suck them in completely. What I saw in Cochrandale in 1991 was zoned out junkies on the park benches, walking zombies in the playgrounds, and dealers as young as 10 years old peddling pot for the big men who stayed back in their apartments and counted the cash. I saw parents so degraded by decades of alcoholism and drug abuse that they watched with dull amusement as their 8-, 9-, and 10-year old children drank malt liquor and experimented with marijuana. And I saw the first wave of cocaine babies born, strange creatures that cried all the time, couldn't stand to be held, and wouldn't even look their own parents in the eye. What the hell is going to happen to these, I wondered? And if this goes on much longer, what's going to happen to this whole society?

Not long after that, I headed to the library and picked up a book on starting a non-profit organization. Though I'm not a lawyer - just a high school graduate with a few military courses in riot control - I did the paperwork, paid my $75 incorporation fee, and put in my application for 501(c)(3) status. When the application came through, I put some of my own money in a bank account as the first donation to Kids for Kids.

When I got down to Cochrandale and started talking my idea around to the residents, I got the first of my pleasant surprises: The people there, even many of the old drunks and druggies who roamed the parks in bored stupors every day, were thrilled with the idea of an organization to keep young kids off of drugs. I told the little kids that anyone who wanted to could join the group, and that there would be trips to Cedar Point, Sea World, and maybe even Washington, D.C. for those who stayed off of drugs. For these kids, some of whom had never left Cochrandale in their lives, even going to Pittsburgh was a frightening prospect, and going to Ohio or D.C. was too deliciously terrifying to pass up. So by the end of a few weeks of visits to the projects, I had 40 kids pledging to stay off drugs, and more importantly, to help keep each other off the stuff, too.

Then I set about setting up my network of contacts, from parents to local priests, to teachers and school administrators, to the old folks who sat around on the benches all day and just watched. If any of my 40 kids started using or dealing, I would know about it, fast. But none did, I believe, because the thrill of being a part of the world proved more powerful than the allure of a bottle or a pipe. When we went to Sea World, the look on the kids' faces when confronted with splashing dolphins and seals and killer whales was just so different from the dull, pleasureless stare of the junkies, that I knew I'd hit the mark. And then the roller coasters at Cedar Point, and the monuments in our nation's capital - the kids suddenly knew that there was a great, big, bright world outside of the projects, where not everybody was on a downward spiral. But, I reminded them, it could only be enjoyed properly by those who made the decision to stay off drugs. Even the car trips to these places, across the hill country of Pennsylvania and into the rolling farmland to the east or west, were eye-opening experiences for the kids. They never knew all of this was out there. They never knew anything but the projects, and maybe a slice of blighted Duquesne.

And I took them on one other trip, too: the drug tour. We started out in Cochrandale, where the dealers worked the stairwells and playgrounds; where the blissed out and strung out hung out or passed out on park benches and stairways, and where paranoid users peeked from heavily curtained windows with eyes wide from drug-fed fear.

Then we bussed off to Shuman Center, the local juvenile detention facility. There they got to see what it's like to be stuck in a tiny cell with no right to come and go, and to walk halls full of fear among the big and violent offenders there. Then we checked out the Allegheny County Jail, where over 80 percent of the inmates were in on drug-related offenses. The kids went through the process of being checked in, given a number, and locked up in the ancient cell blocks of what soon after became the old, abandoned county jail. To top off the drug tour, we stopped at a local cemetery, the last stop on most junkies' long, hard trip.

After that tour, I heard one of the kids tell his mother, "You don't have to worry about me doing drugs, mom." All the work was suddenly worth it. My strategy had worked. I hadn't tried to scare them with overblown horror stories, or bombard them with slogans like "Just Say No." I'd just taken them around and let them see it for what it was. And in doing so, this old ex-mill worker had kept one kid out of the grip of substance abuse - at least for a little while.

The folks in the projects, especially the kids' parents, swore by Kids for Kids. Even the dealers gave it grudging acceptance. They knew that I wasn't out to bust them - just to show the kids that there was another way. I never had any problem with them, and when we held neighborhood concerts, some of them actually helped carry the ice and serve the soft drinks.

Unfortunately, almost nobody else in Duquesne was so helpful. Reverend J.T. Pike was the only one out of the city's 23 ministers who took the time to work with me. The school district wouldn't have anything to do with it. They wouldn't even let us use their facilities. The police and politicians weren't just disinterested - they were downright hostile. Even the NAACP president, Rev. Betters, told me he couldn't help. "I'm afraid to go up to Cochrandale," he told me. "They have guns down there." I pointed out that he had The Bible. "Those guns are stronger than this Bible," he said. Hearing that I wondered why he'd decided to be a holy man, rather than a gangster. Needless to say, I never went to Rev. Betters for help again.

People from outside of Duquesne, like Reverend Pitts of Pittsburgh's Powerhouse Church, who toured the projects with me and pronounced it "Satan's hell hole," wondered how I could operate in such an abyss of despair. County Commissioner Barry Napps offered his support for my Christmas campaign to raise funds for toys, and the newspapers wrote about our concerts and field trips in glowing terms. But some, I really believe, felt threatened by the idea of 40 poor, black project kids staying off drugs. I would soon find out who the real enemies of the drug epidemic were - and weren't.

I contacted the chief of police, the mayor of Duquesne and the state legislators by mail and phone, and made them aware of our efforts. None ever offered me a whit of support. Even a request to the mayor's office to fix up a playground on Cochran Street was ignored. Federal money for rebuilding playgrounds was flowing into white neighborhoods all over the county. The newspapers happily put shining monkey bars and merry-go-rounds in white Polish Hill on the front page. But in black Duquesne, where the kids really needed an alternative to the streets? Our cries were met with silence.

I don't know if it was coincidence or not, but about the time Kids for Kids started making an impact, the Adams family moved in next door. I suspected right off that they had an arrangement with the police. My wife and I would see officers, some in street clothes and some in uniform, exiting their home at very early hours of the morning. For a while, we wondered why cops kept coming and going at such odd hours. We didn't yet know that Ms. Adams could often be seen down on McKeesport's Walnut Street, flagging down lone men in cars. A police cruiser was never far off, but somehow Adams stayed free.

Her sons, one in his twenties and the other in his late teens, were a constantly worsening nightmare. The two increasingly got into fights, played music until all hours, drank and did drugs in public and shattered what calm was left with the sound of discharging guns. After their arrival, residents talked about a rise in drug sales and car break ins. One by one, those neighbors started moving away, frightened that our street would descend into lawlessness like so many others in blighted McKeesport. In late 1991, 19 homeowners petitioned to have the Adamses removed from the neighborhood. But nothing was ever done. Except for their early morning visits to the Adams residence, the police continued to ignore Centennial Street.

No, the police never gave them a bit of trouble. And one day when I came home after driving into Pittsburgh at around 11:30 at night, I found Randy Kemp, the sometime boyfriend of one of Mrs.

Adams's daughters, on the edge of my lawn shouting drunkenly and waving a butcher knife around. He shouted his intention to "get me" in retaliation for the petition and our futile efforts to get the police to bring order to our street. As Lillian ran into the house to call the police, Kemp came after me, chasing me repeatedly around the car and waving the blade around like a madman, his stinking, alcoholic breath raining curses down on the back of my neck.

But as he rounded a corner of the car, Kemp tripped, and I guess my Marine instincts kicked in. I was on him in an instant, wrestling the knife away, and when I got it, I put a gash from the middle of his forehead down to the middle of his cheek. He'd tried to kill me, and he got it good - it took 50 staples to put him together again. But though it was my life which was threatened, my property which was invaded, and my wife who called the police, when the cops finally came, it was me, not Kemp, who was slapped with a charge of aggravated assault. It didn't matter who started it, and the cops didn't bother to look beyond Kemp's story.

I eventually beat it on the basis of self-defense. Still, I shouldn't have had to pay my good money to some lawyer for simply keeping my family safe from a drunk with a knife. But I was Leon Grey, the guy who was getting the projects all excited with this Kids for Kids stuff, a black man getting some positive attention in a community that was getting blacker every day. The police and the political powers that be had me in their sights.

That began a campaign of intimidation which hasn't ended to this day. Before long the Adams boys, Vincent and Larry, regularly came after Devon and Curtis. It was more than a typical neighborhood rivalry, the kind which is just part of growing up and might end in a bloody nose or black eye. It seemed to me like a plot to run us out of the community, orchestrated by some cowardly power happy to use these pawns next door to instigate problems on our previously peaceful street. When the Adams boys caught Devon alone and beat him with a tire iron, I knew this was something far more insidious than just youthful animosity. Still, I didn't know how serious it would eventually get. Maybe I was a little naïve at the time, but I contacted the police, and urged them to investigate.

They interviewed Devon, but never bothered to talk to Lillian or myself. After that, they did nothing. No investigation, no arrests, no interrogations, nothing. My daily phone calls to Juvenile Detective Tom Josephs were met with dull excuses: "We're looking for Adams," he'd say, "but we can't find him." I'd tell him that Vincent Adams was right next door, but that wasn't good enough.

Finally, Curtis and I spotted Vincent in a car in front of the house, and chased him down, while Lillian called the police. After a foot race through the McKeesport Streets, past three cops who did nothing to apprehend the wanted Adams, Curtis caught up with him in a women's abuse center, where he took his best shots. I was following in a car, and arrived seconds later, and the cops seconds after that. "I'm sick and tired of doing you all's jobs for you," I told them, as I handed Adams over. "Take this nigger out of here, before I kill him." The cops wanted to arrest me. But I told them, not today, boys. Not today.

Vincent got six months in Shuman Center, the county's juvenile detention facility, but his brother Larry was never arrested or charged. And the only reason even Vincent served any time at all is because Curtis and I chased him down and handed him over. That's when I knew for sure the Adamses were police informants, with that unspoken protection only snitches have. So I decided to take my complaints to the streets.

I planned a protest in front of the McKeesport Police Department, an unprecedented act in a community in which the police aren't much different from a Third World goon squad. All over the Valley, the McKeesport cops were and still are known as a ruthless bunch of enforcers for the political machine. All through their history, they've been linked to numbers running, drug dealing, prostitution, robbery and extortion - the kinds of activities left to organized crime in most towns. A lot of black men have been found dead in McKeesport's jail cells, and a lot of others have been brutalized and beaten without provocation.

So my family talked about maybe shedding some light on this, and talked it around the neighborhood. Although a lot of people agreed that the cops were crooked, few were interested in standing in front of the station with signs. When I mentioned it to a few of the youngsters in Kids for Kids, though, all sorts of sparks started flying. Many of these kids and their families had seen police indifference, unfairness, or outright hostility before. Now some of those young people I'd helped out wanted to come to my aid. It felt good, like I had friends after all. Truth would come from the mouths of babes.

In retrospect, letting those kids join me in front of the station on a warm May day was a mistake. Sure, we got some media attention on the problem of police neglect of the black community, something that had been a non-issue in the Valley and even the whole region before that. The protest also raised awareness about the corrupt practices of the McKeesport Police Department. But the media portrayed it as a protest by Kids for Kids, rather than a protest by Leon Grey that happened to involve a few of the Cochrandale 40. From that time on, my organization was marked.

Chapter 4

Valley of Darkness

My protest against McKeesport's finest started three months of hell which eventually led to the collapse of Kids for Kids and my own flight for my life from the Valley. Twelve hours after the protest, my nephew and Derek Goodman's brother, Corey, was dead, the victim of a shooting. The media made the suggestion that the protest and the shooting were somehow related, but I told them I couldn't see a connection. How could they be connected, unless the police or their proxies killed Corey? Still, the police took weeks to arrest the suspects, who eventually turned themselves in. To this day, it's unclear why Corey was shot down.

For weeks after the rally, I was constantly followed by police cars. My wife was also trailed, and my sons were carefully watched by quiet cops in stationary cruisers. I rightly assumed that this was a first step in a concerted effort to intimidate me, but I wasn't going to back down that easily. Instead, I sold my car and picked up a used one, just to throw them off. Then, within weeks, I sold that one and bought another. And another. During that couple of months I bought and sold five cars in an effort to confuse the cops who now accompanied me everywhere.

But I couldn't trade myself in, and every cop in McKeesport seemed to know me by sight. I suspect they posted my picture on the top of their most wanted list, though I hadn't committed any crime. That made it dangerous to even be out on the streets, but I wasn't about to hide behind the locked door of my home. Back then I would jog five or six miles most mornings, a habit held over from my Marine days. Some days a car, marked or unmarked, would follow me the whole way, or just appear at different points in my route. And one day, as I crossed at an intersection, a cruiser screeched out from behind a bend and swerved my way, so I had to scramble and leap up on the sidewalk to avoid being mashed into that big Chevy's metal grille. I just caught a glimpse of the crew-cut, four-eyed, white mother fucker before he sped away, and I won't soon forget the twisted snarl on his thin, pale lips.

That wasn't the last attempt on my life. One day shortly thereafter I was sitting at home when my phone rang, and a man identified himself as Froggy DeMarco. "Leon Grey?" he asked.

"Yes."

"Umm, Mr. Grey, I heard about your protest. I have some information on some McKeesport cops who are torturing black kids on a vacant lot on my street. Are you interested?"

"How'd you get my number?" I asked. I've always kept an unlisted number.

"Your friend, Officer Kelly gave it to me." Kelly was an older, black McKeesport cop who was quietly sympathetic to my cause. "So, you coming up, or what?"

"Yeah. Where is it?" He told me, and invited me to meet him up at his place. Just come up from the alley behind the houses and meet him in his garage, he said. From there we could proceed to the lot and investigate.

"Yeah, okay," I said, a little warily. "I'll be up in a little while."

"Okay, Mr. Grey," he said. "I'll be waiting for you."

But instead I got on the phone to Officer Kelly. "Who is this Froggy DeMarco?" I asked.

"Oh, Froggy," Kelly said. "He's one of Chief Beltree's good friends. They're real close. He always comes down to the station and bullshits."

I thanked him and sat down to think it over. It didn't add up; a friend of the chief's, calling me, the police department's public enemy number one, about police brutality? But as I pondered, the phone rang again. "Aren't you coming up?" DeMarco's scratchy voice asked.

"Yeah, I'm coming," I said. "I'll be there in a little bit."

I told Lillian that I was going to go up, at least check it out. The whole thing sounded suspicious to her, too, and she tried to convince me not to go. But my curiosity was aroused, and when that happens, there's no turning me back. I just needed to know what these cops and their friends were trying to pull now.

"Well then you aren't going up there alone," she said, and convinced me that it would be better if she drove the car. Her face wasn't as well known in McKeesport as mine. So I grabbed the camcorder and we headed off to DeMarco's house.

On the way up, I got to thinking. There's no way Kelly would have given that guy my number, and it's unlisted. How did this guy find it? Of course, everybody knows cops can get unlisted numbers from the phone company. So it might mean that he was in cahoots with McKeesport's finest on this, intent on setting me up in some way. Only later, after talking to my sister Marie about this strange affair did I realize that DeMarco's son was my mother's doctor. He might have gotten the number that way. But by the time I thought of that possibility, it was already long clear who DeMarco's accomplices were.

Contrary to DeMarco's orders, we bypassed the alleyway behind his house and headed down the main street. I spotted DeMarco's house and noticed a car parked out front with a bunch of antennae sticking out of it and two guys in the front seats. As we drove by, me peeking over the dash and Lily bravely holding her head high so as not to look suspicious, I caught a glimpse of their faces. I'd seen them before. Having lived in McKeesport for 15 years, I knew those faces, and they were City of McKeesport detectives. At the end of the street we turned around and circled back. The two were still sitting in the cruiser, talking quietly to each other.

We proceeded down Grandview and noted that there was no vacant lot. That pretty much did it for Lily, who wanted to get the hell out of there, but I asked her to take a quick ride down the alley behind DeMarco's house. I'll never forget what I saw as we cruised down that narrow way. DeMarco's garage door was half open, and a lantern shown next to it. In the yellow light that pierced the deepening twilight, sitting sideways in an overburdened lawn chair, was a heavy-set man in a white T-shirt and jeans. The yellow light glinted off of an object he held loosely at his side. As we passed, it took the shape of a pistol.

"Lily, let's get out of here," I said, and we high-tailed it down the way and back toward our side of town. "That was a set up," I told her. "I get out of the car, he shoots me full of holes, the cops run back in time to set up the evidence to look like I was robbing DeMarco's house. The headline in the McKeesport Daily News reads: 'Drug Crusader Shot Burglarizing House.' Just another brother shot trying to take from the white man what is rightfully his."

The incident angered me deeply. I wrote letters describing what had happened to the chief of police, my congressman, the FBI, the ACLU and the NAACP. Nothing was done; no investigation by the FBI or local police, no action by the NAACP, nothing.

Chief Beltree wrote back saying his officers weren't trying to kill me. The ACLU told me to write to my senator, governor, mayor, and on and on. Somebody from the FBI called me, but never did investigate my complaint. It was clear I was on my own.

About that time we both started wondering aloud if we shouldn't just get out of McKeesport, maybe flee to the suburbs like much of the rest of the middle class - white and black - had already done. But after talking it over, both Lillian and I agreed that this was our home, and that was something worth fighting for. I told her I wasn't interested in running away from these clowns, and she agreed. Besides, they'd taken their best shots at me, and I was still standing. But about that time, somebody decided to go after my sons.

One day early in that summer of 1992 Curtis had just come home from school and exited the car, when Vincent Adams ran out of his house with a knife in his hand and a gun in his pants. "I'm gonna kick your ass just like we did your brother," he shouted, but Curtis wasn't one to run. He knocked the knife out of Vincent's hand and would have stood his ground and beaten his ass, right in front of half the residents of the street. But as Curtis laid into him and forced him up the street, Larry Adams ran from the house with a gun in his hand. Curtis, intent on Vincent, didn't notice. But thank God the neighbors did, and a few of them cried out, "Watch out, Curtis, he has a gun!" Now, that was a little more than Curtis was used to. There'd been plenty of little scuffles since the Adamses came to town, but never before had they come after my sons with a gun. Curtis ran for the woods. My wife, who was standing on the porch watching the whole thing, screamed for me to come, fast, and I shook off sleep and ran down the stairs. I reached the porch in time to see the whole crazy procession.

Vincent chased after Curtis, and Larry trailed behind him, and I took up the chase after them. As Curtis made the turn on to Cornell Street, Larry shouted, "Get out of the way! I'm gonna cap him," and took aim and squeezed off three or four shots. But he didn't give his brother enough time to move, I suppose, because he put a bullet square in the middle of Vincent's buttocks. Curtis sped off through a woody strip and on to the street behind ours, as the Adams brothers howled in disappointment and pain. Vincent rushed off between two houses on Centennial, howling in pain from being capped in the ass by his older brother Larry.

I ran back home to get my gun. If I had to kill somebody to protect my sons, I thought, so be it. Lillian was broken up and afraid for our lives, but a phone call came in from Curtis saying that he was at a neighbor's house, and unhurt. Curtis asked if he should call the police. "What are they going to do?" I asked.

Lillian was fighting off tears, but she had to get to work, and I offered to drive her. But as we stood thinking on the porch, an Officer Nixon of the McKeesport police drove up and walked right up to my porch, demanding to search the house for Devon, immediately. Nixon wasn't in uniform, but I recognized him as a cop who lived nearby. He hadn't asked for Curtis, mind you, but Devon. I asked on what charges. He said, "Vincent Adams is alleging that Devon shot him." I told them Devon wasn't home, which was true.

"I have to enter to search the premises," the cop said.

"Do you have a warrant?"

"I don't need a warrant," he answered. "I have probable cause. Now stand aside, Mr. Grey."

Two more cops pulled up. "After how you guys have treated me and my family, there's no way I'm going to let you search my house without a warrant." I wasn't about to let these cops - members of the same force that had now tried to kill me twice - into my home without a search warrant. I knew Devon wasn't running around shooting Adamses, whether that would be justified or not. He was off at my sister's house, working on a remodeling project.

"Kiss my ass and get off my porch!" I told Nixon, as the two other cops, Thomas Sears and Tom Josephs, got out of their cruiser and approached. Lillian and Devon's girlfriend Tiffany stood on either side of me. Peeper and his three-month old puppy came up along side of the house, and damned if that puppy didn't start barking at Josephs and Nixon. I was told later that Officer Josephs picked the puppy up and slammed him to the concrete, and told Peeper that he'd shoot the pup if it didn't shut up. But at the time I was concerned mainly with my own life.

Because by this time Officer Nixon was up on my porch, with

Josephs close behind him. "My men found a gun up on the street and a man down," said Josephs, a short and stocky cop with a ruddy face. "We're bringing Devon in for the shooting. You badmouthed the McKeesport Police Department," he added, sneering out of one side of his little mustachioed mouth, "and you can bet we're gonna go hard on your boy Devon."

That was enough to convince me not to cooperate with these Fifes, if I hadn't known already. "Back off!" I told them. "My wife needs to go to work." I stepped down off of the right side of my porch, the side opposite of the one which the cops had mounted. As Nixon repositioned himself, I threw open the car door. Lillian, still up on the porch, started screaming hysterically.

"She's not going anywhere, Grey," Officer Nixon said, pulling his gun and getting into a shooting stance. "Halt, or I'm going to shoot. Put your hands up on the car!"

"Go ahead and shoot!" I yelled, as I thrust open the driver's side door of my 1991 Buick Regal. At that point my anger at the situation got the better of me. McKeesport's finest had refused to prosecute the snitches who'd beaten my son, they'd tried to run me down and if that wasn't enough, they tried to entrap me in a deadly plot. And now these no-good bastards were after my middle son on some bogus, bullshit charges. I immediately slammed shut the driver's door of my Regal and wildly rushed at the trigger-happy Nixon and the .357 Magnum he was aiming right at me.

"Go ahead, mother fucker, and shoot me!" I screamed, as friends and neighbors up and down Centennial Street gawked in horror.

I walked steadily towards that drawn gun, that single black hole which threatened to pump hot metal into my guts, and those two human eyes, flickering from fear to anger toward a building thrill to kill.

I didn't care, and kept marching toward Nixon, silent and snarling. I would have walked right up until that barrel poked me in the chest or blew me away, but a hand fell on my shoulder. I turned, and saw Officer Gene Keating behind me.

"What's the problem, Mr. Grey?" he asked, in a calm and reasonable voice. "Why won't you let these officers search your house?"

"I asked the motherfucker for a warrant," I told him. "He ain't got one." It was hard for me to speak, I was so feverish with rage at

Nixon. But this guy seemed concerned, and I wanted badly for someone to understand.

Keating apologized for Nixon's behavior, but told me I should just stand aside and let them search my house. As we debated the point, I saw Nixon push Lillian out of the way and barge into the house, followed by Josephs and Greenwood. I followed, and as they rushed through my house opening closets, cabinets and dresser drawers and terrifying my grandchildren, I screamed bloody murder. Another pair of cops rushed in, and by the time it was over, Chief Dan Beltree showed up on my sidewalk. I tried to tell him what had happened, but the chief didn't want to hear it. He just walked on by.

They eventually concluded that Devon wasn't there, and left. They never asked me where Devon was, but instructed me to turn him in if I saw him. I got a good laugh out of that.

It would be a long time before that image of the barrel of Nixon's cocked pistol staring me in the face stopped haunting me. Why did I march toward what could easily have been my death, with my wife watching and three kids depending on me for support? Did I want to die, I wondered? Was I so obsessed with saving face and being the tough guy that I was willing to throw away my life over it? Or was that Marine mantra, "Mean, green killing machine," still directing my actions? I tried to work these questions out with a psychologist over the months and years after the incident. Post traumatic stress syndrome, he called it. By the time I'd gotten close to resolving it, plenty more would happen to fuel my inner rage.

I resolved to sue the McKeesport police - a department so poorly trained that its officers threatened citizens with death merely for demanding a warrant - for violating my civil rights. I went to 15 lawyers, all of whom told me that challenging the cops on this was futile. Finally one took me on and filed suit, but he blew it so badly that Judge Thomas dismissed the case. I could have appealed, or gone after the lawyer for malpractice, but by that time my son and cousins had become the victims of the most notorious case of police brutality in Allegheny County history, and my energies were focused on seeing justice done for them.

Meanwhile, Curtis called from a neighbor's house and told us he was shaken up and would be home later. I went out to my sister La Rue's house in Duquesne to pick up Devon. He'd been out there working side by side with a Braddock police officer, helping to remodel La Rue's porch. I told him he was a marked man, but there was no way I was going to turn him in to those fascists. I told him to stay with my sister La Rue, to remain inside and to tell no one where he was.

But on the way home, I was stopped by a black lady police officer. She asked me if I knew where Devon was. The cops were through pissing around with me and my family, she said. My son was to be hunted down and killed, either by the old "resisting arrest" method, or as a "suicide" once in custody. She recommended that I turn Devon in direct to the juvenile detention facility, Shuman Center, as soon as possible. "If he's spotted on the streets of this town," she said, "they'll try to kill him."

So I called Chuck Newton, a lawyer I had used before and who Ron Jackson had recommended. "Take him directly to Shuman Center and turn him in there," Chuck said. "Do it now. And put him in the trunk for the ride over. Don't even let the McKeesport cops get a glimpse of him. He's a fugitive now, and they could justify just about anything if they caught a glimpse of him." He offered to meet me there.

So the next day, I stuffed Devon in the trunk and took him to Shuman Center. Chuck Newton met me there and arranged Devon's surrender. Poor Devon, just 15, was frightened and upset, mad as hell that he should have to sit in a cell for a crime that happened when he was miles away. But Chuck assured us that this was the only way to keep Devon out of the hands of McKeesport's finest. Besides, it would be a short stay, he promised.

The charges they booked him under were attempted murder and aggravated assault, and due to the severity of those charges he was put in solitary for ten days. The newspapers wrote it up as a case of an armed and dangerous shooter, the son of Leon Grey, anti-drug crusader, wanted for shooting a neighbor. After I took him in, the papers characterized it as a family feud between us and the Adamses, where it was really a calculated attempt to take revenge on a family for daring to question the power of the McKeesport police. No attempt was made by either the police or the papers to interview people on our street who saw the actual incident, or to get our side of the story. Judging by the quotes in the papers, the cops had already made it up in their minds that Devon was the shooter, and the media was buying it hook, line and sinker. If I had any respect for either the law or the press, it disappeared that week.

And of course the preliminary hearing, where Devon's innocence was proved and the charges were thrown out, wasn't written up by any of the papers. Nor did the cops ever apologize for falsely accusing my son and dragging his name through the muck. Chuck Newton and I had a dozen witnesses come in to testify that Devon wasn't even in the City of McKeesport that day, but rather he was out at his Aunt La Rue's house in Duquesne working on a deck that whole day. The clincher, I believe, was the Braddock cop he was working beside all day. Neighbors from our street testified as to what really happened, and confirmed that it was the Adamses, not Devon or Curtis, who started the fights and did the shooting. The judge waited until the Adamses were out of the court room, then dismissed the charges. But neither the police nor the district attorney ever investigated any further, and the Adamses were never charged for attempting to kill Curtis or for perjury. To me, that was just further confirmation that the whole thing was orchestrated by the police.

The Adamses, to my amazement, reacted with righteous indignation to the dismissal of the charges, howling about injustice while the judge called for order and pounded her gavel. Outside of the courthouse, they showered threats on us, promising to kill us, firebomb our house, slash our tires. I dutifully reported that to the McKeesport police. Needless to say, nothing was done.

We took the matter to the assistant district attorney, who told me I was harassing him by bringing it to his attention. He told me to get out of his office and never come back, in fact, and threatened to have me arrested if I did. We were troublemakers in McKeesport, he told us. He wasn't going to do anything for us.

By that time the assault by the police and the press on my family was well known in the community, though of course it wasn't covered as such in the papers. When I sent out press releases and invited the media to come out and hear my story, only KDKA TV covered it, and they censored it down to nothing. They ran video of me talking into their microphone, but droned out my voice with their own narration that never did get to the point.

The truth still spreads mainly by word of mouth, especially in

McKeesport, where the Daily News might as well be called the McKeesport National Enquirer. That rag is nothing more than a media arm of the political powers that be. But word of mouth is still a powerful tool, especially in the black community where it may well be the most reliable method of distributing information, in spite of all of its flaws. I started getting calls from people throughout the community who were fed up with the McKeesport cops. Some gave me information about numerous beatings and even the hangings of two young black men, which never came to light in the press or justice system. Others told me that in their neighborhoods, the cops weren't just ignoring the burgeoning drug business; they were participating in it. I carefully wrote up each call for future reference, and locked them away in a set of filing cabinets. When the evidence mounted, I put in a call to the local office of the Drug Enforcement Agency, and gave them an anonymous tip that McKeesport police were dealing drugs. I don't know that anything ever came of it, but to this day I wonder if my call might have been traced, and if it might have had something to do with what happened a few weeks later.

In the middle of all of that there seemed to be a glimmer of hope coming from the political arena. Bill Clinton was running for president, trying to end 12 years of Republican rule. I've never liked Republicans. They've never seemed to be anything to me but a bunch of well-dressed rednecks out to make things hard on the blacks and the poor. The worst parts of my life - first the shutdown of the mills, and now the persecution by the McKeesport police - occurred during Republican administrations. Now this guy from Arkansas was apparently on the verge of kicking George Herbert Walker Bush's butt. And on August 9, 1992, Bill Clinton came to visit little McKeesport.

I was determined to see him, even though it meant going to the little town square next to the police station. Maybe I would, by some freak turn of events, have a chance to speak to the man, to tell him what was going on in this backward town. Who knew? So I and a few family members headed down at the appointed time, and while the crowd was milling around waiting for the candidate's arrival, I plunged into the mob and jockeyed for a good view of the stage.

The place was crawling with secret service, identifiable by the alert, "make my day" look in their eyes and the curly little cords running from their jackets up to their earpieces. At one point I made eye contact with Officer Josephs, the cop who'd told me that the McKeesport police were going to go hard on me and my son because I badmouthed his precious troop of Barney Fifes. I saw him lift his radio to his mouth and look away. I tried not to think much about it. But a few seconds later I was suddenly sandwiched between two secret service men, one in front and one in back, asshole-to-bellybutton. I thought for a moment I was back on parade deck at Paris Island. These guys mashed up against me so hard we were like an Oreo Cookie, only in reverse. The chocolate was on the inside.

"Do you have a problem?" the one in back asked. "What are you doing here?"

"Problem? No, I don't have a problem. I'm waiting to see the candidate," I said. It felt like I was going to pee my pants. These guys, I knew, weren't Mon Valley's finest. They were serious professionals who'd just as soon use your ass for target practice as shake your hand.

"Why don't you get the hell out of here?" one suggested.

"Well, I really did want to see Mr. Clinton," I said.

"Just get the hell out of here before I lock you up," he answered.

"Yes, sir." I squeezed out from between them, and headed back to the car, where I stood a while talking with Officer Kelly. When Clinton's speech was over, my wife and my friend Bill Wright came out of the crowd and the three of us got the hell out of there. I never did catch any of Clinton's speech, much less get a chance to educate the candidate on the unreported underbelly of American policing. Now I know it wasn't that big of a loss.

By that time I felt like a man under siege in my own town, a political prisoner like the ones the U.S. government said were locked up or under house arrest in China and Russia. I had to get away. So on August 15 we left McKeesport for a week in Port Clinton, Ohio, where we frequently vacationed. It's a little town out on a sliver of land jutting into Lake Erie, about half way between Cleveland and Toledo. The breezes off of the lakes keep it comfortable all summer, and there's plenty of boating, fishing, swimming and plain old laying around to do. It seemed like a good place to get away from the stifling heat of McKeesport, the odor of chemicals floating up from the remaining mills, and the worsening oppression. We were determined to get some R and R, to and get in touch with ourselves as a family again, before returning to the war.

But on the second day up, at 11:30 p.m., the phone rang. It was my sister La Rue. "Buster, I have some bad news for you," she said.

I could tell from her voice that something was very wrong. I felt my guts twist. "What's up?"

"Buster, the chief of the McKeesport Fire Department called me. He told me you had a house fire. Every room in your house is burned up."

Shit. My heart sank just as my temper rose. The fucking cowards hadn't been able to take me on face to face, hadn't been able to stare me down even with a gun pointed at my chest. They'd been unable to frame my son, beaten as they were by the gaping holes in their own pathetic detective work. But the day I left town, seeking only a week's respite from the war, they'd gone after my home. Cowards. It didn't surprise me though. The Adamses had been threatening to firebomb our house on a regular basis ever since we'd gotten Vincent arrested for beating Devon. And judging from prior experience, they wouldn't have to worry about the police getting in their way.

"The fire department called me to ask your whereabouts," La Rue went on. "They said you had a house fire and all the rooms are burned up pretty bad." She had also informed the fire department of the frequent threats to burn the house down made by the Adamses. They hadn't expressed any interest.

I decided the fire department and the house and everything else could wait. I was on vacation, and frankly didn't see any reason to cut it short. The damage was done, so what was the sense? The next day I did call the insurance company and told them what had happened. But I wasn't about to just break off my vacation, or upset my wife and kids.

So I decided not to tell Lillian and the kids. This was their vacation, and although it was ruined for me, it wouldn't be ruined for them. Lillian kept asking me what was wrong, why I seemed so aloof, so distant. I just told her it must be the stress of the last few months working its way out of me. Only on the drive home did I pull over and tell her that our house had burned. Something inside of her seemed to break. First a coma-like shock, then anger and then tears came one after the other on that long ride back.

Back at home, I found that the lock on my side door was broken, with scratch marks on the door frame like a jimmy leaves, though nothing about that appeared on the police report. Nor did anything appear there about the chickenwire fence between our house and the Adamses' place being bent badly just across from that door. The structure of our house was reasonably intact, but every room was singed from floor to ceiling. Everything we owned was spilled all over the place, every drawer pulled out. The drop ceilings I had painstakingly put up were even torn down. My stereo and some of our jewelry were gone. Oddly, my papers, including those pertaining to Kids for Kids, were safe in the metal filing cabinet - except for one odd exception: the files containing witness reports of the criminal activity of the McKeesport police. Those were gone.

The neighbors, who had stood watching the blaze, told me that the police had been running in and out of the burning building even before the fire department came. It was unusual, we agreed, for police to venture into a burning building. Whatever they were doing in there, it sure didn't appear on the police report, either.

Several insurance adjusters interrogated me to no end, asking me all kinds of questions about how long I'd had this vacation planned, why I went when I did, my financial situation, my enemies. Finally I asked them, "Guys, do I need a lawyer for this?"

"Need a lawyer?" one answered. "For what?" The implication I heard in his voice was that only the guilty needed lawyers. I'd seen enough to know that wasn't true.

But I went on and answered their questions, and eventually provided them with receipts, hotel bills and camcorder tapes proving that we were all up in Port Clinton when the dirty deed was done. The insurance company ruled it arson and paid the claim without finding the firebug. The police, they noted, were first on the scene of the fire, but didn't do much in the way of an investigation. That being the case, it was well nigh impossible to catch the culprit.

I was willing to rebuild my home, which was all paid up. It was my right as a man, as an American, and as an ex-Marine, to live where I wanted to, I reminded anyone who would listen. But that event pretty much convinced Lillian that we were in danger in McKeesport. Our children were in danger. I couldn't let my manly stubbornness, she reminded me, endanger Devon, Curtis and Peeper. Even the insurance adjuster, when he heard about all of our problems with the local police, advised us to forget about rebuilding and just get the hell out of the city. So while we stayed with one of my sisters, we started shopping for a new home, outside of the Mon Valley where I'd lived all of my life.

We settled on Monroeville, a giant suburb of Pittsburgh just outside of the Valley. Again, I was bouncing my head against color lines, because Monroeville was, and is, pretty much lily white. And it became clear pretty quickly that the real estate agents were only showing me certain areas, little crannies of suburbia where people of color were let live. I asked about other areas, but was invariably told, "That area is out of your price range." And maybe it was true. But it felt a lot like it had with that old lady up on Grant Street in Duquesne, the one who'd said, "I can't rent you this apartment. See, you and your wife are black."

For better or worse, we ended up in one of Monroeville's little pockets of color, an area called Garden City. I wanted an in-ground pool, plus a paved driveway and two-car garage, and that's what I got. Supplanted from the Valley, I let Kids for Kids fall by the wayside. Other than a dragging legal action I did nothing to further my feud with the McKeesport Police Department. For a year and a half I tried to live my life in relative tranquillity, just doing my job, plus caring for my kids and sometimes Devon's growing brood. Things weren't the same, though. I had never before seen the need to keep weapons in my home. But after what we'd gone through back in the Valley, I started stocking up. When those old tensions bubbled up again, I took my AK-47, TEC-9 or shotgun out and rained metal rage on targets up at a shooting range in Warrendale, north of Pittsburgh. It was, relatively speaking, a peaceful time.

It was during that time that I got around to writing to my senators and congressmen and state legislators. At the height of the McKeesport police department's effort to run me out of town, I contacted the local NAACP and ACLU chapters for help. Both told me that there was nothing they could do, their hands were tied, but had I written to my Congressman? So I finally did, in October of 1993, outlining the whole series of events, communicating the pain my family suffered at the hands of the chiefs of police and reiterating the slanders published by the McKeesport Daily News.

"I am charging the McKeesport and Duquesne Police Departments with the following misconduct violations," I wrote.

"Conspiracy to murder me and my children, civil rights violations, slander, harassment, intimidation, terrorism (Gestapo tactics), denying this family police protection and service from criminal elements, filing false police reports and documents, false arrest and imprisonment, conspiracy to arrest and imprison me and my children, biased police investigations, conspiring with criminal elements to murder and harm me and my children."

I followed up my letter with phone calls to the offices of my senators, congressman, and state legislators. My representatives in Washington and Harrisburg never directly returned my calls, but their aides told me, "It sounds like a state problem. We can't get involved." My state legislators told me it was a county problem. They couldn't get involved. And the county? They suggested I take it up with McKeesport Mayor Lou Dunn. Yeah, right!

So that was pretty much as far as I took my search for justice. Until a bunch of Clairton cops apprehended and brutally beat my son and two nephews early in the morning on March 6, 1994. That shattered the peace, and now I'm not sure it will ever be restored.

* * *

When my sister Marie called me in tears and told me that our boys were beaten, the sensation that everything was spinning out of control felt unpleasantly familiar. But unlike the war in McKeesport, this time I'd been caught off guard. When Devon was in solitary down at Shuman Center for a crime he didn't commit, I felt helpless, but at least I knew the facts and I knew where my son was. All of the sudden I had no idea where he was, what the circumstances were, or who held the power of life and death over my boy.

Marie told me that her information came from Tyrone Morris, a black Clairton constable who had transported the three cousins to Jefferson Hospital. "He also told me that I should get a lawyer because the boys were beaten up very badly by the police," she said.

"Our kids were beaten?" I yelled. "Why were they beaten?"

"I don't know why. But Constable Morris told me that they were accused of shooting at a car driven by an off-duty police officer on Route 837."

"Why would they shoot at an off-duty police officer?" I asked. It just didn't seem like something those three would do.

"Buster," Marie said, fighting back tears, "you know how the police lie. I don't believe a word of it."

I didn't know what to believe. My son and his cousins weren't gangbangers, and certainly weren't in the habit of shooting at passing cars. And Devon and Derek, at least, weren't the kind to disrespect a police officer to the point of earning a crack on the head. At the time, I didn't know Little Sonny very well, other than having heard that he'd made some poor judgment calls in the past. Still, he didn't impress me as a shooter or a tough guy. All in all, the three weren't angels, precisely, but they were wimps. "Marie, please calm down," I said. "I'm going to call the Clairton police station and find out what in the hell happened to our kids. You stay by the phone and I'll get back with you as soon as possible."

It seemed like a reasonable plan. But as I hung up the phone, rage rushed through me. In my mind, I was in my van, Mr. Justice hanging from my shoulder, on the way to the Clairton station to cap every cop in sight. All of the old wounds, all of the humiliations I'd endured at the hands of the McKeesport cops were opening up again.

"Dad, Dad, come quick," my son Curtis called from the next room. "Devon and them are being talked about on the television. They made the 12 o'clock news."

I rushed over. Sure enough, the anchor was in the middle of a story about three young black men who were "arrested for allegedly ambushing, shooting at, beating and hospitalizing an off-duty Clairton police officer. Sonny Brown, Devon Grey and Derek Goodman have been arrested for allegedly shooting at off-duty police officer Clyde Mimms, who was traveling along Route 837 into Clairton. The three men were charged with aggravated assault, conspiracy, reckless endangerment, possession of a firearm without a license, and receiving stolen property. Grey and Brown are being held in the Allegheny County Jail in lieu of $50,000 bail. Goodman is being held on $10,000 bail."

The anchor never mentioned anything about the boys being beaten, nor that the three young men were taken to Jefferson Hospital. I wondered momentarily, hopefully, if the beating was a fiction, or an exaggeration passed on to Marie by some constable with a chip on his shoulder. But I doubted it. Knowing how the media tended to handle things from my days running Kids for Kids and being harassed by the McKeesport cops, I figured that if anybody had their story wrong, it was those bums.

The name of the cop sounded right, though. The name Clyde Mimms was familiar to me from my McKeesport days. During part of that time he'd been employed by the McKeesport Police Department, though some time in the early 1990s he was given his walking papers. Only once did I have any contact with the guy - when someone broke into my car and Mimms was sent to "investigate." He came to check it out, but never left his car, never examined the shattered glass, and never made an arrest. He probably thought it was hopeless, and he was probably right. Still, he could have pretended to care.

The guy never messed with me, I'll say that, but he had a reputation for cracking heads. I'd heard all about him back when I was running Kids for Kids and serving as the unofficial scribe for the Valley's downtrodden masses. If this was the fucker who'd beat up my kid, it would be all the more satisfying to take him down.

My son Curtis stood there, watching my face turn dark and brooding. "Something isn't right," I said to him. "I find it hard to believe they did something that stupid. Shooting? Devon doesn't have a gun, and I've never seen Derek or Little Sonny with one. And beating an off-duty cop to the point that he needed to be hospitalized? Could those skinny wimps have done that? I don't think so."

"Those boys don't have the guts to shoot a woodchuck," said Curtis.

"Nor did they mention that the boys were beaten, which is the information Aunt Marie is getting." It wasn't too unusual, though, for the media to only report one side of the story. And when one side was the cops and the other side was a bunch of young black men, you could bet it would be the cops' side which would make the news, without so much as an attempt to contact the accused. And because all people ever hear is the cops' side, they naturally start thinking that the cops are always right. That's why juries almost never convict a cop of a killing or beating committed in the line of duty; they're brainwashed in advance by the media.

"I'm gonna call that police department, and when I'm finished I'm going to go down to Clairton and find out what happened," I told

Curtis. I tried to hide the crazy anger in my eyes.

But he'd seen me this way before. "Dad, please don't get into any trouble with those cops over there," he urged. "You know how they try to provoke you, so please be careful. We don't need you in jail, too."

He got up and walked over to me. But by that time my mask was cracking, and I felt the beginnings of tears of rage in the corners of my eyes. "Don't worry about me, son," I told him, putting a hand on his shoulder. "I'm not afraid of those no good Nazi bastards. Son, they have one chance to put their damn hands on me. The best thing they can do is leave me the hell alone. Yaw see, I'm not a toy they can play with or a teenager they can beat on. I'll pull a John Rambo on their asses and do them the way they did those boys. And when I get done kicking their asses, I'll set the whole damn town on fire!"

I was raving now, and Curtis took a step back. "Son, I hope those Nazi bastards do provoke me! I'll teach them a bit about ghetto justice."

Curtis just stared in silence. I knew that he'd appreciated the relative peace of our life in Monroeville, after an adolescence marked by conflict with the Adamses and the cops. Now he saw that peace shattered, and it hurt him. I felt for him.

But over and above that I felt a rising nausea when I thought of those bastards with badges who thought they could beat up on black people like they owned them, like they were still slaves. I vowed they wouldn't get away with this one, and picked up the phone book. Clairton Police Department. I dialed.

"Clairton P.D. Officer Smith here," a white voice answered. "Can I help you?"

"I want to talk to someone in charge," I demanded. "Is there anyone in charge?"

"Right now there is no one in charge, sir."

"The chief is not in charge?"

"Yeah, but not today."

"Look, I want you to get a hold of the chief, because this incident with Devon Grey, my son, is going to spark something that a lot of people are going to regret. This isn't a threat; it's a promise."

Suddenly the self-assurance in his voice melted away. "Incident with your, umm, son?" he stammered. "I don't know anything about any incident."

"Well, if my son was beaten the way it's been explained to me then the officers involved had better stand the fuck by. They're going to have to answer to me. I want your chief to call me right now."

"Okay. I'll try to reach him."

"Tell your chief I'm going to call every media source in this damn town, because this incident should never have happened. Why are police officers beating young black men, sending them to the hospital? What kind of department are you running over there? Is this the L.A.P.D?"

"No, sir, and I honestly can't tell you anything. All I know is that three boys were arrested."

Then the thin dam holding back my anger broke altogether. "Well, you tell the chief of police to call me right now. I am under psychiatric care and at any minute I may snap. Now, if you guys want a mess on your hands, then that's all right with me! But it's not going to be with any kids, but with an ex-Marine and Vietnam vet! You've fucked with the wrong people, so tell your chief that. If he's not man enough to call me, then I'm coming over in a ball of fire, and I'm not bullshitting. This is not a fucking threat, but a warning. The officers who beat my son and nephews will answer to me, and believe me, I am not afraid of dying. I've been to the mountaintop. By the way, why don't you cops beat up those fucking politicians who steal all the money from the people? Why not beat up on Clinton for the way he's doing the people in this country? Why must you fuckers beat up on innocent black kids? Why is it always the black people who you beat and murder? Why do you always consider a black kid a threat, subhuman, or a gangbanger? Just because he's black?"

My questions weren't answered - they still haven't been, in fact. "All I know," said Officer Smith, "is that three guys were arrested for shooting at an individual out of their vehicle."

"Were you there?" I answered. "Did you witness what happened? Because I don't believe it. I know how you people operate. I've had first hand experience with the police in the past and you're nothing but a bunch of liars and criminals masquerading as police officers. You can mark my words that the officers who beat my son are going to have to answer to me. I'm not bullshitting you! If you think that Rambo did a job on that mother fucking town in 'First Blood,' then you haven't seen nothing yet. Let me ask you something, brother: Are you prepared to die? Because I sure am."

"You don't even know who you're talking to!" Smith exclaimed. And in a sense he was right, because I had no idea whether he'd played any part in the beating of my son or not. But he was a cop, and at the moment that was enough.

"I don't give a damn who you are. I am asking you a question: Do you have a cause to die for?"

He didn't answer.

"I didn't think so. Well, tell your chief to call me as soon as possible and thank you very much, sir."

"All right," said Smith, as the phone hurdled from my ear to its cradle, and our conversation was ended.

I didn't wait around, though, but instead went upstairs and grabbed my AK and headed for the door. Would I have stormed the station and taken out everybody inside, thereby becoming the most notorious cop killer in the history of Western Pennsylvania? Quite possibly. Maybe I would have cooled off on the way over there, and left the gun in the van. Maybe I would have walked in and tried to talk it out first. And maybe that would have been so exasperating that I would have gone back out to the van, retrieved my weapons, and then come in, guns blazing. There's no way of knowing.

Ron and Peeper intercepted me just in time, as I reached the door of the van, and I ended up stowing Mr. Justice back in the bedroom closet. The newscast Ron had watched put the incident out on the Ravensburg Bridge, so we decided to start there. We took Ron's 4x4 down Route 837. At that point I didn't know we were tracing the route of the previous night's high speed chase. We passed the Clairton Municipal Building and pulled the 4x4 up short of the narrow, two-lane bridge, dismounted and started walking across.

To this day it frightens me to think that my son was beaten on that particular bridge, and to imagine my nephew dangling over the railing, his face and torso suspended over the chasm below. The Ravensburg Bridge crosses a steep, deep breach in the earth, flanked by white walls of raw stone and dotted with tenacious trees holding for dear life to the cliff faces there. At the bottom it's just wide enough to run two railroad tracks on gravely beds. A fall from this bridge would have shattered bone and pierced flesh and quite likely ended in a lonely death in a cold, unforgiving place.

About half way across the bridge, we found the first evidence of the beating. A series of potholes on the outbound side of the bridge were full of a dark mixture of dirty meltwater and blood. There were also crimson stains on the curb nearby. Ron, who seemed to be doing the thinking for both of us that afternoon, went back to the 4x4 and brought out a camera. "Get it all, man," I said.

Even at midday it was freezing out on that bridge, with the wind whipping down the gorge. What a place this was to be beaten, especially in the middle of the night, in the darkest, coldest hours with little hope of a witness driving by or stopping to check out the scene. I tried to piece together the scene, but it was impossible. Except for the blood, there were no clues as to what had happened - why the young men had been pulled over, how they'd been removed from the car, and who had been beaten when and by how many attackers. I wondered if the blood in the holes was that of my son, Derek, Little Sonny, or all three mingled.

"Buster, I got it all right here," Ron said, tapping the camera. He gripped my shoulder, and stopped my mad pacing back and forth. "You doin' O.K?"

"Yeah, man, I'm O.K. I just want to get some justice. Some kind of justice."

"You think you're O.K. to accompany me into that police station, Buster? Just to ask a few questions. You think you can keep your cool?"

"Oh, yeah, I'll be fine."

"You'd better, because laying into them isn't going to get us any information. You get in their faces, they're just gonna clam up. Got that?"

"Got it. But maybe you oughtta ask the first few questions. I'm not sure how reserved I can be right now."

"Sure, buddy. No problem."

We walked back down the length of the bridge, me wishing there was some way to preserve that bloody scene intact for some judge and jury. But we'd done the next best thing by photographing it. Doing our own investigation felt like the right thing, rather than turning it over to some half-ass assistant district attorney or something. The D.A., Bob Pratt, was nothing but an ex-chief of police, a close associate of the heads of the Fraternal Order of Police, and an all-around apologist for the rogue cops rampant in the county. How could a cop be expected to investigate cops? We would have to get the facts ourselves.

"And then?" asked Ron.

"And then I'm going to take this to the FBI," I said. It was something I'd decided on the way over in the 4x4. "I don't know if we'll get any justice by that route either. But if we're going legit with this thing, then we're gonna go all the way to the top."

We climbed back in the 4x4 and pulled into the back lot of the municipal building. I was amazed at what I saw. The glass door to the police station was marred by a long, thick streak of smeared blood, as if someone's lacerated face had been pushed across it. Nearby, a hard-packed mound of ice and snow was also stained red, especially around and in a bowling ball sized indentation. I was incredulous. Here we were, in the middle of the afternoon, and these monsters hadn't yet cleaned up the blood from the previous night's adventures! Ron took pictures, and then we yanked on the handle of the glass door. Locked. Ron banged on it, and a black head peeked into the hallway from a room off to the right. It was Officer Mimms. I recognized him from back in McKeesport, but was a little surprised to see him. Didn't the news report say he was hospitalized? He looked a little bleary-eyed to me, but his arrogant face showed no sign of injury. I doubted the blood on the snow and door was his.

Officer Mimms ducked back inside, then peeked out again, this time with a walkie-talkie up against his face. Calling in reinforcements? I wondered if he guessed who we were, or if he remembered me from that brief investigation years ago. Then he emerged from his little room, tall and big-chested but with the fear in his eyes of a bully whose bluff has been called. As he approached the door, Ron gently pushed me back, said, "Let me do the talking, Buster. You're too fired up."

I nodded. Mimms pushed the door open a crack, and before he could slam it back shut we were inside, and Ron was in his face. "What happened last night with those three young men out on that bridge?" he demanded. "Those were my nephews, and I want to see the chief now. So you tell us what you know."

"Look, my chief isn't here. He told me not to discuss this case," he said, his right foot dancing forward and back.

"Well, if you don't want to talk about it, then I'm going to get the FBI to investigate. How do you like that prospect?"

Officer Mimms turned and ran back into the room he'd earlier peeked out of. We heard a bolt turn. He'd locked himself in. We walked up and peered in a window, saw the big, bad cop hiding under a table with a walkie-talkie up against his face. The police station was, by all appearances, at our mercy.

But just then a squad car pulled up outside, and in rushed a white cop with "Smith" printed on his nameplate. He was a short guy, with a big gut and a nervous way of shifting his eyes around. This Smith was the one I'd spoken to on the phone, and he seemed to know immediately who we were. Maybe Mimms had radioed him. "Umm, can I help you?" he asked.

"Where's the chief?" Ron asked.

"Fishing," said Smith.

"Fishing?" Ron asked, incredulous. "The man is fishing in the middle of the winter?"

Smith twitched. "Oh, wait, he went to take his daughter somewhere. Out of state."

"A minute ago, he was fishing," Ron said.

And Officer Mimms had said that the chief had told him not to talk about the case. So the chief, who was either out of state or out casting his line on some lonely, wind-swept lake, knew about the incident. How dumb did these Barnie Fifes think we were?

"Who beat those three boys last night?" Ron asked.

Smith backed up, started waving his hands around. "I didn't have anything to do with it!" he protested. "I wasn't even on duty last night."

It was ridiculous in the most disgusting way, seeing these cops lie and deny and make general idiots of themselves under interrogation by two men simply in search of the truth. I could hold my peace no longer. "It stinks in here!" I heard myself shout. "You cops stink. It stinks! Stinks! Stinks!"

Smith hurried past us and disappeared into some side room, no doubt to call in reinforcements. "You guys think you're some kind of Wyatt Earps," I shouted after him, "that you can do what you want. Well, you're wrong!"

Ron grabbed my shoulder. "Buster, it's time to go," he said. I knew he was right. We were on their turf now, armed only with a lot of questions and a minimum of knowledge. As much as I'd have liked to give them hell right then and there, my time had not yet come. I let Ron coax me out of there and into the 4x4, and he hurried me home.

* * *

That afternoon, I took an anguished call from Marie and another from Devon, who was still locked up in the Allegheny County Jail. He filled me in on the details of the high speed chase, the use of the Camaro for target practice by the Fifes, the kicking, the beating, the terrorism and torture. "We got a ride to the hospital with Constable Morris," he said.

"Why didn't the police take you guys to the hospital?" I asked.

"They said they didn't have enough cars to take us," Devon answered. "I think Morris said it was a guy named Clyde Mimms who beat us, a black cop who used to be a McKeesport police officer. Soon as he saw us, Morris said, 'I see you boys have had a run-in with Clyde Mimms.'"

But it wasn't just Mimms, he told me. It was also the two white cops who'd kicked, beaten, harassed and threatened the three young men. And it was the other Clairton and Jefferson Borough cops who'd stood around watching, or laughing, or goading their sadistic colleagues on. And it was a system which allowed these monsters the power to make their own laws, write their own codes of enforcement, come to their own verdicts, and administer their own punishments on the citizenry, and particularly the second-class citizenry called black America. I vowed war on Mimms, the other cops, the Clairton P.D., and the whole structure of authoritarian rule in the Mon Valley and America itself. The next day I would not only go to the FBI and the courts, but I would launch a media crusade and a one-man campaign against all of the forces which allowed my son to be shot at, kicked, beaten to unconsciousness while handcuffed, threatened with death and tossed in a cell without medical treatment. I'd see where justice could be found.

Chapter 5

The Truth Comes Out

They say everyone gets 15 minutes of fame. For a lot of young black men, that 15 minutes consists of a few seconds on the evening news, in handcuffs, and a write-up on the police blotter page of the local rag, complete with grainy mug-shot.

That's how it could have been for Devon, Derek and Little Sonny. In fact, that's how it was for the first few days after the beating. News reports on the case referred to them as the three blacks males who'd fired on, injured, beaten or even hospitalized an off-duty Clairton police officer. While I calmed anxious relatives and arranged to bail Devon and Derek out of the ancient Allegheny County Jail, the cops were out putting their spin on the story, weaving fictions that, through the media's laziness, became the printed record.

Most people assume that printed record is the truth. Acquaintances and co-workers to this day remember those initial press reports above anything else. "Oh yeah," they say, "those kids who shot at the cop and got arrested." Little do they suspect that those newscasts and articles were built on fabrications by a news media that is lucky if it can get one side of the story right, let alone seek out the other.

After Devon called from the Allegheny County Jail, I got out the phone book and started burning up the lines. All weekend, it seemed, I was leaving phone messages. I put in some 10 calls to Clairton Public Safety Director William Abbet and a dozen others to local TV stations and newspapers, all of which went unreturned. By Monday I'd made the $50,000 bail for Devon and the $10,000 for Derek by putting up my house as collateral, and my sister Marie was in the process of putting her house up to cover the $50,000 needed to get Sonny out. Devon and Derek would be released that day, and I was determined not to let that event go unnoticed. After a flurry of phone calls I finally got Ralph Destry, a TV reporter from KDKA TV-2 who I knew from back in the days when he covered the steelworkers' union.

Destry had heard of the case. "Yeah, people have been calling the station, wondering what happened there," he said. "Wasn't that police officer, Mimms, taken to the hospital?" he asked.

"That's a fucking lie," I answered. "Man, those cops have manipulated you people in the media, and you've bought it hook, line and sinker."

"Well, what happened then?" Destry asked. I told him that it was the three accused men who were taken to the hospital. My voice rose in anger as I related to him what Devon had told me over the phone from the Allegheny County Jail. My son had been beaten by one Clairton officer, kicked in the face repeatedly by another when he was told to bend over and remove his boots, and threatened at gunpoint by a third. My nephew had been beaten with a shotgun, kicked and dangled over the edge of a bridge. The two would be released later that day, and their bruises were still fresh.

"Oh, my God," said Ralph. "You're saying that they were kicked, punched and threatened at gunpoint by police officers? Are you alleging police brutality?"

"You're damn right."

"And your son is going to be released today?" he asked.

"Yes."

"Can you tell me what time? I can have a news camera there."

"Some time after 6 o'clock. I'll call you when I know more."

"Please do, Mr. Grey. This sounds like an interesting story for KDKA. Do you think your kids will mind being interviewed for the cameras?"

"They're not going to mind it. Come on down Ralph. The Clairton police are saying that nothing happened, but we saw enough blood on that bridge and outside the station to know that something hideous happened there."

That evening, Devon and Derek staggered out of the county jail. The guards, I later learned, had warned Devon that the media was outside, and that he'd better not say anything to them.

"Kiss my ass," Devon told them. "I'm gonna say what I want."

And he did. As Devon was walking down the steps, he shouted, "Look what the cops do to black people in this country!"

Devon and Derek then told Destry and the camera about the chase and the beatings both on the bridge and inside the police station. It was the first time such accusations had really gotten any media coverage in Western Pennsylvania, and it shocked the region. But more shocking than the words were the images of two young men just out of police custody, their faces blotched with bruises and their scalps marred with bald spots where tufts of hair had been ripped free. Derek's hair stood straight up in every direction, as if he was Don King's little brother. Devon's ears were black and a quarter-inch hole had opened up on the right side of his swollen nose. Pittsburgh and environs, with their long history of reverence for the police, hadn't seen film like this before.

The Clairton police had told the media and the people lies. They'd done nothing less than try to cover up the heinous crimes committed by the cops on that bridge. They'd tried to portray the incident as just another instance of a noble police officer surviving an encounter with the dark forces that plague violent society. Destry told me that when he called Abbet prior to interviewing Devon and Derek, Abbet had told him there was no story there, that nothing happened. But those images of Devon and Derek blew a hole in that illusion. Something had happened to these young men while in police custody - the pictures didn't lie. Western Pennsylvania would be forced to consider the possibility that the police, rather than being the solution to our society's ills, might be part of the problem.

It felt like the right first step. We had to get the truth out in front of the people. The Clairton police, it seemed, weren't interested in cooperating, or even in speaking with me and the young men. If they had returned our calls and done something more than wring their hands and say, "Nothing happened," I might never have gone to the FBI or media. As it was, if justice would be done, it would be the result of dogged persistence on our part and public scrutiny intense enough to keep the government from sweeping this under the carpet. But seeing them before the cameras with their faces discolored, looking ragged, hungry and tired as goddamned POWs released by the Viet Cong, made me sick to my stomach. At that moment part of me wished I had gone the other route - the route I'd been headed for a few days back, before I was intercepted in my driveway by Ron Jackson and Peeper, and convinced to put the AK-47 away.

I'd taken this route instead, and at least Destry seemed interested. The 11 o'clock newscast led with the young men's story. Destry stressed that the beatings were "alleged" and occurred after the boys allegedly fired on a police officer - wording which made us shake our heads in disbelief. "Alleged?" Curtis said. "How can they show film of those boys' faces and say the beatings are alleged?"

The boys' personal effects were still inside the Clairton Police Station, so we had no choice but to go back into the belly of the beast. Ron Jackson picked up Devon, Derek and myself and we headed on in, unsure of what we would find or how we'd be received. All I could think of, walking up to those glass doors, was the blood stains I'd seen on the snow. And as we entered, the image flashing through my mind was the barrel of a gun, resting right between my son's eyes.

We went up to the window and gave the three names to the cop there. He was a puffy-cheeked little guy with a rodent-like manner. You could almost see long whiskers sticking out from both sides of his pursed mouth.

As he walked back to get the wallets and things they'd seized, Derek grabbed my sleeve. "That's the dude who kicked Devon in the face and kicked me in the balls," he said. "The karate kid."

"Looks more like Mickey Mouse to me," I said. I turned to Devon. "You agree that's the one?"

"That's him. Told me to take off my boots and then kicked me in the face when I leaned over to do it. Twice."

Ron Jackson nudged me away from the window as the Mickey Mouse cop returned. I got a look at his name plate: D. Rahis.

He passed the few small items under the glass. "Anything else I can help you with?"

"Sure," said Ron Jackson. "You tell your boys that I got the three men they beat out of jail. I'm sure you all thought they were going to be in jail until their injuries had healed. You thought because they were black, their families couldn't make bail. Well, that didn't happen. We aren't going to let this go unnoticed."

"Hey, look, I wasn't even on duty that night," Rahis said. "I didn't have anything to do with any of ... whatever happened."
"You'll wish you didn't."

That first night, Curtis and Peeper rallied around their brother in their own quiet way, staying close to him and listening to his nightmare story. They've been lucky enough not to have inheriting my explosive disposition. While I got outraged and burned up the phone lines and stomped around the house, they showed solidarity with their brother in a peaceful way. I suspect growing up with the heat from the

McKeesport cops and their proxies the Adams's somehow tempered my sons, made them resistant to tragedy. I hope that quality serves them well, though I wonder whether the kind of anger I feel isn't bottled up somewhere deep down inside them, waiting to burst out.

Yes, we'd been through the fire and the flood before. But this one, I could tell, hurt Lillian more than even the torching of our home had. The sight of her beaten son and the news report left her pale and silent, seemingly robbed of both her color and her voice. For me, putting the incident into words was a way of gaining a feeling of control and understanding. But for Lillian, things are different. To speak of these body blows her sons and family have endured is to relive them and to confirm their reality. So she keeps silent, holds it all inside, files it away for future reference and moves on.

It's been a long time since I was fooled by the idea that the police were there to protect and serve, so the actions of Clairton's finest weren't entirely surprising. McKeesport had taught me that a confrontation with the police wasn't the end of the world, though you were always outgunned, outmanned, outmeaned and outmediaed. The war which the cops waged against me after I formed Kids for Kids had prepped me for this, though nothing could quite ready me as a parent for seeing my son in such a pitiful state, from the blood-filled whites of his eyes to his blood-blackened ears. When I looked at him, what little hair I had on my head stood on end. I was prepared to die to make things right.

But I was overjoyed to have him back, bruises and all. I was glad he was alive. He could easily have been killed. We sat down at the dinner table and reviewed the events of the night of March 6. "Dad, we didn't do anything," he said. "That Mimms guy was drunk, and he tried to run me off the road. When he couldn't pass and my car backfired, he started firing at us. And when we went to get the cops, they tried to kill us."

Devon was always a gentle child, with a soft, warm handshake and a way of looking you right in the eye without seeming to issue a challenge or a threat. Though he could fight if cornered, he was never one to go looking for a rumble. So when he told me that he and his cousins didn't provoke the three cops who beat them up, I figured I was hearing the truth.

"Dad was real mad at those cops," Peeper told Devon. "He was gonna take his rifle down to that station, before me and Uncle Ron stopped him."

I told him how close I'd gotten to my own personal Armageddon, and his eyes glazed over a little. Then something in that picture - me, his dad, lugging an AK-47 out to the van and intent on going down in a blaze of glory - struck him as funny, and he started to laugh. It was a slow, jerky, unstoppable laugh from the belly, which steadily transformed into a good, long cry.

I started tearing up myself. "Devon, I would have given my life to have come upon the Ravensburg Bridge and seen Mimms and those no good mother fuckers beating you and Derek and Sonny. The coroner would have had a busy night picking bullets out of their asses, I'll promise you that."

I told him that at no time was I more ready to die than when I heard about the beating he took. When they sent me to Southeast Asia, the Marines had done all they could think of to turn me into a killing machine, ready to explode upon impact and take as many of the enemy down as possible in a self-destructing conflagration. And back then I was gung ho on the outside, but some nagging voice inside of me insisted that the mission just wasn't legit. Muhammad Ali had said the black man had no business being in Vietnam. It wasn't the Viet Cong who were calling us niggers. No such doubts tormented me when it was my son I was fighting for.

Devon nodded. "I'm glad you didn't do it, Dad," he said. "I'm glad you're ... still here. To take care of your wife, and Peeper." His voice kind of trailed off. He was obviously still numbed by the experience. His voice was a monotone as he recounted further details from the night of terror. He told us about the care he'd gotten at Jefferson Hospital. He'd demanded the hospital staff take Polaroids of their condition, and though the staff had seemed none too anxious to get in the middle of a police brutality case, they obliged. "I remember what you told me, Dad - to always get pictures taken if you're in an incident with the police," he said. Those pictures, I said then, would come in handy when we next go to the media and then the FBI.

"To hell with the media and the FBI," Devon said. "Little Sonny and Derek and I decided we're going to go right at the root of the problem - those cops."

I didn't have to ask what that meant. The same feelings of vengeful hatred were strong in me. But now I played the role of the voice of reason. "I know how you feel. But right now, as it stands, the next few weeks, months or years of your life will be living hell because of those cops. If you three go and do something foolish, it'll be more like the next few decades. I don't have time to go visiting you on death row. So let's stick together here. I've got a plan."

* * *

Early Tuesday morning I got on the line early and alerted all the local media I could think of that I would be having a press conference later that day in my driveway. Suddenly people who wouldn't return my calls just a day before were thrilled to hear from me; KDKA's scoop, the first televised interview with victims of police brutality in Western Pennsylvania in anyone's memory, was big news. Later that morning, when I stepped out into my driveway, three camera crews, a bunch of radio guys with mikes, a host of notepad-toting reporters and a half-dozen photographers were there to listen.

Again, Derek and Devon told their story. They didn't embellish. If anything, the two of them and Little Sonny have understated the events of that night when faced with the bright lights and insistent questioning of the press. Still, they told an engrossed press corps about the high speed chase and the subsequent terror on the bridge and in the station.

Then the hot lights turned on me. I told them that Clairton Public Safety Director Abbet had opted not to take my calls, so I would be taking the matter to a higher level.

"Will you bring the allegations to District Attorney Bob Pratt?" someone asked.

"We're not going to Pratt," I announced. I'd gone there before, when the McKeesport police were doing everything they could to stomp me out, and they'd treated me like I was the criminal. "The DA's office is nothing but the legal arm of the cops. Pratt is an ex-cop, his office works with cops all the time, and I think he has a conflict of interest. Pratt will just sweep this thing under the rug. We're going straight to the FBI. And if things don't work out, those renegade cops are going to have a war on their hands."

The press seemed interested, and a few of the newspaper people hung around to talk with us after the TV folks drove away. I encouraged them to get to the bottom of the story, but at the same time chewed them out for running the cops' tall tales without even making an attempt to contact the three young men. By the time they left I thought I might have done my part to push them to look a little deeper next time, and to consider the possibility of actually contacting the young men they regularly branded as criminals, rather than just taking the cops' word for it.

But the next morning the papers continued to identify my son and nephews as "the three suspects." They also had Derek and Little Sonny as brothers, an error they would repeat again and again, in spite of my phone calls to correct it. The Pittsburgh Post-Gazette led with Abbet's promise to investigate the charges of brutality. Abbet the intrepid investigator who never did get around to interviewing the victims of the beating, announced that day that, "I would venture to say that my investigation probably is not going to please the actors" - meaning Devon, Derek and Little Sonny. The story didn't recount the details of the beating until more than half way through. Nor did it explain why Abbet was conducting an investigation. The victims never filed a complaint with his department or asked him to conduct any investigation. The only thing I could figure was that he wanted to get the media off his back long enough to prepare a cover-up.

The McKeesport Daily News mentioned the beatings only in passing in the third-to-last paragraph of a lengthy article. It was clear that the press, all too eager to listen when they were face to face with the three men, were none too eager to tackle the issue of police brutality.

The reports angered me, but I had other concerns. Devon was having constant headaches, and Tuesday night I took him to Health America. There our celebrity status caught up with us. A little girl, standing by her mother, pointed up at my bruised son and said, "Mommy, that's the man I saw on TV last night."

Devon smiled weakly. "She saw me on TV, but she didn't say anything about the cops beating me up," he said. Then it struck me that I could parade them before the cameras time after time after time, and to most of the people in the Pittsburgh region, they'd still be a bunch of black kids who got beat up, and probably deserved it anyway.

"Who beat you up?" asked Dr. Frank Casey immediately upon us stepping into his office. Devon told him what happened, and he seemed genuinely concerned, asking first about the extent of the beating and then about whether there was any kind of investigation ongoing. We told him what we could about both, and he prescribed some medication for Devon's red eyes and nagging headaches. "I'll get you set up for an MRI in Oakland," he said, "to make sure everything's OK inside that head and neck. And we'll get you a referral to a specialist to look those eyes over."

"What about his ears?" I asked. "Are they going to stay pitch black forever?"

"I doubt it. That's probably just broken blood vessels, and there's really nothing I can do about that. Give it a week. It should heal on its own."

That was relieving. On the way home, Devon joked that he'd worried he'd be stuck with these pitch black ears forever. It wasn't all that funny, but I laughed and laughed. It was the first joke I'd heard him tell since the night of the beating, and my mood proved contagious. Our laughter rocked that van all the way home.

It was a little like old times, like back when he was a kid and rode with me in my dump truck on hauling jobs. The hauling was a side business, so I could bring my first born son if I wanted, and often I did. He'd sit there trying to peer over the truck's high dash, then turn to look out the door window at the cars way below. "Look at those cars way down there. They're so small and we're so big!" he'd announce, and laugh. Sometimes I'd let him shift the gears while I worked the clutch. Then on off days, when I was neither working at the mill nor hauling, we'd go fishing. Sometimes Curtis came along, and other times it was just Devon and me - Peeper was too small then. We'd go down the Youghiogheny River or up to Pymatuming Lake and dip our rods in and wait. But mostly we'd just eat our packed lunches and drink pop and joke around. What we caught, we'd throw back.

Though we'd never really become distant, adolescence and the teen years had the same effect on us that they have on every family. Children grow older, seek independence. Strange frictions develop, and a painful sense of separation sets in. As a parent, you wonder if you'll ever have that old closeness back again. If there was a silver lining to Devon's experience during those early days after the beating, it was the renewed closeness between us. Our roles seemed simple again: He was my son, and as his father it was my role to help protect him, no matter who or what the enemy might be. Sure, there would be times we'd disagree and drift apart. But I was sure, as that van rumbled back toward home, that we'd always come back together again.

* * *

That week we didn't get so much as a phone message or a post card from Public Safety Director William Abbet. So on March 16, I cautiously advised my son and two nephews to file civil rights violations charges against those officers involved in the torture. After a few days of thinking about it, Devon, Derek and Little Sonny went out and filed complaints with both the National Association for the Advancement of Colored People and the American Civil Liberties Union. I cautioned the trio not to get their hopes up too high. After all, it was the NAACP and ACLU who failed to investigate my complaints a few years ago against the McKeesport Police Department. I truly didn't have much confidence in either the NAACP or ACLU, but something had to be done with those three sadistic cops who tried to kill my son and nephews in the City of Prayer.

Days later, to my surprise it would be the NAACP that would step up and take action. The NAACP brought the beatings to the public's attention by showing up at a city council meeting and demanding answers from Public Safety Director William "Bud" Abbet.

"Heinous and outrageous" is how the ACLU described the Grey, Goodman and Brown beatings, but they stopped short of making any commitment to the three cousins to investigate their complaints against Mimms, Rahis and Sanalas.

Friday I called the FBI's office in Downtown Pittsburgh and announced my impending visit. "We've been expecting you!" said the receptionist, a Ms. Holly, when I introduced myself. I guess she'd seen me on TV. She put me on the phone with a man who identified himself as Special Agent Bill Gunn of the FBI's civil rights division, a specialist in police abuse cases.

"Bring the boys on down, Mr. Grey," Gunn said. "We've been

expecting you. I saw the young men on TV. I'm not going to rush to judgment until I investigate, but you're welcome to bring them on down to file a complaint."

It was a much different response than I got in 1992, when I'd called the FBI to report the activities of the McKeesport Police Department. Then I'd just gotten the run-around, and nothing had come of it - no interviews, no investigation, no charges. Maybe something had changed there. Or maybe I was witnessing the power of television coverage. In either case, we packed into my van and headed into the arms of America's most powerful law enforcement agency.

On the way into Pittsburgh I got to see the three cousins together for the first time since the calamity. They didn't talk much about the beating itself, and that somehow relieved me. If they had been back there making sure their stories matched, I'd have turned that van around. Instead, it seemed they were past the point of dwelling on what had happened, and had moved on to the question of why, and whether they were going to get any justice.

"I'd just like to ask that Mimms guy and those white cops one question," said Devon. "Why'd they have to beat us? Why'd they have to hold you over the edge of the bridge? Why wasn't it enough to just handcuff us, bring us into the station and charge us with some trumped up shit?"

"The dude was drunk," said Derek. "You smelled it. He was a damn distillery."

"I can still smell it," said Devon.

"I'll tell you what, I think he was more than drunk," said Little Sonny. "I think the dude was on some heavy shit. I mean, he was acting bizarre."

"He didn't even break a sweat running back and forth around that car, beating on all three of us," Devon marveled. "He was geeked on something. That nutball was stoned out of his head. I thought that maniac was going to kill us."

"The horror stories that you guys have been telling me about Officer Mimms are heinous. I've decided to rename that crazy bastard," I said. "As of today, I'm going to start calling him Clyde 'The Maniac Cop' Mimms. That bastard is definitely a candidate for Prozac."

"It's dope, I like it, Uncle Bus," said Little Sonny. "Maniac Cop Mimms! Right on."

Derek and Devon chuckled.

"You're funny as hell, Uncle Bus," said Derek. "Hey, unc, do you think Officer Mimms is going to be pleased with his new name?"

"To tell you the truth, I don't give a flying fuck if he likes it or not. Piss on him, his mammy, and the City of Sinners. They can all kiss my bi-racial ass!"

I was glad they weren't talking about vengeance. For those guys, whose combat experience consisted primarily of being on the receiving end of the gunfire and fists, revenge would be the fastest way to a long jail term or an early grave. In the darkest corners of my mind I still hadn't put aside my own desire for quick justice; not by a long shot. But I had committed to a peaceful plan, and I was glad they were on board.

"Remember," I told them, "this FBI is going to be working for us, not doing the cops' work for them. So if they start asking about guns and about the lies these cops are feeding the media, just remind them that you're here to discuss the violation of your civil rights, and that's all. There's criminal charges against you on the other stuff, so you'd do best to save that for a court of law. If they start pressuring you to confess to some crime that you didn't commit, get up and walk out. They probably have the meeting rooms bugged."

We parked and headed to the northeastern corner of Pittsburgh's Golden Triangle, where the Federal Building stands, and took the elevator to the Federal Bureau of Investigation's suites. There the receptionist treated us like long-expected holiday guests, offered us coffee, tea or soft drinks and ushered us into a conference room where we were made to wait.

The boys mulled about and watched people bustle by in the hallway outside the room. But my mind was far from there. I was back in the '70s, back at Deer Lakes, in northern Pennsylvania, where I used to go to watch my idol, Muhammad Ali, work out. Ali knew something about fighting on foreign turf - hell, he fought in Zaire. He knew how to take on a larger opponent - George Foreman, for example. And he knew that the battle is often lost and won in the space between the two combatants' eyes.

Ali usually won that battle, and I remembered his trick: Rather than stare straight into the opponent's eyes, he focused on the nose. The guy bobbing and weaving a few feet away would think Ali was staring him right in the eyes, and would try to meet the Champ's gaze. But staring at a man's nose is a lot easier than staring him right in the eyes, so Ali always won. And he who wins the battle of wills, more often than not, wins the war.

That's the mood I was in when the door frame was filled with a short, stocky guy, gray and a little baggy around the eyes but with the bounding gait of a rookie. He puffed his chest out into the shape of a barrel, extended his meaty hand and announced, "Hey! My name is Special Agent Bill Gunn. I'll be handling your son's case."

I pushed out my own chest, gripped his hand and yanked it roughly toward me, looked right at his nose and announced, "Hey! My name is Leon Grey, and you people have a problem!" And you know - he blinked!

Something changed in his eyes. "Yeah, I know," he said, pulling his hand from mine. "I saw the boys on television. Who was responsible for putting them on television, anyway?"

"Look, it doesn't matter who put them on television," I said. "They're down here to make a civil rights complaint. As far as I know, the FBI is supposed to take that complaint, not act as their media advisor."

Gunn took a step back. He seemed to be evaluating his options. Admittedly, I was doing the same. Gunn's question about the television appearance had the smell of a cover-up. I wondered if Devon, Derek and Little Sonny felt the same, but when I looked back, they seemed to be struggling to suppress grins.

"All right," said Gunn. "You're right. We're going to take each of you aside and take a statement. We'll proceed from there."

Gunn led Derek off, while other agents took aside Devon and Little Sonny. I suppose I sat there for 10 or 15 minutes before Devon and Sonny were led back in. They said the agents had asked them to describe what happened on the bridge and in the station, and they'd done so, and the agents wrote it up and had them review and sign it. That was it. From what the boys told me, the agents seemed totally disinterested in the car chase and in Maniac Cop Mimms' behind-the-wheel marksmanship practice, and instead concentrated almost completely on what happened on the bridge and in the station. They were particularly concerned with when the handcuffs went on and when they came off, and what happened in between. That was about it. So we sat there and waited.

And waited. "What the hell are they doin' to poor Derek?" Sonny asked.

"Maybe they're beatin' him again," Devon said, half-joking.

"I doubt it," I said. "He's already been beaten once. I don't think they'll beat him again. Besides, they seemed scared to death of us going on television, and we already proved we can get on the tube."

"Oh, man, Uncle Buster, I liked the way you handled that," said Little Sonny. "When he asked you who put them on TV, you told him where he could stick that."

"They asked me the same thing," said Devon, "about who put me on TV. I told them the TV people came to me. Nobody had to put me there."

"I got the same question," said Little Sonny. "Only I told them I was never on TV, because by the time I made bail, the news people weren't interested anymore. It was already old news."

We continued to wait, until finally I went and asked the lady at the front desk what was taking so long. She buzzed back to Gunn's office, and he told her that he needed more time, 10 or 15 minutes at least. I told Devon and Sonny, and we decided to get some air, and took the elevator down to street level. Down on Grant Street we paced around a bit, wondered what was taking so long and watched the traffic flow; lawyers' cars, bankers' cars, judges' cars. That's all there were down here any more, just cars full of people in suits, rather than streetcars full of folks in hardhats and work shirts, like there were when I was just a kid.

We went back upstairs and Derek still wasn't out. "I bet they locked him back up," Little Sonny kept muttering. "They gonna work on him and get him to testify against us. They done locked him back up." I tried to ignore him, and finally Gunn and Derek came back out. Derek was grinning.

"Can I have a few minutes with you?" Gunn asked me.

"Sure."

We headed down the hall, and I wondered what he wanted with me. My heart started beating harder. But then I decided not to let this guy intimidate me; After all, my tax dollars pay his salary, and he's here to serve me, I thought. So when we got to his tidy office, walls lined with diplomas and awards, I leaned across his desk and looked Gunn in the face.

"Look, let's dispense with all of the bullshit," I said. "You know those cops beat their asses. Let's just get that niggah down here and those two white Barnie Fifes. Put 'em in a room with me for five minutes and I'll take care of their asses, and we'll forget about the whole damn thing."

He laughed and shook his head. It was a nervous laugh. "Hey, I sympathize with you, Mr. Grey. I'm a parent, too. But you know we can't do that. We'll handle this, and I assure you, Mr. Grey, that no stone will remain unturned." He paused. "I know you probably don't trust me very much right now. I'm law enforcement. I'm a police officer, in a way, and we all took the same oath to protect and serve, me and Clyde Mimms and every other cop and agent. But I don't like the fact that if what these boys say is true, they were beaten while they were handcuffed. Mr. Grey, I must be honest with you. I do see something terribly wrong with this picture. Do you know what I'm talking about?"

"Yes indee-dee I do," I said. "From day one I've been wondering what in the hell happened to resisting arrest? If these boys earned that beating, why didn't the cops make that charge? Is that what you're talking about?"

"Yes, Mr. Grey, that sends up a red flag to me. When I get to Clairton one of the first questions I'm going to ask is why no resisting arrest charges were filed."

"Yeah, what's up with that, Agent Gunn? Hell, Stevie Wonder can see that my son and nephews were beaten. How can those three cops justify a head full of stitches, a broken finger, bruised ribs, multiple abrasions, contusions and black eyes with no resisting arrest charge? Those tales the cops are telling about my son and nephews falling on ice are nothing but lies. My son was very vocal about who kicked his ass, and let me tell you something, it wasn't a sheet of ice."

Then I leaned forward. "Agent Gunn, I am demanding justice. I want those three bastards in jail where they belong. I'm angry and upset. Trust me, I don't want to have to go to Clairton and kill anyone or burn that damn town to the ground. I want justice and I want it right now, not tomorrow."

"Please, Mr. Grey, calm down!" he said, leaning backward as if to put some distance between himself and the heat radiating off of me. "I don't have all the facts. It's going to take some time. Let us help. You getting in trouble with the law will not help them one bit."

I sat back, suddenly aware again that I'd chosen to play it his way, and for the time being, I'd have to play by his rules.

"Do the boys have a gun?" Gunn asked.

"I have never seen them with any gun," I answered. "Look, I know them well. I've known all three for a long time. I have no reason to think they have or had a gun, and I've never seen or heard tell of any of them packing one. They aren't violent young men. They've never belonged to gangs, and they don't have violence in their past. I can't claim to know everything there is to know about them, but this stuff just doesn't make any sense. Something's wrong. It just doesn't make sense."

"So you don't believe they fired on Mr. Mimms prior to the incident on the bridge?" he asked.

"Mr. Gunn, having known Devon for all of his life and Derek for many years, and having had Little Sonny over my house plenty of times over the last six months or so, I don't think they have the guts to fire on a chipmunk."

He gave a little snort. "So why do you think the beating occurred?"

I thought for a minute. "From what they tell me, that niggah was drunk. If he really did think he was fired on, then he might have done it out of retaliation. Cops are vindictive. He also probably thought it would impress his white colleagues. Those white cops probably saw an opportunity to beat on some niggaz and joined in." I decided not to tell him about the car backfiring. That information, I felt, could be crucial in proving my son's innocence, and at that point I didn't want it to fall into anyone else's hands, even Gunn's.

Gunn closed by asking me what medical treatment Devon had obtained since his release, and I told him. He was through questioning me after about 10 minutes. Then he looked me straight in the eyes. "I know you're angry. Justifiably so. Just don't do anything stupid. If you have any problems, you can call me anytime. But let us handle this."

I looked him in the nose. "I hope you will handle this. I hope to

God you will."

I walked together back to the conference room. Little Sonny, Derek and Devon seemed upbeat, and greeted Gunn with nods and smiles. I sat down and he thanked us all. He said he would be setting up a file and investigating further. He might need to conduct further interviews later on. We should keep him apprised of anything that happened in the criminal case against the young men.

"Also, I'm sure the Clairton police will be doing their own investigation," Gunn said. "Please cooperate with it in every way possible."

"If they are doing an investigation, it sure isn't like any investigation I've ever seen," I said. I told Gunn how my 10 calls to Public Safety Director William Abbet hadn't been returned. The boys confirmed that they'd heard nothing from Clairton's finest. And I recited for Gunn the quote from the newspaper, about how "the actors" probably wouldn't be happy with the results of the so-called investigation. "Let me ask you this: What kind of investigation opens up with a statement of which side is or isn't going to be satisfied? I would be happy to cooperate with them, but they won't cooperate with me. That's why I'm down here, in your face."

Gunn shook his head again. "OK. But if they do conduct an investigation, it would be in your own best interests to cooperate. To not cooperate would give them an excuse not to do anything, and would make it look like you had something to hide."

Whatever. There were handshakes all around, and then we left.

"Looks to me like those cops are going to jail," said Little Sonny, as we piled into the elevator and dropped toward Grant Street. "I don't figure that's a very friendly place for a cop. I hope those five-o's like having their assholes enlarged."

His cousins laughed nervously. "I'll believe it when I see it," said Derek. "I never seen a white cop put another white cop in jail yet, and two of those cops were white."

"Whole thing has to go before a judge and jury before anybody goes to jail," Devon added. "Think a judge and jury's going to put cops in jail for beating on us?"

"When I get me the best lawyer in the county and have him put me on the stand and tell my story, boys, that jury's gonna be in tears," Little Sonny said. "They'll want to cuff those cops and lead 'em off to jail themselves. Don't you think, Uncle Buster?"

We trundled out into the blustery late winter day. "I got a funny feeling," I said. "That guy Gunn seems OK. It seems strange to me that he would ask who put you on TV, and he had no business asking about my guns, that much is true. But I think he cares, in some way. And I think he was being straight with us about doing a thorough investigation."

"So you think they're going to jail?" Devon asked.

I stopped in the middle of the busy Grant Street sidewalk. In Pittsburgh, that piece of pavement is a chasm between the towers of law and high finance, which have divided up between them what was left of the town when steel died out. Nobody in any of those towers, from Oxford Center to One Mellon Bank to that rusty titan, the USX Tower, gave a damn about what had happened to us, I felt, and those were the people who pulled the strings. "Do I see them going to jail? No, I can't say I do. I just can't see that happening. Not in this county."

We got back in the van and headed for the Mon Valley, where I would drop off Sonny and Derek before taking Devon home with me. As we got closer to Route 837, the high spirits created by the visit to the FBI evaporated and the agitation level in the van rose. "Why didn't they want to know about that damn magistrate, that Raymond Locke?" Little Sonny asked. "Why weren't they interested in the failure of those cops to get us medical treatment? I mean, it was that constable who finally had to take us to the hospital."

I asked what he was talking about. The three then related what had happened the morning after their encounter with the Clairton cops. They were roused by Officer Rahis, who announced that the "good-for-nothing-niggers" had a "date with the judge." "You niggers are going down for a long time," he added. "I hope you no good bastards rot in jail."

Then Rahis and the other white cop, the one who'd put his gun to Devon's head, entered their cells, handcuffed them, and marched them through pools of their own blood and out of the holding area. Their socks left fat, red exclamation marks down the concrete hall, punctuated by little scarlet periods and commas where the blood from their open wounds fell. Two open cuts on Derek's head continued to ooze blood, which dripped down his face on to his now-crimson shirt.

Sonny, too, continued to drip from the shotgun-barrel-shaped lacerations on top of his head, and could barely stand up straight for the pain in his ribs. Devon's eyes were swollen almost completely shut, his ears were ringing and when they wrenched him upright, he nearly crumbled to the floor.

"I asked them whether they were taking us to a hospital," Sonny said. "They said no, there weren't enough officers to transport us to any hospital. We were going before the magistrate, and then to jail." Devon and Derek were placed in one cruiser, and Sonny was taken by Rahis. "He told me I had one last chance to be a good guy and tell him who fired the gun, like my buddy Derek did," Sonny told us. "If I did, he said, he'd see to it that I only got probation. I said there was no gun. They'd made a mistake, and picked up the wrong people. We hadn't fired a gun at anybody. In fact, we were fired at. So he lost it. He starts screaming how he could make sure I go away for a long, long time, and 'Have it your way, you ungrateful little fucker,' and on and on. It was like he was trying to play good cop-bad cop with me, except he was playing both."

The three groggy, aching men were dragged into the courtroom of Clairton Magistrate Raymond Locke. "OK, you niggers, sit your black asses down and don't give me any shit," Rahis told them before the magistrate came in. "I'm a cop and I can beat or kill your black asses and get away with it. I'm a cop, and cops do that all the time. So don't you black bastards test me." The implicit message, of course, was this: If you complain about being beaten, it'll only be worse for you next time.

When the cops wandered out of hearing range, the cousins had a chance to talk. They looked each other over, and Devon noticed that Derek was crying. "You all right, cuz?" Devon asked.

"Oh, not exactly," Derek said. "But at least I can't see myself. Man, if I didn't know it was you, I couldn't recognize you. You look like the damn elephant man."

"You do look like shit," Sonny added. "Those bastards are going to pay for what they did to us."

"When they take these handcuffs off, I'm going after those damn cops," Derek said. The words set off a searing pain in Devon's head, and he felt tears building in the corners of his eyes.

"Just be careful," said Sonny to Derek. "You ain't in such good shape yourself. Man, I can practically see inside your head. You're still bleeding. I don't know if you're ever gonna stop."

"I think I need stitches. Problem is nobody seems willing to take us to the hospital. I think they'd just as soon see us bleed to death, right here in the courtroom. You know, Sonny, you've got one hell of a shiner."

"But it's my side that's hurting. I think they broke some ribs." They watched quietly as Magistrate Locke listened to the cops and filled out the paperwork. When Rahis and the other cop finished talking, Sonny called out.

"Mr. Locke, sir."

No answer. He didn't look up.

"Your honor, please, can I speak with you."

Locke kept his nose in his papers, continued to write.

"Sir, we're hurt. We need medical care. These cops beat us up."

He seemed to pause in his writing, but didn't look up. Then he continued to write, turned to two nearby constables, and said, "All yours, boys."

"He wouldn't even look at us," said Sonny, back in the van. "We tried to tell him we needed help, that we'd been beaten. He kept his nose buried in his paperwork and didn't even respond when we called out to him. That fucker didn't even care that we'd been beat. Didn't care if we bled to death right in front of him in the middle of his courtroom."

"He treated us like so many dogs," said Derek. "Like nothing but a pack of stray dogs."

"And it wasn't him decided to have us taken to the hospital - it was the constable."

That constable was Tyrone Morris, who happened to know the parents of all three cousins. Without any instructions from the magistrate, he and Constable Dobie Walker took them to a car and drove them to Jefferson Hospital. In the car, Morris was quiet, and didn't express much sympathy for his injured charges. But in the hospital waiting room, with Walker out of earshot, he bent down close to his handcuffed and shackled prisoners.

"I hear you guys had a run-in with Clyde Mimms," he said. "He's a bad ass. He's been thumping people up here for years." He looked at their swollen and cut faces and shook his head. "I'm sure you'll sue his ass so bad, it shuts down the City of Clairton."

Morris took Marie's phone number from Derek and called to let her know where her son was. Marie then called me.

I wondered how people like Tyrone Morris could work for the same system that employed Raymond Locke. Morris was a sympathetic man, willing to risk the ire of the system by taking injured men to the hospital instead of the jail and by calling their families, after that had been denied them at every step of the process. Raymond Locke had proved himself to be a monster - because that's what a person would have to be to just sit impassively in the face of such obvious human misery. Like the Clairton Fifes, the Jefferson Borough cops and the media, Locke had showed not one ounce of humanity, compassion or sympathy. As I pulled that van on to the Parkway and aimed it east toward Duquesne, McKeesport and Clairton, I was filled with a desire to plow the big blue beast right through the front of Locke's courtroom and just expose it for the pathetic sham it was.

Later, I learned that Locke was a former Clairton police officer. In a sense, that explained it. In another sense, that explained nothing at all.

* * *

"Dad, it's for you," Peeper yelled from the next room. I heard a groan from the kitchen - we were about to sit down to dinner, and, as usual, the telephone was beckoning. "It's Choke."

Why, I wondered, would Peeper's barber be calling at the dinner hour? It wasn't like he was due for a haircut yet. He'd just gotten one a week before.

"Buster Grey here."

"Buster? Hey, how's it goin'?"

"It's goin', man. It's goin'. So what's up?"

"Hey, sorry to bother you, but I was cutting this guy's hair today, and the subject of the beatings your people took in Clairton came up. And he said he was sitting practically right next to Clyde Mimms the night of the beatings, and Mimms was drinking."

"No shit Maniac Cop Mimms was drunk. But this guy was sitting right next to him? Who is the guy?"

"Name's Steve. I gave him your number - I hope that's OK. But

I don't know for sure if he'll call you. He seemed reluctant to get involved."

"Steve what?"

"Just Steve. He doesn't want me to give out his last name."

"Whatever. Everybody wants to whine and complain, and nobody wants to get involved. Well, since you're in the business of giving out phone numbers today, you mind giving me his?"

Choke gave me the guy's pager number. I thanked him and hung up. Lillian was calling me for dinner, but I told her I needed to make a quick call. I dialed the number, then when the beeps came, I punched in my own.

My phone rang within two minutes. "Hello."

"Hello. Who's this?"

"Who's this?"

"Who's this? Didn't you page me?"

"Guess you got me there. I'm Buster Grey. You Steve?"

"Oh, Buster Grey! Yeah, I'm Steve."

"Yeah. I hear you saw Clyde Mimms the night my son was beaten. Any truth to that?"

"Yeah. I was meaning to call you, just didn't get around to it yet. Sorry."

"No problem. But where'd you see Mimms?"

"Down the Wee Bee Back Saloon in Homestead. Dude was sitting two barstools down from me, with Michele Blunt and his cousin Dana Bell, and another white lady."

"Drinking?"

"What else you do at the Wee Bee Back Saloon? He was hittin' it pretty hard."

"Beer? Shots?"

"Hmm. I don't know what he was drinking. But he was going pretty steady from about nine or ten o'clock until the bar closed."

"So when did he leave?"

"Just before I did, which was after last call. It must've been around 2 in the morning."

That would put him on the road at about the time the Camaro was fired on. And the only sensible way from Homestead to Clairton was down Route 837. Steve's story seemed consistent with the facts. "Was he drunk?"

"Well, y'know, who can say for sure? He drank a lot, that I can say."

Steve went on to tell me that he knew Mimms well. He grew up in the house behind Mimms in McKeesport, and though he never much liked Mimms, he didn't have any kind of vendetta against him.

"Steve, this thing's going to trial, one way or the other," I told him. "Those cops are pressing criminal charges against my son and nephews, and we're going to file something against them, I can tell you that. Would you be willing to testify?"

"Hell, man, I don't know. Can't you find someone else who was at the Wee Bee Back to testify?"

"Do they keep a sign-in sheet?" I snorted. "Look, you saw Maniac Cop Mimms drinking. You know what happened to those three boys. They were beaten, terrorized and tortured. Are you going to just sit back and let this kind of shit happen, or are you going to do something about it?"

"Look, man, I know the guy, and he knows me. I don't want to get into it."

"You afraid of retaliation?"

"No, I ain't afraid of the guy. I just don't want to get involved."

"Shit. It's people like you who allow this shit to go on and on and on. You've got to come forward with this information. That's the only way this kind of thing is going to stop."

We sat silent on the phone for a minute. "Look, if I can testify, I will," he said. "I'll get in contact with you. I won't promise anything, but you have my beeper number."

"Yeah, OK." I made sure he still had my number. We quickly said goodbye, and hung up. I realized when I did that I never did get the guy's last name.

I would have one more conversation with Steve, weeks later while trying to round up witnesses for the preliminary hearing. He would tell me then that he didn't want to get involved, that he had too much to do, too much to fear and too many things that somebody could come and take away. Later I would pass a man on my way into Choke's for Peeper's haircut and Choke would tell me, "That was Steve, the guy who saw Mimms in the bar!" And I would run back out just in time to jot down the license plate number of his receding vehicle.

When I told Choke that this Steve refused to get involved, he shook his head. Choke's a guy who knows what's going down. He's an ex-member of the Nation of Islam, a serene man who's aware of the problems the poor man and the man of color face in America. "Man, I don't get it. The guy could strike a blow against this kind of oppression. He could come forward and do something about it. He talks big, but he won't do it. Steve's a pussy, I guess."

Choke then told me his last name: Timmons, Steve Timmons. "Maybe you can track him down and convince him to testify, or somebody could subpoena his sorry behind." When, years later, I would finally find an attorney with enough gumption to track Timmons down, his answer would be the same: "I don't want to get involved."

Just like the folks who drove by when my son was lying, bloodied, on the ground and the reporters who were too lazy to search for the truth and the magistrate who wouldn't look up from his papers at the battered "suspects" in the middle of his courtroom. Sometimes I wonder where the concept of right and wrong has gone. Sometimes, people today make my guts twist.

Chapter 6

The Fix Is In

A day or two after the visit to the FBI, I took the cousins out to Knukles's Garage to pick up the car. They stayed in the van while I checked it out. Sure enough, the old thing had two bullet holes, about an inch apart and on a diagonal, in the bottom left side of the spoiler. To me, it was physical evidence that the cousins' story was accurate; a cop had fired on the car. I checked under the car, but couldn't locate any further damage from the bullets, nor the bullets themselves.

Old Nick Knukles followed me around the car, nodding and grunting. I asked him if he or any of his employees had seen any part of the beating, or had even seen the young men lying on the ground when they'd come to pick up the car. "Nope," he said. "Didn't know nothing about no beatings until I saw you on the news the other night. Didn't even know that a cop was shot at until I saw that on the news. I figured it was just another drunken driving case."

"Cop wasn't shot at," I said.

"No? Huh. Inneresting."

"These look like bullet holes to you?" I asked, sticking my pinkie finger into the round punctures in the spoiler.

"Hmm." He bent down to look at them. "Could well be. Could be."

"Hey, can you give me a slip or something which confirms that these holes were here? So nobody can say that I took the thing home and punched holes in it?"

"Sure." Knukles wrote up a receipt with a brief description of the holes, and even drew a tiny diagram showing their configuration. "Will that do ya?"

"I think so." I circled the car again. "Hey, know what? Did the police do up any kind of report on the damage to the car? Have they been by to look at it or write something up?"

"Not that I know of."

"Would you mind calling them to see if they did write anything up, or if they're willing to make up a report? My insurance might ask for one. I mean, if it would be too much trouble, just say so."

"No, no trouble at all."

I followed him back to his office, where he dialed up the station and asked for Abbet. The dispatcher put him through right away - in marked contrast to the run-around I had been getting. "Yeah, Bill, I've got Leon Grey here looking at the Camaro. ... No, he's not causing any trouble. He's been a perfect gentleman. ... Well, actually, he'd like a police report on some of the damage to the car. ... You'll send somebody over? Great. Thanks."

I wandered back over to the van to tell the boys what was happening. "So a couple of Clairton cops are coming out to check out the Camaro," Derek mused. "Wonder if they'll try to finish us off."

"I wonder if they'll recognize you from TV, Dad," Devon said.

"Could be. Could well be."

"This time they won't get us in handcuffs quite so easy," said Little Sonny. "I don't think I'm gonna let anybody handcuff me for the rest of my life."

Quick as that the cruiser pulled in; Knukles's place was just across the Ravensburg Bridge from the station. Two white cops jumped out. I was disappointed and relieved at the same time that Maniac Cop Mimms hadn't made the trip. One of the cops was a medium height guy with real close-cropped hair and the beginnings of a bald spot, and the other must've been about 6'6" and had a mustache. I met them at the car.

"What can I do for you, sir?" asked the short one.

I read his name plate: E. Sanalas. "I'd like a police report on the two bullet holes in the spoiler of this car," I told him, and pointed.

"Is it your car?"

"It's my son's."

"And where exactly are the holes?"

I went down close and he joined me. I put my pinkie finger through one, then the other again. "Bullet holes."

He examined them. "Looks to me like somebody drilled those holes," he said.

"Nobody drilled holes in this car," I said. I turned to Knukles. "Did you drill holes in this car?"

"I didn't drill no holes."

Sanalas looked long and hard at the two holes, then down at the pad in his hand. "I'll note their presence and your opinions, as well as my own, in the report," he said, and he began to write.

As he took notes, I heard a "pssst" sound from the van, and saw Sonny gesturing for my attention. I walked the 30 feet across the parking lot to the van, and the three of them gathered at the door. "That's the cop who put the gun to Devon's head," Little Sonny said.

"The tall one?"

"No, the short one. You get his name?"

"Yeah. E. Sanalas. You recognize the tall one?"

"Naw, never seen him before. But the short one, he was beatin' me up, too."

I headed back over to the car. So this was the man who'd held a gun to my son's head and told him he could kill him without consequence. Though it was a cool day, I felt fever heat rising through my body. Everything from my toes to my jaw tightened up. That long-dormant Marine instinct to attack surged forth, and I figured if I tackled him quick, I could get a few licks in before the other cop shot me. But that wasn't the way I'd chosen to go. Stay the course, I told myself. Stay the course.

"What's your full name, officer?" I asked him.

"Edward Sanalas," he said, meeting my gaze. I could tell by his eyes that he knew that I knew. He had a bulldog-like face, with little crevices and pock marks all over it. I committed it to memory.

He had a little Polaroid camera around his neck, and now he turned it on the spoiler. Snap. Then he took a step in my direction and leaned conspicuously toward the car. But at the last second, he turned it on me, opened the shutter, then shifted it back toward the car. I suspect he didn't think I noticed. But I managed to sneak in a cheesy grin.

Sanalas peeled off the protective backing and grimaced. He did the same with the second shot. I took a step toward him.

"Didn't come out," he said, shoving them into his breast pocket. "This camera isn't working right."

"What a shame," I said, smelling a cover-up in the making. "That truly is unfortunate. Can I have a copy of that report, at least?"

"Oh, this isn't the formal report. Just notes. I'll take this back to the station and type up a formal report. I'll mail you a copy."

"Whatever you say. Please do." He left quickly, and I was glad for that. I had work to do, like getting the car over to Firestone for a diagnostic test to see if it was liable to backfire. And then there was finding a lawyer, so I could take this cocky cop who dared put a gun to my child's head and lay him low.

I never did get his report. I'm still waiting.

* * *

We saw Gunn just one more time in those early months - when he came to my sister La Rue's house to take a look at the Camaro. We met him there, and I stayed just long enough to watch the FBI photographer shoot a roll, mostly of the bullet holes in the spoiler. Then Gunn started interviewing the boys again, and I took off.

That week Devon received notice that the charges against him and his cousins would be heard on May 23 by District Magistrate Raymond Locke, the fine public servant who had ignored their pleas on the morning after the beating. We'd been talking about getting a lawyer on and off since Devon had come home, but now was the time to move on it.

Little Sonny was already in touch with Larry Vicious, a black lawyer with offices in Pittsburgh who'd defended him back when he had that bad habit of stealing cars. Vicious had negotiated him through a series of plea bargains which had resulted in minimal jail time, and that had been fine by Little Sonny. This time, though, Vicious pledged to get the case thrown out pronto. "He says there's nothing here," Sonny told me. "No fingerprints on the gun. No nitro test on our hands. No independent witnesses. Larry says this thing's a crock and it won't hold up."

Derek went along for the ride. He had two juvenile delinquencies on his record, both for drug possession, but he didn't have a regular lawyer for that. It seemed sensible that Derek and Sonny would have the same attorney; that way, it wouldn't become a contest between the lawyers of who could save his client first by sending the others up the river.

Derek and Sonny decided to hire Vicious for the civil case we'd be filing against the Clairton P.D. But something told me not to use him to defend the criminal charges. Vicious is about medium height, with glasses and a squirrelly mustache. He speaks with a deep voice, so he sound like a giant over the phone; maybe that's why he seems so small when you meet him. He's warm in person, and kindly enough, sure. But maybe that's why neither Devon nor I felt like trusting him with a matter that could profoundly effect my son's future.

I called Ron Jackson. As a jail guard, he sees lawyers come and go, and gets a feel for which of their clients tend to walk away whistling Dixie, and which ones tend to stick around the big house a while. "You've been good for advice so far," I told him. "You think I should get Attorney Jipenstein to represent Devon for the criminal case?"

Attorney R.W. Jipenstein had helped me out in McKeesport, when the cops there were bearing down on me and framing my sons. He was based down there, and knew the judges and cops of the Mon Valley as well as anyone. He was white, which could be a plus when going in front of the mostly-white jury pool of Allegheny County. And he had a good reputation.

"No way," said Ron, to my surprise. "Jipenstein's one of those old Mon Valley lawyers who's seen better days. You think he's going to aggressively defend a case which makes the Clairton cops look like a bunch of stupid brutes?"

"Hey, if I pay him to, he will. Besides, he's a defense lawyer. He goes up against cops all the time."

"Yeah, but not like he's going to have to in order to win this case," said Ron. "Check this out, Buster; whoever finally puts this case to bed is going to have to use those beatings to do it. He's going to have to show those cops for the monsters they are. Otherwise, who is an Allegheny County jury going to believe? Cops or three black youths?"

We went back and forth, and after listening to Ron I tried to reach a few local renegade lawyers who'd proved their willingness to challenge the system. There are 7,500 lawyers in Allegheny county, but most of them are corporate shills or known ass-kissers. Apparently, though, the few good ones were already in demand, because I couldn't get a return call out of either of the two.

In the end I hired Jipenstein in spite of Ron's advice. I had a lot to learn about lawyers. It wouldn't be long before I would start learning it.

Our first meeting with Jipenstein was a quick one. We signed the Power of Attorney, and then he spent about five minutes with Devon and me and took some notes on the arrest and the beating. He said he knew Mimms and was aware that the guy had some problems, but he couldn't really talk about them. As for the other officers involved, the Clairton cops who'd kicked and threatened the cousins and the Jefferson Borough cops who'd stood and watched, Jipenstein didn't seem interested in them.

"We'll get the names of the officers after the trial is over," Jipenstein said.

I screamed that we would get the names and get them now. A trial could take months, I pointed out. Little did I know how long it would actually take before the commonwealth's case against would finally be put to rest.

No lawyer I would deal with, in fact, would show the slightest interest in the other perpetrators. Vicious went as far as discouraging Derek and Little Sonny from working with the FBI investigation. If we hadn't fingered the cops, I don't think anyone ever would have.

A sixty-ish man with a bad hairpiece and a moderate manner, Jipenstein suddenly didn't seem like the guy we would need to take on the power of the police. In fact, he told us out front that he wasn't interested in handling our civil suit against the Clairton police. "I have too many dealings with the police departments down there to start suing them," he said. "I'd be glad to defend you against the criminal charges. I'll line up someone else to handle the civil matter for you. I need a thousand dollars up front to represent Devon at the preliminary hearing."

"What for?"

"Well, for one, I need $150 for transcripts. The other $850 is my fee for representing him."

Whatever.

The greatest victory the dynamic duo of Jipenstein and Vicious would win for us would be their first - getting the case out of the courtroom of Magistrate Raymond Locke. Locke had already proved his bias by sitting silent while the cousins bled in the middle of his courtroom. He'd slapped an excessive $50,000 bond on two of the three - a ploy, we thought, to keep them in jail until their wounds were healed and the physical evidence of the brutal beating was gone.

In addition, as we would learn later, Locke was ex-Clairton cop. And this man would determine whether there was enough evidence to take the case Downtown? I didn't think so. Jipenstein made some calls and got the case transferred out of Locke's courtroom. From what he said, Locke didn't mind. He didn't want to have anything to do with it anyway.

Trouble was, the case was moved from ex-Clairton cop Raymond Locke to ex-McKeesport police chief Thomas Raley. Raley, if I remembered right, had been Maniac Cop Mimms' boss for part of the time he was policing McKeesport.

I got on the phone to Jipenstein. "Did you see what these jokers did?"

"I saw it, Leon."

"Raley used to be Mimms' boss. This is no better than Locke."

Of course, he was aware of the connection. If anybody knew who was who and who'd served where in the Mon Valley, it was Jipenstein. "Leon, I've already talked to Larry and we're going to ask President Judge Damian Simple to change the venue for the preliminary hearing again. I think we have a right to a magistrate who hasn't had any connection to Mimms' career. I think moving it to Raley was just an honest mistake."

If so, it wasn't a mistake Judge Simple was willing to correct. Jipenstein and Vicious went before the king of the judges and made their arguments and pleaded and prodded and pointed out conflicts of interest. Simple listened patiently, then spoke. "Raley is a good magistrate, and I trust him to be able to handle the case," he said. And that was that.

For me, though, that was the first sign that the fix was in. The three cousins were threatening to blow the lid off the dirty secret that cops beat people. That was something the justice system couldn't afford to see happen. The police are there to protect the power of the powerful, defend the property of the propertied and keep any threats to that power structure in a state of fearful submission. They are the militant arm of the status quo - and the status quo is the money men, the politicians, the media, the judges and even the lawyers. Most of all the lawyers. When the police are threatened, I would soon learn, those forces close ranks like the lips of a Venus flytrap. The fix was in.

An early victim was Wendy Thomas. When the TV showed three young men with bruised and swollen faces and the newspaper carried allegations of beatings on a frozen bridge, much of Clairton did what most towns do when their cops are called to the carpet: They rallied around the boys in blue. The exception was Wendy Thomas.

Thomas was the city manager of Clairton when the three cousins were beaten. While Abbet predicted that the actors wouldn't be satisfied with the results of his investigation and told the papers that the allegations were impossible because Rahis and Sanalas had been through eight hours of sensitivity training, Thomas quietly did her own inquiry. Then Thomas did the unthinkable: She used her powers as city manager to suspend Mimms, Rahis and Sanalas indefinitely, and recommended that they be fired.

The uproar was immediate. Abbet and Clairton Mayor Lou Costello condemned the decision. The cops got lawyers to appeal the suspensions. Clairton City Council expressed its doubt about the decision. And within a month of the suspensions, Thomas resigned under pressure from the mayor and council.

Sanalas served a 10-day suspension. Rahis and Mimms stayed home from late April through the end of September. At that time council reinstated them and, declaring Rahis' suspension to be retroactively reduced to 30 days, handed him $5,696 in back pay. Rahis promptly went on sick leave and then resigned.

Maniac Cop Mimms' time off wasn't exactly trouble-free. In August, Clairton cops were called to the home of his estranged wife, where her boyfriend told them that Mimms had just pistol-whipped him and put a gun to his head. The suspended officer told his colleagues that it was all a lie - his wife's friend had walked into a closet door. Mimms was never arrested, and apparently the incident didn't make much of an impression on Clairton council. Mimms' suspension was cut to 90 days, entitling him to $1,792 in back pay. He continues to work his beat in the City of Clairton.

* * *

After one postponement, the first step in the criminal case against my son and his cousins finally rolled around on June 2. The media would be there, and I was determined to put the story of the out-of-control cops in their faces yet again.

Local rapper Doc Boogie had recorded a song about the case, and we played it over and over from a boom box on busy Fifth Avenue in Downtown McKeesport, right in front of Raley's chambers. Doc Boogie, my sister La Rue and I wore shirts printed with, respectively, "Maniac Cop Sanalas", "Maniac Cop Rahis" and "Maniac Cop Mimms." The three of us passed out fliers with the lyrics of the song on them and told anyone who would listen what had really happened on that icy road and that lonely bridge in Clairton.

And we got an earful, too, as McKeesport residents came up and told us about their own run-ins with Maniac Cop Mimms, which all too often had ended in threats, intimidation or violence. "How can that dude be a poll-lease officer? He cops drugs from me 24-7," said a drug dealer. "Clyde Mimms is my biggest customer," boasted a local white prostitute.

I'd heard rumors of Mimms' uncontrolled rages and criminal behavior, but at the time, I didn't know the half of it. Years later, when I pried open the FBI files, I would find that Clyde Maniac Mimms had a record of criminal activity likely as long as anyone he'd ever arrested.

It started even before he became a cop.
On August 19, 1987, according to McKeesport Police Department records, Mimms was charged with simple assault for beating one Curtis Harper's leg with a baseball bat. The incident, which happened on August 12, according to the police reports, put Harper in the hospital for two days.

That knowledge apparently didn't deter the City of McKeesport from hiring Mimms as a police officer a year later. He took his oath of office August 8, 1988, the records show. And for about a year, his supervisors rated him highly, though they noted that he was a little shy for a cop.

On December 12, 1989, one Danielle Ura Seals filed a police report alleging that Mimms raped her. McKeesport police investigated the claim and declared it unfounded.

According to the records, that was just the beginning of a spate of troubles which would eventually see Mimms pushed from the force. On January 23, 1990, police reports say, Mimms allegedly kicked out the window of his ex-wife Wanda Cummings's car and assaulted the man she was with, Derrick Smith.

More domestic trouble followed. On June 29, 1990, police records show, Mimms was parked near the old McKeesport Tube Works having an argument with his new love interest, Paula Smith. When Daniel "Danny Boy" Wright happened by, Mimms got out of the car and the two scuffled. Mimms fired a shot, and when police arrived, they found Wright bleeding from a wound above his eye. Mimms said his gun went off accidentally.

Mimms filed charges against Wright, but dropped them three weeks later. In a July 17, 1990 memo on the incident, McKeesport Police Chief Daniel Beltree wrote that Wright should never have been arrested. "Mimms was off-duty, had been drinking, and was engaged in an argument with his girlfriend, Paula Smith, when Wright wandered onto the scene," Beltree wrote. "A witness, Lloyd Turner of JennyLind Street, came to see me after the incident and is very willing to state, wherever may be necessary, that Mimms initiated the confrontation with Wright."

The memo went on to call Smith "a convicted felon, prostitute, and drug user."

According to police records, Wanda Cummings's car bore the brunt of Mimms' aggression again December 22, 1990, when he saw his ex-wife with one Jody Ann Price. Mimms brandished "a weapon" at Ann Price, the report says, and Ann Price and Cummings ran back into a bar, fearful of being shot.

On July 8, 1991, a police oficer was called to an apartment for a domestic dispute between Mimms and Smith. The report says that Smith refused to confirm to the officer that Mimms had threatened her with a gun, but then said to Mimms: "If you wouldn't of put that gun up against my head this wouldn't of happened."

On August 19, 1991 Mimms was temporarily relieved from duty for eight weeks of treatment for what the records describe as drug and alcohol abuse. Records show he complied with the treatment, but didn't think he had a problem.

On December 2, 1991, a police report indicates, a McKeesport man named Derek Murphys reported that an "intoxicated" Mimms repeatedly drove past his house, brandishing a gun, and on one occasion got out of the car.

A letter by city Solicitor John Bloch to Beltree and McKeesport

Mayor Lou Dunn dated December 30, 1991, said the incident involved use of a weapon against the general public "while under the influence of alcohol or drugs."

"It is clear that Officer Mimms' conduct has indicated a possible alcoholic problem, a tendency for violence and a continued history of gun related incidents," Bloch wrote.

Some time later, Mimms was given an ultimatum to either leave McKeesport's finest or be fired, and he resigned. On Jan. 16, 1993, he was hired by Clairton for $8 an hour.

There, records show nothing until that night of March 6, 1994, when Mimms snapped again and beat and tortured three young black men on a frozen bridge.

As I was handing out fliers I happened to look across the street and saw a familiar figure striding down the opposite side of Fifth Avenue: It was Special Agent Bill Gunn. He eyeballed me, but didn't stop. Instead he turned and walked into the Executive Building, McKeesport's version of an office tower. A few minutes later I saw his face and a few others watching us from above. I wondered what the hell the FBI veteran was doing up there. If he came for the case, he should be in the courtroom, shouldn't he? A few minutes later a guy in a suit came out of the building and crossed the street, and grabbed a flier from La Rue.

I later heard that Gunn was supposedly teaching a seminar on police brutality in McKeesport that day. Ironically, the cops who sat in on his seminar probably learned a lot more about police brutality than any of the spectators at the preliminary hearing just across the street, where three victims were on trial for a trumped up crime, but the subject of their beating turned out to be taboo.

We continued to pass out our fliers and share the story with whoever happened to pass by; but as the minutes went by I started to notice a new presence. Two of McKeesport's boys in blue were slowly inching down Fifth Avenue toward us. I looked up, and saw Gunn still in the window. Was he there to protect me, or watch my untimely end? I wasn't sure.

As the cops worked their way down the sidewalk, I pointed them out to La Rue and Doc Boogie. "Don't start anything," I said. "I don't think they're trying to memorize Doc's lyrics or anything; I think they're out to intimidate us the hell out of here. I don't like it, but I don't want any confrontation today, either. If they tell us we're breaking the law, we'll just move down the road."

Pretty soon they were right beside me, asshole to belly button. I turned and nodded. "How you guys doin'? Are we breaking the law here?"

"No, you're within your rights," one said. "You're not breaking the law."

I didn't ask them why they had to stand close enough to be our shadows if we weren't doing anything wrong, and they didn't do anything to get in the way of our leafleting, nor ask us to turn the music down. But their presence was felt, and La Rue quickly headed into the courtroom.

Our new friends stayed with us until someone snatched a purse right across the street from where we were standing. They took off in pursuit of a real crime.

When the hearing started, the cameramen and print journalists quickly moved into Raley's packed courtroom. I suspect that the seat of justice in humble McKeesport had never seen such a spectacle. Every one of the 30 folding chairs was occupied, with Derek's and Sonny's mothers sitting right in among Mimms' family and the media hordes. The three cousins stood against one wall, dressed in their best suits. Devon wore a black jacket and pants, Derek a purple tie and slacks, and Sonny a shirt dripping with different colors and a solid tie. Though I believe at this preliminary hearing they were already skeptical about their chances of receiving a fair trial, their dress and demeanor, at least, showed respect for the court.

That wasn't enough for some people. Before the hearing newswoman Brenda Safety of the local TV-2 walked down the aisle announcing that the three "looked like gangbangers and should go to jail for what they did." Sonny's mother Arnella, who happened to hear the comment, didn't think that was the kind of attitude a journalist should have before listening to the evidence. "How do you know what gangbangers look like?" Arnella shouted, getting right in Safety' face. Safety apologized, saying she didn't mean anything by it, and the incident ended. But her offhand comment spoke volumes about the assumptions the supposedly unbiased media brought to the case.

Assistant District Attorney Ronald Zarewcyzewski led off by

telling Judge Raley that his first witness would be one of those charged - Derek Goodman. Goodman, he explained, had told Mimms out on the bridge that there was a gun, that it was Little Sonny Brown's, and that Sonny had fired it. And inside the police station, under interrogation, he'd confirmed it and signed a statement to prove it.

The so-called confession was a one-page document written in a handwriting foreign to all three cousins, with strange references to someone named "Toby" sprinkled throughout. Zarewcyzewski said he would have Goodman testify in confirmation of the contents of the confession, and only to that.

"Are you going to let your client testify at this hearing?" Raley asked Larry Vicious.

"No, your honor," Vicious said, and that was that.

Zarewcyzewski then called Clyde Mimms. Mimms lumbered up to the witness stand and plopped into the chair. He's a big man with a cocky look in his eye and a way of speaking which brings to mind cold corn syrup. The A.D.A. had him go through his resume and asked him if he'd ever fired a gun in the course of his work as a police officer. Mimms denied it. Next he had Mimms confirm that he was driving down Route 837, or River Road, on the early morning of March 6, 1994. Then suddenly, Zarewcyzewski was stopped by a hacking cough.

"You need a drink of water, Mr. Zarewcyzewski?" Raley asked him.

"No, it's something that will continue all day, judge," he answered.

"You sure? We can get you a little glass of water."

"No, I'm fine, thanks."

Zarewcyzewski then led Mimms through his description of the fateful night. It was dark. There were only two cars on the road, Mimms' Pontiac Sunbird and the black Camaro. Mimms was on his way home with his girlfriend, who at the time was pregnant with his child, he said. He was in a hurry, so Mimms pulled up on the Camaro.

"The black Camaro was going kind of slow," he said.

"What do you mean by slow?" Zarewcyzewski asked.

"It was going under 35. So I decided I was going to pass. I went out into the left lane, and tried - "

"So this is just a two lane road?" The A.D.A. interrupted.

"A two lane road."

So in spite of the solid double yellow line and the icy conditions, Mimms tried to pass.

"I got out a little ahead of the black Camaro and the Camaro sped up right beside me."

"What do you mean, sped up?" asked Zarewcyzewski.

"It moved a little faster. I had moved out a little in front of it, and it moved a little faster and got up right beside me."

"Were you able to get in the other lane?"

"No, not at that point, because it was right beside me. I couldn't get in the other lane."

"Did you look over to see who was in the vehicle?"

"I looked over, but the windows were tinted."

Then, Mimms said, the Camaro suddenly bolted ahead. He moved back into the right lane. "They went up so far, and then I guess they slowed down again," he said. "The driver-side door came open."

"From the moment you got back in the proper lane to the moment you say the driver side door opened up, how much, how far was it, what was the distance?" asked Zarewcyzewski.

"About 7 or 8 car lengths."

The A.D.A. switched gears. "Did you have a weapon on you on this day?" he asked.

"Yes I did."

"And why is that?"

"Uhh, I always carry a weapon when I'm off duty, with everything that's going on nowadays."

"Where was the weapon at this point?"

"On the seat of the car."

"When you got back in the proper lane, did you pull the weapon out at that point?"

"No, it was still between the seats of the car."

The driver's side door of the speeding Camaro hung open to the freezing night. "When the door came open, all I saw was muzzle flash coming back my way."

"From where?"

"From the driver's side door of the Camaro."

"The driver's side door. The front door. Did you see anybody in the

car at that point? Was there movement in the car?"
"No, I couldn't see."
"You believe it was a gun being fired?"
"Yes, I know it was a gun being fired."

Mimms knew muzzle flash, he said; he'd seen it before. Two or three times, he said, flashes of fire leapt from the open door of the speeding Camaro. Rather than slow down or turn around, though, Mimms took his pregnant girlfriend for a ride.

"At that time I got my gun out from between the seats, stuck it out the driver's side window and shot it once up in the air."
"Up in the air?"
"Up in the air."

That got the message across, said Mimms. The shooting from the Camaro stopped. Still the Clairton cop drove on, trying to get the plate number off of the car. When the Camaro turned from Route 837 up residential Maple Street, Mimms said, he followed it. When it ran red lights and stop signs in residential Clairton, he did so too. When it spun around on a side street and headed back down Maple toward 837, so did he. Only then did he get close enough to see the plate, and his girlfriend jotted the number down on her hand.

There the shooting started again. "Down near the bottom of Maple and State, they had made the left, going north on 837. And at that point they opened the car door again -"
"What door opened up?" Zarewcyzewski asked.
"Driver's side."
"Did you see who fired?"
"Couldn't see who fired."
"Describe what happened."
"He started shooting at me again."
"How many times?"
"I don't know."

Again Mimms wasn't hit, and he shoved his gun out the driver side window again and returned fire. He emptied his gun of the five remaining bullets there. When the Camaro turned South on 837, Mimms turned north, in the direction of the police station. For the Camaro drivers, though, Mimms told the judge, it wasn't over.

"The car was turning around, coming after us," he said. So he gunned it back to the station, and the Camaro disappeared in his rearview mirror. It didn't fire another shot, and Mimms pulled into the municipal building parking lot.

"As I got out of the car and was approaching the door, Officer Sanalas and Officer Rahis were coming out. They had gotten calls about shots." As if on cue, the offending Camaro drove slowly by the municipal building. Mimms jumped in the car with Sanalas while Rahis led the way on his own. Rahis drove around the Camaro, Mimms said, and it stopped. Mimms jumped out of Sanalas' car and "approached" the passenger side door.

The three young men winced. At this point, they all knew, Mimms smashed Derek with his shotgun, dragged him from the car, beat him, kicked him, held him over the edge of the bridge, and smashed his head against the curb. The terror of that night started replaying itself in their minds. But nothing of the sort would come out of Maniac Cop Mimms' lying mouth on this day.

"We got them out of the car and then arrested them," Mimms said "Did they open up the door, did you open up the door, or what?" Zarewcyzewski asked.

"I opened up the door."

"When you first opened up the door, were you able to determine who was in what seat? First of all, how many occupants were in the vehicle?"

"Three."

"Only three?"

"Yes." Mimms then identified Goodman as the one in the passenger's seat. The driver, Grey, was, "the guy in the black suit." In the back seat was Brown, who he identified as the one "in the multi-colored shirt, standing between Mr. Goodman and Grey." The suspects were identified for the record.

"Okay, what was your next line of action? You opened up the door."

"We took them out of the car and arrested them."

And there, abruptly, is where the direct examination ended. I guess it was only natural that the Assistant District Attorney would stop short of the beatings, the terror, the gun to Devon's head. It was our lawyer's job to dredge through that muck and show this officer of the law for the thug he was. Attorney Jipenstein stepped up to the plate.

Jipenstein started off slow, asking Mimms when that day he had worked, where he had gone after work, and on and on. Turned out Mimms had worked the 8 to 4 shift, then headed home. He'd stayed home a while - he didn't know how long. Then, he claimed, he'd taken Mishelle Blunt to his cousin's home in suburban Penn Hills - he didn't know exactly where. After spending a little while there, he headed for his home in Clairton.

"After work I went home, then I went to my cousin's house, then I went to go home," he claimed.

Of course, I'd passed the tip I'd gotten from Steve Timmons on to Jipenstein. "Had you been in any establishment in Duquesne or Homestead prior to being on River Road that night?" he asked.

"No," said Mimms.

"You're sure you weren't?"

"Sure."

"Okay. Now when you were in your cousin's home and when you were in your home, did you have anything to drink?"

"I had a beer at my cousin's. Along with dinner."

"One beer? Did you have any alcohol?"

"I just said one beer."

The cousins shook their heads. This man on the stand had been breathing fire-water three months ago when he'd apprehended them. If it was one beer he'd consumed, it must have been one huge beer.

Jipenstein pointed out that Mishelle Blunt had been subpoenaed to testify at this hearing, but hadn't showed. He then led Mimms through a description of the chase scene. The big, slow cop showed increasing annoyance as he was forced to go over the route again, where the shots were fired, where the Camaro had turned, why he'd continued to follow it.

The old lawyer kept up his friendly, we're-just-here-to-get-at-the-facts demeanor. The cousins wondered whether he would catch Mimms up in his lies, expose him for the fraud he was and end this vindictive prosecution here and now. Instead, the proceeding bogged down into an argument between the lawyers about when Mimms was or wasn't able to see the Camaro's license plate number, why he wasn't able to see it earlier than he was, how dark a dark night is, and on and on and on.

Jipenstein jumped back to the supposed party in Penn Hills.

"Mishelle, had she had anything to drink in your presence, during the time you were at your house and at your cousin's house?" Jipenstein asked.

"Not at my house. I can't recall if she had anything at my cousin's house."

Jipenstein asked if Blunt appeared to be impaired in any way, and Zarewcyzewski jumped up to object. Again, the A.D.A. and the defense lawyer went on and on about relevance and hearsay objections. Raley sustained Zarewcyzewski's objection, and told Jipenstein to take his cross-examination somewhere else.

Jipenstein took it straight to the bridge. He asked Mimms what happened. "[We] got out of the car, slipped on the icy bridge," he answered.

Did you have weapons drawn when you approached the car?

"I had a shotgun," Mimms said. "I'm not sure if anyone else had weapons drawn. I wasn't paying attention."

"Where did that come from? The police car?"

"The police car."

"That's a standard weapon that you carry in the police car?"

"Correct."

"The passenger in the front seat got out of the car? Or did you have to assist him in getting out of the car?"

"I'm not sure. I think I may have assisted him in getting out of the car."

Derek smiled grimly. Maniac Cop Mimms had an interesting idea of how to assist someone, he thought. His thoughts were interrupted, though, by Zarewcyzewski, who leapt from his seat.

"Your honor, at this point I'm going to object. The direct examination stopped at the arrest. This is beyond the scope of the direct examination. Also it's beyond the scope of the entire complaint. If you look at all the charges that were filed, and the amendments that were made next week, there's no resisting arrest, there's no disorderly conduct, there's no harassment as to any of these defendants, so I think the question is beyond the scope, it's irrelevant."

The A.D.A. was trying to stop the defense from taking any testimony on the beating and arrest. Jipenstein stepped toward the bench.

"Your honor, this isn't a fishing expedition," he said.

Raley frowned. "Mr. Jipenstein, please. I'm going to overrule the district attorney's objection. I'm going to allow you to continue, but, you know, we've spoken about this already. We're here for these criminal complaints against these three defendants. We're not here for any subsequent action which may or may not transpire through the course of this thing. ... This is not a civil liability case or a lawsuit. ... If I start hearing questions that I don't believe are relevant or pertain to why I'm here and why this court has to here this case, I'm going to stop it. Do you understand?"

"Absolutely," said Jipenstein. "The arrest is an essential part of this incident."

Zarewcyzewski objected again, but Raley made it clear he was going to let Jipenstein go for the time being and see where he ended up. The court's attention returned again to Mimms, and Jipenstein brought him back to the bridge.

"What activity occurred between you and he at that moment?"

"We stood outside the car." Mimms choked slightly as he said it.

"Was he cuffed?"

"No."

Again Zarewcyzewski jumped up and objected to any further questioning about the arrest. The Commonwealth of Pennsylvania's tactic was clear: They would fight tooth and nail to keep any testimony regarding the beatings out of any proceeding. They would call my son and nephews shooters or thieves or conspirators, but they would allow no mention of out-of-control cops who beat citizens with shotguns, kick them with heavy boots and hold pistols to their heads in sick imitation of Russian Roulette.

Raley listened to Zarewcyzewski's objections. Then, to everyone's surprise, he shot them down. "Overruled. Go ahead Mr. Jipenstein."

"Where were they then taken?" Jipenstein asked.

"To the Clairton Police Station," said Mimms.

"How long were you at the scene before they were taken to the Clairton Police Station?"

"About 10 minutes. However long it took to search the car."

"Now while they were searching the car, were you in charge? Did you have all three of them in your custody? Were they in front of you? You only had the one?"

"Just the one."

For a third time Zarewcyzewski jumped up to object, and for the third time Raley overruled him.

Jipenstein asked Mimms if he had any reason to think that the young men were inebriated, and he said he didn't. But suddenly our attorney reached a line he appeared unwilling to cross. He didn't ask Mimms anything about the beatings. He didn't bring the testimony to the front of the police station, where Mimms pummeled Devon's head into a heap of hard-packed snow. He didn't venture into the station, where Derek was intimidated into signing a false confession, where Little Sonny was beaten and put in submission holds, where my son was threatened with execution and kicked in the head. He just stopped.

Larry Vicious came up next, and the cousins wondered if he'd mop Mimms up. Maybe Jipenstein and Vicious would work as a tag team, one setting Mimms up and the other dealing the crushing final blow. Instead, Vicious led an increasingly testy Mimms through another description of the events of the day prior to the chase.

Then Vicious asked whether a trained policeman is supposed to fire back when fired upon. Mimms' answer didn't make much sense, though. "Yes, you are trained, being that you are so close to that curve, as Mr. Jipenstein referred to, I did not want to fire any rounds in that direction for fear that someone might be coming around the corner."

"Did your vehicle or the vehicle of the defendants get stuck in the snow at any point while you were in pursuit of them?" Vicious asked. "Yes, their vehicle got stuck after they made the left on to Reed Street off of Shaw," Mimms answered.

Devon wondered whether Vicious would ask him about how he got out of the car, slinked sidelong down the street toward the snow-bound Camaro, held his pistol at the ready and growled, "I'm gonna kill you motherfuckers!" For months he'd tried to forget that night, though he'd had to dredge up the memories for the FBI, the media and inquiring relatives and friends. Now, to hear the events of that night recounted in this edited, sanitized manner made him sick. He wanted to take two steps to the right, grab Mimms around his fatty neck and shake the truth out of him.

But Vicious instead asked him who'd searched the car on the bridge. "Officer Rahis," said Mimms. And during that search, Vicious asked him, did you have any interaction with Mr. Goodman?

"We had some words," Mimms said.

"Where?"

"I believe on the bridge. And again at the station."

"At the station. And did your person that you took out of the car make any statements to you that were reduced to writing?"

"Not to me."

That was it for Vicious. The Assistant District Attorney then called John Rahis to the stand, and the Mickey Mouse cop who'd claimed to me he hadn't even been working on the night of the beatings took his seat beside the judge. Zarewcyzewski had him testify that he found a .25 automatic, nickel-plated pistol with one live round in it and an empty .25-caliber magazine in the car. The gun, he said, was reported stolen from Glassport. Rahis claimed he "got a verbal from the lab that the gun was operable."

To the amazement of the defendants, their lawyers stipulated that the gun was operable. Jipenstein said that if the written report came back different, they'd withdraw the stipulations. Defense had no further questions for John Rahis, the cop who'd shot at the car and practiced his karate skills on Derek's groin and Devon's head. He stepped down.

Jipenstein then launched into what Raley would later call "the best performance I've ever seen you make in my courtroom." He pushed for dismissal of all charges involving Mishelle Blunt, because she had failed to show up for the hearing. The A.D.A. protested, but Raley dismissed the charges, without saying whether they could be filed again.

Jipenstein then honed in on the criminal conspiracy charges. The testimony, he said, "certainly can't constitute criminal conspiracy. ... I submit there is absolutely no concerted action of these people. Sitting in a bus with a bus driver that's crazy, being in an airplane with a pilot who does something, certainly does not constitute a conspiracy on the part of the passenger."

Vicious jumped on the bandwagon. "There is absolutely no testimony showing that my two clients furthered any attempt to do anything as far as the automobile is concerned that is driven by Devon Grey."

Devon wondered if he'd be left shitting in the wind. But the

A.D.A. seemed to see the problem he'd face if Jipenstein and Vicious successfully de-linked the three cousins' cases: Since Mimms didn't see who allegedly fired the gun, it was an all-or-nothing proposition for the prosecution.

"Mr. Jipenstein's argument may not hold water for the reason that, sure a bus driver and if you're a passenger in a car with a wild and crazy bus driver, that's not the situation," Zarewcyzewski blurted. "Look at the relationship of the parties. Three gentlemen in a car. In a car, not in a bus where you have strangers, passengers coming in with a bus driver. ... Three gentlemen in a car, knowing one another, going somewhere together, is a lot different."

Then Zarewcyzewski launched into what would come to be known as the "pass the gun" theory. "Who's the one that actually shot? Had the gun in his hand? Who's the one who did the shooting? It could have been all of them. ... Any of those three very easily could have had that gun and could have been doing the firing. ... But who's shooting the weapon? It could have been any of the three. And circumstances will show that."

Jipenstein seemed almost gleeful as he jumped to the boys' defense. "Your honor, let me respond to that. It's almost like we're in a commission hearing to see who killed Kennedy. There might have been a conspiracy. I don't know, your honor. But we have to take the testimony that they gave. We didn't put their testimony on; they did.
"They have a magazine in the front seat, by the driver. They have a gun described to be in the rear portion of the driver's area. They have a door opening when the car is in movement. It's the driver's side. The car doesn't veer, it doesn't do anything. A hand - apparently, I'm not even sure I recollect he saw a hand, but he certainly saw some flash from the driver's side. Now to say, to even permit a conjecture - conjecture isn't permissible at this level, either; it's mere suspicion.
"Three people were in the car. Do you want to say that Clyde Mimms firing a weapon out of his car, which might have been a crime for an off-duty officer, is Mishelle Blunt guilty of a conspiracy?"

Devon felt the hair stand up on the back of his neck. Now that was lawyering!

"Three people got out of the car. They were in the car at 3:00 in the morning. If that's a crime, then on that particular night you have to pick up half of McKeesport."

"The district attorney in his argument has just said to you, 'I don't know who did it,'" Jipenstein continued. "If there happens to be some cocaine in the front row of this room, that's being occupied by 20 people, are you going to say who did it? Are you going to allege that I'm just as responsible as the man who might be nearest it? I'm not even sure that the man who might be nearest to it is necessarily guilty of the crime. It seems to me that there is no evidence of recklessly endangering. Certainly not against three people. ... You can't have everybody responsible when the testimony from you is that from one place came several shots."

Vicious chimed in, and again he seemed intent on cutting his clients loose at Devon's expense. "There's no act by the passenger, there's no act by Mr. Goodman," he said. "They have no overt act by anyone, other than the fact that Mr. Grey was the driver. They don't even know that he was driving. There's no testimony about who was driving, because they couldn't even see in the car."

"During that time everybody could have played rotating chairs," Jipenstein added.

Suddenly, the middle of the courtroom audience erupted into shouts. Mimms' mammy, it seems, had made a comment that the three defendants should go away for a long time. Arnella Brown, who was sitting behind her, answered with, "Quiet down! Your son almost killed my son." Now the two women were standing in the middle of Raley's court, shouting in each others' faces as journalists scrambled to write it all down and Raley pounded his gavel.

"Quiet!"

The mothers calmed down and slowly, warily, took their seats.

The A.D.A., who by this time looked like a hunted animal, closed by arguing that all three should remain charged with the crimes. After all, he said, Devon had control of the car and the door. Little Sonny had access to the door, and the gun was found in the back. And Derek, he said, could easily have reached across the front of the '78 Camaro and fired out the driver's side door. He ridiculed what he called Jipenstein's "musical chairs" defense. And suddenly the theatrics were over, and everyone in that room was looking to Raley for the word.

"There's a lot of speculation here," he said. "But what is not speculation in the eyes of the court is that there was a gun fired at Officer

Mimms. I'll hold the charges," he said. The matter would go Downtown. "But I will say, Mr. Jipenstein, that was the best performance you've ever put on in my courtroom."

I was still outside when the doors swung open and chaos poured out into the street. First came Little Sonny, the media right on his heels. "Yo, man, we was robbed!" he shouted. "It was all lies. Mimms and Rahis told a bunch of lies."

Then came Derek, another pack of reporters surrounding him. "Yeah, I knew the case would be held for court," he told them. "They'll do anything to prove this wasn't police brutality. We feel police brutality is common in our neighborhood. That's why people want an all-out war with the police."

Then came Devon. He was less vociferous than the other two, so there were fewer press people around him. Someone asked him if he thought it was a fair hearing. "I guess it was fair," he said, and shrugged. "I don't know."

Finally there was Jipenstein. He dodged the reporters and found his way to me. "They held the charges."

"I know."

"Raley didn't have the balls to throw it out," he said. It seemed strange coming out of his mouth - like he was trying to talk my language, talking down to me. "But I think I got enough out of Mimms to get it kicked out Downtown."

"I hope you're right."

He hurried off to answer press questions, and I drifted to the edge of the mob. I ended up next to a TV reporter who'd apparently grown tired of fighting through the swirling press hordes and was just standing there, maybe waiting to see if a riot broke out. "What'd you think?" I asked him.

"What do I think? They should have kicked that out. They didn't have anything on them," he said. Then he seemed to notice my T-shirt. "Who are you?"

"I'm the father of Devon Grey."

He seemed startled, and didn't say anything else. But that was enough; I was mad. If this guy, who had no reason at all to be biased about the case, thought it should be kicked out, then it must be more than fatherly subjectivity which made me feel that this prosecution was a crock of shit.

All around there was craziness. The media rushed around as if they were really important, when I knew well that they would report the same old crap: the "suspects" were held for trial for shooting at a police officer, and after the hearing they "alleged" being beaten. Inside La Rue has cornered Rahis and chased him out of the courtroom, down some stairs and out on to Lysle Boulevard, a scene which would be captured on camera and replayed on the evening news. I saw Mimms peeking through the doorway, and when we made eye contact, he turned tail and ran upstairs.

We all got together after the hullabaloo died down and talked about what had happened. Some thought Jipenstein was brilliant, others thought he blew it. Everybody thought Vicious had asked stupid questions when he'd opened his mouth at all.

But the crux of the matter was that my child was going to trial for allegedly shooting at a police officer, and as of yet nobody had said a thing in court about what had happened to him. Like the police reports, the preliminary hearing had carefully avoided all mention of the real crime - the one perpetrated against Devon, Derek and Sonny. It was a one-sided affair, carefully censored by the judge with the full acquiescence of the so-called defense lawyers, and tailor-made to protect Maniac Cop Mimms' credibility.

My son was caught up in a Kangaroo Court determined to convict him and protect the men who'd beaten him. I was paying thousands to defend Devon against a full-speed-ahead prosecution, while Mimms, Sanalas and Rahis had yet to be charged for any of their crimes. But someone would have to answer for what happened on that bridge and in that station. Though they'd escaped man's justice for now, they would have another date with justice, in the civil court. And then there would be God's justice. I wouldn't want to be in their shoes when that day comes.

Chapter 7

Grand Injury

That summer the criminal case against my son and nephews slowed to a crawl. Bill Gunn all but disappeared. And I hit the streets.

I launched my own private war on the three maniac cops, and my weapon of choice was not the shotgun, but the pen. I put a mug shot of Mimms on top of a flyer and captioned it: "Maniac Cop Clyde Mimms: America's Most Wanted. Alias: God" and then detailed the March 6 beatings. Below that I listed some of the things I'd learned about Mimms' background, and asked citizens to "Check Yes or No if you want Maniac Cop Clyde Mimms to protect You." Another flyer showed the battered, blackened faces of the three cousins and detailed the handiwork of Mimms, Rahis and Sanalas.

Thousands of these flyers went up on light posts and bulletin boards all over Clairton. The three cousins and I launched quick strikes through Clairton, posting our flyers in a long swath through the heart of the community and dropping off handfuls in bars, restaurants, laundromats - anywhere people were gathered with time on their hands. Sometimes the cops would follow the trail of paper, tearing down the flyers as they went. At times they were no more than 30 seconds behind us, ripping them from light posts and running into business establishments, asking, "Any fliers here?"

What they could find, they tore up, crumpled or shoved in their pockets. Once they got so close that we could see Maniac Cop Mimms' and Sanalas' faces contorted in rage. But they never caught up to us, and we left Clairton in a cloud of smoke and a torrent of laughter.

I went on two black radio talk shows - Debra Webb's show on WAMO and John Chapman's on XCXJ. The family led three demonstrations in the City of Police Brutality, Clairton. One evening I led a pack of demonstrators, mostly friends and family, in a march on Clairton City Council. We entered the council's weekly meetings, holding signs saying, "Mimms and Rahis got to go," and "Abbet is a racist." I could see the mostly white leaders of mostly black Clairton fidgeting in their seats.

When the meeting ended and Mayor Lou Costello asked if there was any other business, Little Sonny got up to speak about the beating. Costello, an older white guy with a face like a peach left out for days in the sun, barely let him get out two sentences before he started pounding his gavel.

"This is neither the time nor place for this!" he hollered. The incident was under investigation, he announced.

Little Sonny sat down, and I got up.

"I'm here to tell you that we are not going to go along with this," I told the assembled council members, citizens and reporters. "We as black people are not going to be treated as we were 40 years ago."

When I told them I was here to give them a warning about relations between their police department and the citizenry, Costello lost his cool. "This meeting is out of order!" he yelled, banging his gavel. He started shouting about how he wouldn't stand for people coming into his meetings and making threats. I told him it wasn't a threat, just a warning. Then I asked him where Public Safety Director William Abbet was.

Abbet, who had been sitting off to the side, stood up.

I walked toward him and he toward me. "You are a coward and a liar!" I told him.

"I am not a coward and a liar," he answered, then turned to Costello. "Do you want me to escort him out of the room?" he asked the mayor.

"Please do," Costello said. He slammed the gavel again and declared the meeting adjourned.

"This is supposed to be America, this isn't Haiti!" I shouted. I told them how in a democracy, public forums were places where peoples' viewpoints could be heard.

Then Abbet and I were in each others' faces, shouting, he threatening to have me removed, me saying why don't you go ahead and try it. This was the man who was trying to cover up the beating my son and nephews took on that bridge, the man who was doing everything he could to protect Maniac Cop Mimms, Rahis and Sanalas from justice, and I was just a hair away from pounding him into the wooden floor of that tawdry little council room. It could have come to blows but my sister La Rue got between us. "Don't do it, Buster!" she said. "They just want you to get violent so they can have an excuse to haul you off to jail. Don't give them the satisfaction."

She and a few other family members dragged me away. We protested outside for a little while, and I remember this white cop, couldn't have been more than 20 years old, watching and probably wondering what the hell he'd gotten himself into. I told him he'd better not hang out outside, that it was too dangerous; go back into the municipal building where it's safer. He did.

Clairton's brand new city manager happened out of the building, and I walked up and introduced myself. He said his name was Ken Strong, and handed me a card. "I wasn't on board when the beatings occurred," he said.

"I know. Whatever happened to the old manager, Wendy Thomas?"

"Well, she had a disagreement with the mayor over suspending Mimms and Rahis."

"So did he push her off the job?"

"Basically," he said, rubbing his nose. "He's told me and the council members that 'it's us against them,' and that we've got to reinstate the cops."

"Us against them," I repeated. "That's the one true thing I've heard out of Clairton since this whole thing started. It's us - Devon, Derek, Little Sonny and their families - against the whole damn establishment. Costello, the FBI, the media, the lawyers, the commonwealth - the entire establishment seems arrayed against us."

In the newspapers the next day, Costello was quoted as saying I was "going to jail" if I held another demonstration. I wondered when they'd passed a law that speaking at a public meeting was punishable with jail time.

It was apparent Costello was turning a blind eye to the truth and justice. He would go on to enable the reinstatement of the Mimms, Rahis and Sanalas, three crazy men who called themselves police officers.

The insults from Clairton just fueled my information campaign. It was sweet revenge, good clean fun, and it kept the public informed, but we knew no number of fliers or radio appearances would ever put the three cops behind bars. Nor would it send a message to other cops who might be tempted to beat and torture people on frozen bridges and in chilly brick edifices. For that, we needed the FBI.

Gunn called early in October and said that his preliminary investigation was complete. The Department of Justice had decided to convene a federal grand jury to hear the case. "We're going to subpoena you to testify," he said.

"Me? Why bother with me? I wasn't there. I didn't get beat."

"I know, I know. But you initiated the first contact with the FBI, and you seem to know the most about the case."

"Well, whatever. I'd be glad to testify. But what about Devon, Derek and Little Sonny?"

"We intend to call them later. What we've got to do now is interview you in preparation for your testimony. I'd like to bring by two Justice Department attorneys to talk to you. One is local and the other is flying in from D.C. for this."

It seemed they were giving the case a high profile. I asked him who the Justice Department was going after. Would it be just Mimms, or would they go after Rahis and Sanalas, too? And would assault or attempted murder charges be pursued?

Gunn danced around the question. That "had to be determined." He didn't say by who. I let it go.

We set up an appointment at my place for Oct. 13, and Gunn said my subpoena was for Nov. 1. He said he'd also subpoenaed Marie Goodman, and would meet with her separately. She was the first to hear of the beatings, he explained. I gave him directions to my house and got off the horn.

I shook my head and went to tell Devon, who'd been living with me since March. "Seems they've finally got things moving, seven months after you were beaten. But why would they be so interested in me?"

"Who knows, Dad. You speak well, and you know all the details of the case. Maybe they just want you to soften up that grand jury for Derek, Little Sonny and me."

Maybe. I waited for them to call again to set up an appointment with the real victims, but that call never came.

October 13 rolled around, and I prepared coffee and tea for my expected guests. I tried to figure out how to act with them. I could be Leon the Fighter, like I was with Gunn, and stare them right in the nose until they blinked. Or I could be Leon the Outraged, like I was outside of Raley's chambers and in front of the media mob. Then there was Leon the Teacher, like I was back in the days of Kids for Kids. And there were others, versions which had been dormant ever since the McKeesport cops first set their sights on my family, something which suddenly seemed a long and weary time ago.

While I waited, a friend called to tell me what had been reported in that morning's McKeesport Daily News. Mimms was facing charges of harassment for allegedly shoving a McKeesport woman on September 26, and for bruising the young child she was holding. A hearing on the case would be held in private, the newspaper reported, in front of District Justice Thomas Raley on October 27. The paper also reported that in August, Clairton police filed an incident report against Mimms for allegedly pistol-whipping Paula Smith's boyfriend, but nobody ever pressed charges.

Thank God for the FBI, I thought. Somebody's going to get this guy off the street.

The time for the appointed visit came and went, and the coffee sat getting stale. I fidgeted as 15, then 30, then 60 minutes passed with no Gunn.

I thought about calling the FBI, but was worried that I might be on the phone when Gunn called to explain. Then I was seized with a desire to go outside and run, just run, like I used to do back in McKeesport. Run from this private war with the police. Run from this FBI investigation which I couldn't control but was forced to rely on. Run from the whole damn country. Then as 60 minutes late turned to 90 and morning edged toward afternoon, I had a more practical impulse - to go do the shopping Lillian wanted me to do before she got home.

I was headed for the door when the phone rang. "Leon, this is Bill Gunn. Sorry, we're going to be a little late. We got lost. How do we get to your place from Business Route 22?"

I gave him the directions - again - and put down the phone. Lost for an hour and a half in Monroeville, huh? That was either a blatant lie or evidence of utter incompetence. I wasn't sure which was preferable. The man had probably gotten busy with something else and hadn't thought to call me. When you're the FBI, I suppose, you assume that people are going to wait.

Gunn's maroon sedan pulled into my drive, and I breathed deep to try to control my anxiety. When the three marched into my house

I tried to be cordial and professional, but I must've come off as a bundle of nerves. I didn't know what to say when Gunn introduced attorneys Constance Cass of Pittsburgh and Peggy Liu of Washington, D.C. I forgot to ask to take their coats until they had them in their hands and were looking around desperately for some place to throw them.

There was no sense asking if they'd had any trouble finding the place, so I mumbled a few words of greeting and led them into the kitchen. We sat down at the table and Gunn had me go through my involvement with the case. Cass and Liu asked a few questions and took notes. Cass was an enormous white lady who seemed to frown all the time. Liu was a slender, pretty woman of Oriental descent who met my eyes and shook her head as I described the swollen face, black ears and bright red eyes with which my son emerged from the Allegheny County Jail.

"There's no dispute, they were beaten," Liu said. "We saw the pictures taken at the hospital. Those men were beaten." She looked over at Cass. "We've got to get a guilty verdict on Mimms."

"And what about Rahis and Sanalas?" I asked her.

Cass frowned. Liu looked over at Gunn.

"We may have a shot at Rahis," said Gunn. "I doubt if we can get Sanalas."

Gunn said he was in the process of trying to match the gashes on the pictures with the barrel of the shotgun that was in Sanalas' cruiser that night. "If they match, Mimms might face attempted murder charges," he said.

I was glad for that. Mimms certainly tried to kill my son and nephews and hurt them badly. If nothing else, he'd been utterly unconcerned with whether the three men in his custody lived or died. For that matter, neither had Rahis and Sanalas.

But a pattern was emerging. These two whites and this Oriental woman who talked like a white wanted to nail this black cop Mimms to the wall, but hemmed and hawed when the two white officers were mentioned. If it were mine to decide, I would have crucified Rahis and Sanalas on either side of Mimms. As it was, I thought I could make out faint hints of the sweaty, adrenal stink of a lynching.

Suddenly, Cass shoved a flier showing the three beaten men in my face. It was one of my "Maniac Cop Clyde Mimms" posters.

"Do you have any idea who has been posting these?" she blurted out, as if she'd been struggling to hold the question in the whole time she'd been at my table.

I glanced at it and threw it back across the table at her. Out of the corner of my eye I saw Gunn bury his head in some piece of paperwork. "I don't know anything about it. I've seen these around, but I don't know who's been putting them up. Not that I blame them. If I had the money to buy space on billboards, I'd buy up every one in the City of Clairton and put up signs saying, 'Police brutality is alive and well in the City of Clairton,' and I'd put a picture of Maniac Cop Mimms up there beating three black men with a shotgun on the Ravensburg Bridge."

She looked at me with something like disgust in her eyes. I could feel the words "smart ass nigger" floating, unspoken, in the air between us. Gunn seemed stunned. It struck me that these people could never really understand what I felt. Back in McKeesport, police had searched my house without a warrant. They'd harassed my kids and sicced their informants on us. I felt they were responsible for two attempts on my life and the arson fire which destroyed my home. They'd brutalized my son and two nephews. To Gunn, Cass and Liu, these were civil rights violations and they had a professional responsibility to pursue them. But to me, they were something more - attacks on my family and on myself, and a continuation of centuries of mistreatment of people of color. These professionals from the FBI and Justice Department might know the law, but they would never understand how these violations of my family, my security and my dignity felt.

Cass put the flier away. "Well, Mr. Grey, if you do find out, please tell them to stop. Somebody's going to cause a riot if they're not careful. We're going to try Mr. Mimms before a grand jury, and there's no need to try him in the streets."

I thought about pointing out that he'd tried my son and nephews in the streets, found them guilty and exacted his sentence right then and there. But I said nothing.

Cass frowned and went on. "Mr. Grey, do you think the beating your son and nephews took might have had anything to do with the problems you had with the McKeesport police?"

Now I was the one who was shocked. I'd never told Gunn about those days. Seemed these folks had done some homework.

My mind rewound to 1993, the year when we were refugees from the Mon Valley cops and their snitch proxies. I remembered a phone call and a gruff voice which claimed to represent the FBI. The bureau had gotten word from the NAACP that I'd been a victim of police persecution, the voice said. Did I want to come down and file a formal complaint? I'd said I'd think about it.

I'd told Lillian, Ron Jackson and a few other confidants, and all agreed: It could be a trap. I might never come back. I never did call back the voice from the bureau. Only now did it occur to me that it must have been Gunn.

I didn't let on. "The last few years I was in McKeesport, Mimms was on the force," I said. "But I never had any specific problem with him. I have no reason to believe that this beating had anything to do with the McKeesport stuff. I guess anything's possible, though."

"So if this man had no grudge against your family, why do you think he beat them so badly?" Cass asked.

"Mimms was drunk, and he made a mistake that night." I told them about Steve Timmons and the Wee Bee Back Saloon, and Gunn scribbled frantically to keep up. What I didn't mention was that the car had a problem with backfiring, and I had the tests from Firestone to prove it. That night on Route 837, when Devon hit the gas to try to escape an erratic driver, that Camaro had backfired, and an alcohol-impaired Mimms apparently mistook the car's complaints for gunfire.

At that moment, I didn't trust them enough to give them that piece of evidence. My son still had a criminal case against him, and I didn't want this key part of his defense to somehow get back to the district attorney. These people were playing like they were on my side, but they were still the government. The D.A. was the government, too. I figured they all ran into each other in the corridors of power, talked, went out for coffee or scotch, and played golf together on Saturday mornings - the FBI, the D.A.., the judges, the cops, and even our defense lawyers.

"How can I reach Timmons?" Gunn asked.

"You're the FBI. You can get a hold of him quicker than I can. You already did an investigation on me. Now do one on Steve Timmons."

"Look, Leon, we're on a limited time schedule. Do you have any idea how I can reach this Timmons?"

I wasn't about to give Timmons's pager number to the FBI. That just isn't done. But I had to give him something. "Timmons's uncle is the fire chief over in McKeesport," I said. "Try there."

They asked me a few more questions and then reminded me that I had a date with the grand jury on Nov. 1. They started packing up their papers, and I asked them again when the three young men, the real victims, would be testifying. They said they would get in contact with them. They'd keep me posted.

It seemed time was running short. The grand jury, from what they said, was less than three weeks away, and still they hadn't contacted the star witnesses. But I guessed they knew what they were doing. Gunn, anyway, seemed to care about the investigation.

As they pulled out of the driveway, I remembered the coffee and tea. I'd left them on the stove, hadn't even offered my guests anything to drink or eat.

It was probably for the better. I never make coffee, and probably couldn't make a decent cup of the stuff if my life depended on it. I was out of my element there.

* * *

That Halloween night Lillian seemed to throw herself into the strange holiday's customs more than usual. She's always enjoyed the decorating, the costumes, the parade of little children and the handfuls of candy, and this year, with the impending grand jury hanging over the household, she did it with unusual zest. With her own kids a little beyond the trick-or-treat age, she lavished her attentions on Devon's little ones, and took them traipsing through the neighborhood.

I've never liked the holiday, which is a holdover from pagan times, so I was left home to pass out the candy. It didn't help that I was all nerves. A few times I missed the openings in the outstretched sacks entirely and dropped Snickers bars all over my patio, all over the feet of the costumed little beggars on the doorstep.

While many young people headed for parties and used the kiddy holiday as an excuse to get drunk or stoned, Devon stayed home with me. Years back he'd decided Halloween violated his beliefs, whatever those beliefs were. I suspect the whole costume thing disagreed with him, too. Devon had never seemed to have a need to pretend to be something he was not.

"See what you've done?" I said, as I plopped down on the couch beside him. It was eight o'clock, and, in theory, the trick-or-treating was over. "You've got me going in front of a damn grand jury. You guys should be going up there. I don't know anything about no damn grand jury."

"Aww, you know it's just a big conspiracy," he said. "You know how they are, Dad. They don't really want to put those cops in jail."

"Have Little Sonny or Derek gotten subpoenas?"

"I talked with them a few days ago, and they didn't say anything about any subpoenas."

I sighed. "I guess this is going to be another farce. Suppose I'll go in and do my best, but I'm not expecting much."

Nobody else was either. The papers had noted that a grand jury was convening, but weren't able to say much more. The FBI and the Department of Justice were keeping the whole thing very hush hush. Jury selection was closed to the public, as the hearings themselves would be. The press would have to get its information piecemeal from the lawyers. That bothered me. The press hadn't been perfect over the seven months since the beating, but at least it had occasionally gotten the issue out before the public when the likes of Abbet and Raley had done everything in their power to cover it up.

That night when I went up to bed, Lillian was down on her knees beside the bed, praying, as she did every night. Her faith was the rock of our marriage, the thing that got us through the hard times. It kept her on an even keel when the cops or their proxies burned down our house, and it got her through when her son was beaten by the cops and tossed in jail. Her inner strength in turn was the bedrock on which the family was built. If she hadn't been solid like granite, I think I'd have gone off the deep end a long time ago.

Most nights I just plopped into bed and went out like a light. But on this Halloween night I got down beside her and said my own supplication.

It had been a long time since I'd talked to The Lord, and memories came rushing down on me there. I remembered the night when He made Himself known to me and asked me to do something about the tide of drugs and crime in the housing project where I'd grown up. I'd formed Kids for Kids and done what I could, and I think it made a difference in Cochrandale.

Doing The Lord's work there got me no end of trouble from the cops and politicians and their cronies, I realized. That was the beginning of all of my problems with the cops. And maybe it didn't directly cause the beating my son and nephews took on Ravensburg Bridge and in the Clairton police station, but I had a creeping suspicion that it colored our dealings with the justice system. From Raley to the D.A. to Constance Cass and even Gunn, everyone I dealt with seemed to think the Grey family were troublemakers. After all, they'd tangled with the cops before, their logic apparently went. They must have done something to deserve what they got out on that frozen bridge.

"Lord," I prayed, "You've got me in a lot of trouble. But I'm sure You have a purpose for all of this. Please give me the serenity and strength to make it through this trial. And if it be Your will, please give my son and nephews justice through this process I will participate in tomorrow. Although only You know the plan, and I'm with You no matter how this thing is supposed to go, please give me a sign that there will someday be justice, so I can be at peace."

When I was done, Lillian got up from her prayers. "Buster, it's been a while since I've seen you do that. You praying for something special?"

"For a little justice from the Department of Justice tomorrow," I said. "Seems sometimes justice is for 'just us' - just the police and the politicians and the rich people. Maybe tomorrow will be different, but I doubt it. I don't think too much will come of it."

"You shouldn't be so negative," she said.

I told her it wasn't me who was negative. It's just the way things are. It's a world full of negatives. Try to be a positive and they go after your kids, your house, your dignity.

"Just don't you become a negative," she said.

I couldn't think of anything to say to that. I was so much at the mercy of things I could not control, from magistrates to lawyers to FBI investigators and grand jurors. There was nothing to do but hope for the best, and try to get some sleep.

* * *

My sister Marie was a basket case as we drove down to the Federal Courthouse in Pittsburgh. "Buster, what do they want me for?" she asked. "What could they possibly ask? What do they expect me to be able to tell them?" And on and on.

"How should I know?" I finally blurted. "We just have to go in there and answer whatever questions they have, to the best of our ability. Just be cool. Don't sweat it. Never let them see you sweat, like the commercial used to say. If you don't know the answer, just say that. I'd rather not be doing this either, but it's the best shot we have at getting any kind of justice for our sons."

Marie had never been particularly calm, cool and collected, but since her son Corey's senseless death in 1992 she'd been positively frazzled. His death brought her a big life insurance pay-out, and between that and her salary she and Derek lived comfortably in a rented house in McKeesport. They had enough left over to hunt for a house in the Mon Valley. But money couldn't restore Marie's faith in a world which took her son from her and then gave his killers a slap on the wrist.

Derek Goodman Sr. wasn't much help. The only time Marie knew her husband's whereabouts was when he was in jail, or when he showed up at the door looking for a hideout and a handout. So it was just Marie and Derek Jr. and the endless parade of Derek's mostly jobless, aimless friends.

"Since that beating that boy hasn't wanted to do anything," she said as we walked down Grant Street on that blustery morning. "He was going to Connelley Tech. before, and I thought he'd get out and get a job, unlike his daddy. But those cops busted up his finger so bad, he couldn't do the hand work. And they scared him so bad, he doesn't even want to leave the house anymore. So he never went back. Now he doesn't even go out with his friends. He just sits there and plays those damn video games forever and ever and ever."

As we approached the low, long stone face of the Federal Courthouse, a tall, black man walked out and turned toward us. He met my eyes and then quickly looked away. As we passed, he muttered, "Hi," to Marie, then hurried on.

"Who was that?"

"That was Tyrone Morris," Marie said, "the constable who took our boys to the hospital."

I turned, but he was already crossing the street. "He seems to be in a hurry to get somewhere. Too bad. I would have liked to thank him. He's the only person who showed any compassion in the whole sorry, sordid tale. Why do you suppose he took off like that?"

"Probably afraid of you."

"Afraid of me?"

"Yeah. A lot of people are afraid of you, Buster."

I didn't know what to think of that. I was relieved, though, that Morris had apparently been called before the grand jury. He'd thought enough of the three men's plight to take them to the hospital, rather than hauling them straight off to jail. Maybe he could tell the jury about their swollen faces, their open wounds. Maybe they'd believe a man with a badge.

We entered the Federal Courthouse and ran smack into a pair of portly security guards and a large metal detector. We emptied our pockets and went through, and they scanned us with a hand-held wand. This was a lot more security than I'd ever seen at the County Courthouse or at Raley's pitiful chamber. This was the big leagues, where real crooks got tried for crimes against the United States of America, I thought. Real crooks like Mimms, Rahis and Sanalas.

The guards let us through and we boarded the elevator. I was thinking about how the two of us might be the last, best hope to get some degree of justice for our children. After all, Devon, Derek and Little Sonny hadn't yet been subpoenaed or received so much as a phone call behind this grand jury, and I figured that meant they wouldn't be testifying. I wondered how much Marie knew about the beatings. "Does Derek talk much about what happened to him?" I asked.

"When he first got home, he did," Marie said. "He told me all about getting beat with the shotgun, and dangled over the edge of the bridge. And then he was kicked in the groin, too, by that white cop."

As the elevator climbed, I closed my eyes and thought about what Derek had told me about that horrible night. He may have gotten the worst scare of any of them, and I wanted to be able to recount it for the grand jury, if asked to do so. Besides being dangled over the bridge rail, Derek was singled out, separated from his cousins and tortured into a false confession.

Rahis took Derek aside, handcuffed him to a chair and played a weird one-man game of good-cop bad-cop with him. First he tried to sweet talk him into framing his cousins. When that didn't work, out came the sap gloves.

Sap gloves look a lot like leather driving gloves, with a diabolical twist: Between the pieces of leather are either lead strips or sand, which serve both to protect the hand of the user and give tremendous added weight to the blow as it lands. Most police departments have banned sap gloves. Not Clairton.

Rahis laid into Derek with ferocious energy, pounding his head with sap-gloved fists. Cuffed to the chair, Derek couldn't even raise a hand in self defense. Rahis paused only long enough to shout questions at his reeling captive. "Who owned the gun, nigger?" Punch. Punch. "You no good nigger, you'd better start talking or I'm going to beat the shit out of your black ass!" Punch. Punch. "Talk, you little son of a bitch!" Punch. Punch. "I want answers and I want them now! Who fired the shots?" Punch. Punch. "Was it you? Are you the gangbanger? Who owned the gun?" Punch. Punch.

Derek struggled to stay conscious as the blows rained down. He felt his face stinging and swelling at the same time, and thought that if he didn't do something to stop the beating he'd surely die. "I keep telling you," he cried out, as Rahis stopped punching and listened, "I don't know nothing about a gun or a shooting, except some maniac shootin' at us. I didn't shoot no one. You've got the wrong guys. I don't know nothin' about that."

Rahis stared coldly for a minute. "Wrong answer, nigger," he spat, and the gloved fist crashed into Derek's head again. "Don't you have something else to say? Don't you have something else to tell me?"

The world was spinning. All Derek could focus on was the black fist and the face before him, a white face, rat-like and twisted with anger. It occurred to him that if he said what the cop wanted him to say, this might end. But then that would be a lie, and would leave Devon or Little Sonny high and dry.

"All I have to say," he cried, "is that you guys made a mistake. We didn't shoot at no one."

Rahis sighed. "Have it your way, nigger. I'm going to get somebody in here who will make you talk."

He left and then came back with "God," the black guy who'd dragged Derek out of the car, held him over the edge of the bridge, slammed his head to the curb and landed countless kicks and shotgun jabs to his body. Derek shuddered. It was Mimms, of course, though Derek didn't yet know his name or even that he was a cop. Without a word, Mimms delivered a blow to his head. Then another, and another. A fourth sent Derek and his chair crashing to the hard, cold floor. As he cringed there, trying to get his bearings, Derek saw the white cop sitting in another chair, laughing.

"Can't even sit up straight, huh?" Rahis asked. "You'd better get up off that floor, boy. You'll catch cold."

Derek struggled to right himself. The world was spinning and he was cuffed to a chair, but the fear of those boots crashing into his body and head again proved strong motivation. He scrambled with his feet and got back up, then collapsed back into the chair which had become his prison.

Mimms continued to pound him, and Derek lost count of the blows. His head felt like it was tearing apart, and his brain ached so bad he thought it was going to explode. "Man, I'll do whatever you want!" he finally cried out. "Just quit beating my ass."

The blows stopped, and Derek made out snatches of a conversation between his two assailants. He was nauseous, spinning, on the verge of vomiting - it was just like bed spins, but heavily seasoned with pain. Then things were quiet for a time - he couldn't tell how long. He just wanted to get away, to get out of the cuffs, to be somewhere where he could curl up and hold his aching head and cry.

Then suddenly his hands were free, and someone shoved a piece of paper in front of him. "It's a statement of your rights," the white cop said. "Just sign it at the bottom, and we'll take you somewhere so you can get some sleep."

Derek looked at it. The words swam in the blood which dripped into his eyes, and he could make no sense of them. There seemed to be something handwritten on the back - he could see the impressions of the letters coming through. But he was too woozy to flip the paper and read it. Flip that paper and his guts would heave out his mouth, Derek felt. Signing meant no more beating and a place to sleep. He scribbled his signature at the bottom.

"Good boy," the white cop said.

I opened my eyes as the elevator doors opened. Marie was shaking her head and speaking, though I hadn't been listening. "Since that beating there's been this bitter and fearful side of him that I hadn't seen before," she said. "He feels terrible about signing that confession those cops wrote up, but he didn't have any other choice. In the beginning he talked a lot about it, but now he doesn't seem to even want to be reminded of it."

"Same with Devon," I said. He'd really clamed up about it since Raley's hearing. I wondered if they might be a new phase of trying to cope with what happened to them. I couldn't put my finger on it, but something in the cousins' newfound silence worried me.

We stepped off the elevator and saw Bill Gunn standing across a small lobby from us. His eyes seemed to shine as they met ours. "Good morning," he said quietly, with a little wave and a smile. He was dressed in a suit, but it didn't much suit his roundish body and chubby face. He looked like he might be more comfortable in sweats and a parka, out on the streets doing undercover work.

I wished him a good morning. He told us that things were moving along smoothly, and we should be called around 9:30 and 10, respectively. He showed us to a couch near the entrance of the courtroom, and then quickly disappeared.

"He's a little strange, but he seems like a decent man," Marie confided after he left.

"He's all we've got," I said.

We sat out there as a couple of guys in paramedic uniforms were led in, one after the other. Then a pair of Jefferson Borough cops. Then Clairton Public Safety Director William Abbet, who scowled in our direction. I just smiled.

Gunn and Cass kept passing by, and Cass in particular gave us strange looks. I saw them confer, and then Gunn walked up to us.

"It's going a little slower than expected," Gunn said. "You know, there's a cafeteria just a few floors up. If you'd like to wait there, I can come up and get you."

I could read in his voice that he wanted us away from here, where we could see all of the witnesses coming and going. I didn't like that - it was just another sign that things were being hidden - but this was his turf. "Yeah, okay. We'll swing up there for a little bit."

Though we weren't particularly hungry, we went up to the empty cafeteria. Marie ordered a sandwich and I got a hot chocolate, and we sat down. The prices were outrageous, Marie complained, and I said I figured lawyers and judges and witnesses and prisoners were probably the bulk of the clientele, which would tend to boost prices. After all, lawyers and judges had money, and the prisoners and witnesses were, to one extent or another, captive audiences.

After about half an hour, Marie was done with her sandwich and my hot chocolate was long gone. "Let's go back down," I said. "I want to see who's coming and going, and if they don't want me to know, they can come right out and say that."

We headed back down and parked again on our couch. When we'd been there a few minutes, Peggy Liu came out and seemed startled to see us there. She stopped, and I wondered if she would tell us we had to leave. But instead she smiled.

"How's it going in there?" I asked.

"It's going pretty well," she said. "Mr. Abbet wasn't too interested in telling the truth at the beginning, but we caught him in a few lies, and now he's starting to talk. I think we've got a good chance at a conviction."

I said I certainly hoped so, and she hurried on. If Abbet was still in there, then they must really be grilling his ass, I thought.

A few minutes later, Abbet hurried out, looking even more red-faced than usual, and he was in the elevator and gone in a flash. Perhaps "the actors," as he'd called the cousins in his statements to the media, would be more pleased with the results of this investigation than they were with his.

Cass hurried out a minute later and pulled up in front of us. She seemed excited, almost winded. "I think we have a good chance at a conviction here, Mr. Grey," she said. "Please don't go in there and showboat and have us lose this case. The government is spending a lot of money on this, and we don't want anything to ruin it."

I didn't know what to say to that. I just shook my head as she hurried away.

Then out came Gunn. He was flushed, as if he, too, was in some heightened state. I supposed this must be how white people get when they think they're getting justice for Negroes.

As he stood there, a bailiff walked past us holding a shotgun. "That's the shotgun that Mimms used to beat the three young men that night,"

Gunn said. "I subpoenaed it, and when I examined it, it still had blood on it."

"Not surprised," I said. "There was still blood on the municipal building door and the snow when I went to the scene the day after the beatings. These guys aren't much for tidying up."

Gunn told us they were also using Derek's blood-soaked shirt as evidence, then darted back into the courtroom. I wondered if the cops had left that blood on the shotgun by accident, or on purpose as a trophy from their night of ass-kicking. Either way, that kind of thing might make an impression on a jury, I thought. The weapon looked heavy, and the round end of the barrel seemed to match the arc-shaped cuts on Derek and Little Sonny's heads.

It wasn't long before Gunn reappeared and led me into the grand jury room. The warmth of the room hit me and a strange haze momentarily obscured my sight. This room was a weird world all its own, completely divorced from the reality outside. Gunn guided me to a long table, and I took a seat between Liu and Cass. Facing us were about 25 people, two of whom were black males; the rest were white. They were seated in folding chairs on a terrace-like structure with three levels. One of the black men was sleeping and the other seemed to be fidgeting, checking his watch and frowning all the time, like he had somewhere to go. The whites, too, seemed to be in various states of disinterest.

As Constance Cass told the grand jury who I was, it struck me how ridiculous this all was. Three men were beaten seven months ago on a frozen bridge in Clairton, and now this panel would sit in a too-warm courtroom on Grant Street and listen to a parade of witnesses that didn't even include the victims and try to decide what happened. If the Department of Justice wanted to do this thing right, they should have gotten the cops, the cousins and the whole damn jury together on the Ravensburg Bridge at 3 a.m., put a beer in Maniac Cop Mimms' right hand and a shotgun in his left, and seen what happened. This, as it was, seemed to be nothing but a joke.

Liu and Cass peppered me with questions. When did I first learn of the beatings? What did Devon tell me about his experiences? What kind of medical treatment did he need? I answered factually. No showboating.

To my surprise, there was no cross-examination in the proceeding. Instead, Liu opened it up to questions from the grand jury members. They fidgeted. I wondered if they were afraid of me, like Marie said Tyrone Morris was.

But one older white guy cleared his throat. "Sir, how did they threaten Devon?"

I told him how, on the bridge, Mimms said he was God and he decided who came and who went in his hood. That was code for "who lives and who dies," I explained. And I described how in the station, Edward Sanalas put a gun to the middle of Devon's head and told him that he could kill him and no one would ever do a thing about it, because he was a cop.

Then a younger white guy spoke up. "How bad were they beaten?"

I thought about that for a second. "They looked like they went 15 rounds with George Foreman with handcuffs on."

A ripple of interest seemed to course through my audience. They shifted in their seats and murmured. George Foreman, 15 rounds, handcuffs - they seemed to understand that.

Cass handed me a dozen Polaroids.

"Do these pictures look worse than how the young men looked the day they got out of jail?" she asked.

I looked. The four photos showed Devon in the same pose I'd seen in the Polaroids at the hospital a few days after the beating, when I had nearly lost my lunch from seeing how blackened and bloody and swollen he was. But these pictures were different. I looked up, startled.

"These aren't the same pictures I saw when I viewed them at the hospital," I said. "They've been lightened. I saw the originals, and Devon looked like a black blob. These have been sanitized. Doctored. They looked worse coming out of jail than they look in these pictures. They were darker, and there was more blood on them."

"But can you identify the three men?" she asked quickly, an edge of impatience in her voice.

"They're Devon Grey, Little Sonny Brown and Derek Goodman. But -." "That's all we have, Mr. Grey." And before I knew it I was being led out of the room and Marie was being led in. They hustled me out of there so fast I hardly had time to stand up. I think I was still in a sitting position when they deposited me on the couch.

I sat out there in a daze. Something sinister was happening, and I felt powerless to stop it, or even understand it. The Department of Justice was playing a game with my son's best chance at vindication. They weren't calling the victims as witnesses, and they - or someone - had doctored the photos that showed the extent of the beating. It was as if this grand jury wasn't allowed to get too close to anything that might shed light on what really happened out on that bridge and in that station.

It seemed like grand theft justice to me. But why?

I'd done my best in there. I told everything I knew. I was going the legal route, just like Ron Jackson and Peeper and I agreed. I'd cooperated with Bill Gunn and by and large stayed out of the faces of the Clairton cops while he'd done his investigation. If this turned out to be a farce, I didn't know what I'd do.

It wasn't long before Cass led Marie out. She was shaking and rubbing a few stray tears from her eyes as she sat down beside me. "Thanks so much for both of your help," Cass said. "That's all we'll be needing, so I guess you two can head home and get some rest. I'm sure this hasn't been easy."

I shook my head. "How's it going in there?"

"Oh, it's hard to say yet. We have a lot of witnesses still to come."

"Right. So when are you going to call Devon, Derek and Little Sonny?"

"Well, we've tried to get in touch with them, but haven't been able."

That was a lie. None of those boys, I knew, had gotten so much as a phone message. "If you need help rounding them up, I can do it."

"If we need you to do that, I'll call you," she said. "I've got to get back in there."

"I'm sure you do." I wanted to strangle this arrogant lawyer who lied to my face and seemed determined to go through the motions of prosecuting my son's tormentor without doing anything that might actually help win the case. But she walked calmly and confidently back into the stuffy courtroom. This was her game, and the rules were written by people just like her and there was nothing anyone like me could do about it but watch and wait and hope that it accidentally worked.

We left. Waiting for the elevator, Marie said they'd asked her about the same things they'd asked me: when she'd been informed of the beatings, what she'd done, how badly her son had been injured, what he'd told her about the night of terror, and who were the men in the photographs. What else could she testify to? She wasn't there. She wasn't beaten.

We were quiet on the way home, both a little depressed about what we'd just seen. I'd chosen this route, made contact with the FBI, thinking it might be my best bet. Now I felt oddly guilty.

* * *

And then there was nothing. The grand jury ended, but no verdict was handed down. Derek and Little Sonny called me every week or two, asking if I'd heard anything. "What's happenin', Uncle Buster? They gonna put that maniac Mimms in jail?"

"I heard nothin'," I had to answer.

It proved a tough time for Little Sonny. The notoriety the case brought got him fired from a nursing home job and then a temporary services job. "We don't need any bad publicity," one of his bosses told him. Little Sonny found a new job each time - people say he can get a job like a white person - but the firings shook him.

It wasn't as if Little Sonny had never heard that we live in a racist, classist society which kicks you when you're down. But for the first time it really hit home. His mood seemed worse every time I saw him and he started talking about how the world was "fucked up" and "the whole system was prejudiced" and "nobody cared" whether he lived or died or worked or went to jail.

It didn't help any that he was still living in Clairton, and that Mimms was back on the beat. Just two weeks after my appearance before the grand jury, Little Sonny got a visit from his attacker. He was loading a few birthday presents into his car after a quiet, family get-together at his girlfriend's mom's place, when a Clairton cop car pulled up next to it, the window came down, and Maniac Cop Clyde Mimms leaned his head out.

Little Sonny stood by his car, unsure whether to run or call out for help. Mimms sat there in silence and stared him in the face, his eyes full of syrupy hate.

Little Sonny lowered the packages into the back seat. He was afraid to walk around the car, with Mimms just a few feet from the driver's side door, and too spooked to turn around and head for the apartment. So he waited. And Mimms waited.

"Well, what you want?" he finally asked.

"This is my town," Mimms said, his languid eyes still burrowing into Little Sonny's. "I want you to get the fuck out, or it ain't gonna be pleasant."

Mimms sat a few more seconds, then let the cruiser slowly roll away. Little Sonny stayed frozen like a deer in a spotlight until the car rounded a bend and disappeared. Then he slammed the car door, ran around into the driver's seat and hurried home.

By the time he got home the shakes were so bad he could barely fit his key into the lock. Once inside, he rushed to the phone. He picked it up, then put it back in the cradle and ran for the medicine cabinet. Two little pain killers would get rid of those damn shakes. Then back to the phone, where he had Gunn's card. He dialed the FBI, but they said Gunn wasn't in. He punched in the home number scribbled on the back.

"Gunn here."

"Yeah, this is Little Sonny Brown. Man, Mimms just came up to me and told me to get the fuck out of town," he said, struggling not to pant. There was no reason to be this way - he was safe at home, and he didn't think he'd been followed. But he couldn't control it. And the pills hadn't kicked in yet. "Does he have any right to do that?"

"No he doesn't," said Gunn. "This is a free country and you can live wherever you want."

"That's what they say. But what if the guy starts arresting me for some trumped up bullshit, or comes up and starts beatin' on me or shoots me? He's a maniac. He might do anything. How much of a free country is it then?"

"If he harasses you again, I'll arrest him," Gunn said.

"It might be better for you to tell him that. Otherwise, I might be dead before he finds out."

"I will. I'll call him and tell him."

Little Sonny lay down on the couch to wait for the pills. He thought about getting up and grabbing a beer, but a wave of fatigue pressed him to the couch.

He tried to relax, but what Gunn said didn't make him feel all that much better. Like Derek, he'd suffered his own private beating that night in March, and that time he'd spent alone with the cops was what came back when he shut his eyes. The events replayed themselves over and over again. Rahis took Devon to the cell. Mimms and Sanalas uncuffed him and knocked him around, daring him to fight back. When Little Sonny finally gave in to his rising rage and charged Mimms, the off-duty cop put a submission hold on him and slowly ratcheted up the pain level.

Now it was happening again, in a narcotic nightmare like a hundred others before. Little Sonny struggling to wrestle his arm free, screaming, "Get the fuck off of me!" as he and Mimms crashed against the refrigerator.

"Say you a bitch," Mimms demanded, pushing Little Sonny's arm further up his back. "Say you a bitch!"

"Fuck ... you!" Little Sonny spat.

"All right then," Mimms breathed into his ear. He pushed his arm up above the shoulder blade. "Say you a bitch. Say you a bitch, boy! Boy, say you a bitch, or you gonna be my bitch!"

Little Sonny felt things in his shoulder coming apart. He pulled against the unrelenting force behind him. In his mind he saw bone bending, breaking, splintering into a sea of muscle and blood. Still he struggled against the weight behind him, and suddenly he and his captor crashed to the floor.

Mimms struggled to secure the hold again. Little Sonny tried to squirm free, but the big brute was on the back of his legs. He tried to roll out from under him, but crashed into a wall. Then Mimms had control of Little Sonny's right arm again, and started pushing it up, up, up the back.

"Say you a bitch!"

Little Sonny's soul screamed, "NO!" as his body shook with the pain.

"Say you a bitch!"

"No!"

Mimms punctuated each word by ratcheting up the arm a little more. "Say ... you ... a ... bitch!"

"Okay, I'm a bitch!" Little Sonny wailed. "I'm a bitch! I'm a bitch."

Mimms let go of Little Sonny, and he thought it was over. Then suddenly a searing, burning pain bit into his side, and he was helpless, in spasm like an epileptic, his body quivering and out of control. He collapsed to the floor in time to see one of the white cops grinning and holding an electric stun gun.

Mimms got up and pulled Little Sonny to his knees. "Yeah, you my ho," Mimms muttered, as he looked over at the white cop, grinned, and reached for his fly. "Maybe I ought to make you squeal like a pig, too."

Little Sonny looked about him wildly. Were they going to try to rape him? Saying he was a bitch burned him to the core, but he would sooner die than have this brutish asshole's cock up his butt. He wondered if he could grab the white cop's revolver and at least take someone down with him. He tried to get ready to fight, but he had no control of his shocked muscles.

The prick Mimms pulled from his pants was limp. "Man, I gotta take a leak," he said.

"Hey, know what? I do, too," said Sanalas, smiling.

Little Sonny tried to get up, but couldn't muster the strength. And suddenly he was in the crossfire of two lines of urine, the yellow streams hitting his aching torso and bruised legs. His whole body boiled with the humiliation, and he struggled to stifle a scream. That would probably just get him beat again.

What burst out instead was an anguished sob.

Then the streams stopped. Little Sonny shut his eyes against the piercing pain in his head. Then he heard a low chuckle and felt something against his face, and opened his eyes to see a penis brushing across his nose. He moved left in horror, but the white cop's prick was there, and it, too, suddenly mashed into his face.

"You like that, don't you, bitch?" Mimms said.

"Oh, yeah, he wants us bad," said Sanalas.

Little Sonny struggled to get up, as they laughed and grabbed at his pants. Rahis walked in, and Mimms and Sanalas quickly zipped up their pants.

Rahis chuckled. "Let's lock him up."

The big white cop jerked Little Sonny to his feet and dragged him to a cell. He stayed at arm's length, probably trying to keep away from the blood and urine that dripped off of his prisoner. He pitched Little Sonny in a cage and slammed the door shut behind him.

"This is the lady's side of the jail, nigger," the cop said. "Pleasant dreams, nigger."

Mimms, standing looking over his shoulder, licked his lips. "Yeah, you my bitch," he growled.

Little Sonny collapsed on the cold metal slab which was the bed. He rolled and moaned and fought back the urge to vomit brought on by his own fetid stench. He wished he could strip off the bloody, urine-stinking clothes, but it was freezing in the cell, the air as cold as the walls and the bed. Everything stung and stuck to his body and what kind of a way was this to treat a man who'd worked a double shift?

"Man, I made some mistakes," he moaned to himself. "But I paid the price. I been trying to make good. Aww, fuck."

That night and for months after, sleep was no rest at all. Night was a grainy film populated by shotguns, kicking boots, fists and streams of steamy piss. The murky area between consciousness and sleep was filled with a snarling voice calling itself God and demanding, "Say you a bitch, bitch. You my bitch." Sleep, when it came, was broken by screams. When he woke and searched, panicked, for the source, Little Sonny found himself alone.

Days he dragged himself, heavy-lidded, to his jobs. When he'd come out of prison just months before the beating on the bridge, Little Sonny had vowed to try to do it right, to work for his money and to pay for cars rather than stealing them. Now his name was in the papers, his face on the television. "Little Sonny Brown, accused of firing on an off-duty Clairton police officer," the announcers said, and it proved too much for some of the employers who'd considered him a risky hire in the first place.

With Mimms back on the beat, Little Sonny didn't think he'd ever be safe again in Clairton in spite of Gunn's assurances. "Man, if he sees me and pulls me over and starts to rough me up, what the fuck am I going to do? Ask him to let me call Bill Gunn?" Little Sonny asked Devon in one of their many phone calls of that time. "And if he beats me again, he knows he'll have to kill me. Because he ain't gettin' no handcuffs on me, and the only way I'm goin' in that station again is stone cold dead."

"I know, cuz, I know," Devon said. "Maybe you oughta get hell out of Clairton."

"I ain't moving back in with my mom. Where am I supposed to go, man? If I'm gonna run, where am I gonna run to?"

For the moment he ran to the doctor for some more pills to ease his throbbing head and stop the shakes. He begged for stronger medicine, something like Percocet, a prescription drug with enough kick that even junkies liked it. But the doctor wouldn't budge, and kept him on the light stuff.

Still, a couple of pills, a couple of beers and Little Sonny felt better. It even calmed his nerves enough that he could stop thinking about Mimms and go out, have a good time, meet some friends he hadn't seen in a while. Have a few more beers, pop a few more pills. Laugh it up and get really silly. Get busted for drunk driving on the way back home.

The state suspended Little Sonny's driver's license for driving under the influence. That didn't have the desired effect of keeping Little Sonny off the road - he had to drive to get to work, so drive he did. But it forced him to do most of his drinking in the Clairton apartment where he still lived with his girlfriend.

Relations there became strained. "Man, she's always naggin' me," Little Sonny told Devon on the phone. "Little shit, like changin' the toilet paper and puttin' away my shoes. But other shit too. The other day she said I gotta quit drinkin' in the house. What the fuck is that? Can't a man have a beer or two in his own apartment? And what the hell else am I gon do? I can't go to a bar. No way I'm goin' to no Clairton bar, risk runnin' into Mimms or Sanalas. I can't drive. Hell, if the cops stop me driving with a suspended license and smell alcohol, I'll be back in jail."

"Hey, cuz, maybe if you went easy on the drinkin' for a little bit, your lady would get off your case," Devon said. "You ain't supposed to drink while you're on those pills anyway, are you?"

"Ain't supposed to drink when I use the pills," Little Sonny moaned. "Ain't supposed to drive. Ain't supposed to get beat up by the cops. But I am supposed to sit here and wait patiently for my trial for a crime I didn't commit. I am supposed to just accept the fact that this Judge Gibson is gonna preside over a trial to see if I go back to jail. I am supposed to get a new lawyer to replace that damn Larry

Vicious, according to your dad. If I'm supposed to do all that, how can anybody expect me not to have a beer or two now and then?"

When Devon next saw Little Sonny, it seemed like the weight of the world had been lifted. It was a Saturday evening, and Devon and his cousin Porky were over at Derek's place, playing video games and waiting for Derek to either come home or call and tell them where he was. The front door swung open, but instead of Derek, in came Little Sonny. He was swaying a little from side to side.

"You been out drinkin' already?" Devon asked.

"Naw, man, naw. I'm okay." Little Sonny plopped down on a couch, holding his stomach.

Devon looked over at him. He didn't look okay. He looked a little pale even. "You sure?"

"Yeah. I just hafta lay down a minute. I'll be okay."

"You gonna be able to go out tonight?"

"Yeah, well, I don't know."

Devon shrugged and went back to the game he and Porky were playing. Little Sonny had been acting strange lately, but he wasn't sure what he could do about it. The boy wasn't the same as he had been back before the beating, when they'd cruise all over the Mon Valley and even Pittsburgh in that black Camaro everybody called "The Demon." Back then he'd seemed carefree, almost a symbol of freedom to young Devon. Now he seemed like an old man.

After a few minutes, Little Sonny started moaning. "Aww, man, this ain't so easy as I thought it'd be."

"What you mean?"

"Cuz, man, I thought I had it all figured out. I didn't hafta wait for no damn trial. I didn't hafta sit in no courtroom with no white judge. Didn't hafta watch out for cops or get beat again or drive around with no shuspended license. And I didn't hafta listen to my bitch whinin' about this or that or I didn't flush the toilet or whatever. I didn't hafta worry about any of that shit."

"That's cool," said Devon, warily. "How's that?"

"I took about 20, 30 of those pain pills. Figured I ain't never gonna feel no pain again. Came over here to just lay down, take a long, long nap. But it hurts, man. It hurts!" He was grabbing his belly, and seemed near tears.

"You took 20?" Devon shouted.

"Maybe 30."

"Oh, man, we gotta get you to the hospital."

"Aww, shit. I was just about to win, too," Porky said.

The two got up off the floor and helped Little Sonny from the couch. Little Sonny didn't struggle, and even did his best to walk with them.

As they got to the door, Little Sonny stopped walking and just hung there. He'd gained weight, and could be remarkably heavy when he tried to be. Devon and Porky stopped.

"What's with this?" Devon asked.

"Man, I'm startin' to feel better. Let's just hang here for a while."

"No way, Little Sonny, I'm gettin' you to a hospital. Otherwise, those pills are gonna kill you, man, and then where we at?"

"Aww, let 'em. This world ain't worth shit. Got prejudiced people. Got bad cops. You try to do good. They beat you. They wanna throw you in jail again. Fire you. Won't hire you. White judges, white juries. Ain't no use. Better just end it. Not worry no more."

"Man, that's what they want!" Devon blurted. "They want you to give up. They want you to take your pills and die. One less niggah in the world. One less niggah they gotta prosecute and jail. One less witness to what they did to the three of us. One down, two to go."

Little Sonny's head drooped. Devon nodded to Porky and they started dragging him through the door. "Man, wake up! You listening to me?"

"Aww, I heard. One less niggah. One less niggah."

"So you with me?"

"Huh? Aww. One less niggah. That sounds okay. Less niggaz. Less trouble."

"No, man, you don't get it! You let go, that makes it that much easier for them to get us. We all go to jail that makes it that much easier for them to get all the other Africans. Man, you gotta live! You gotta stay on. You're my friend, man, and I ain't gonna let you die. I'll drag you if I have to."

Little Sonny grudgingly started walking along with them. They dumped him in the front passenger seat of his red Chevy Cavalier and Devon took the keys. Porky slid in back.

Devon reached for the volume knob on the stereo. "Try sleepin' through this!" he yelled over at his cousin, as he cranked the sounds way, way up.

The inside of the car came to life with a booming rap beat. Devon looked over and thought he could make out a faint smile on Little Sonny's shut-eyed face. He backed the car out, made a quick three-point turn and squealed down the hill toward the McKeesport-Duquesne Bridge.

Little Sonny hunched over and vomited a torrent of stomach acid and unidentifiable chunks all over the floor mat in front of him.

"Aww, shit, man, can't you wait?" Porky complained.

The stench was overpowering. Devon rolled down his window, afraid that he might lose his own lunch. "Little Sonny, man, roll down the glass. Roll down the glass!"

But Little Sonny was too busy heaving.

"Hey, cuz, wouldn't a gun have been a little less messy?" Porky joked.

Little Sonny leaned back in his chair. "I don't feel too good. Don't feel good. Don't feel good."

In the five minutes it took to get to the McKeesport Hospital parking lot, Little Sonny seemed to get even worse. When Porky opened the passenger side door, he sat there, motionless.

"I don't wanna carry him," Porky said. "He's liable to puke all over me."

"Let's go, Little Sonny," Devon said.

"Aww, hell, cuz. Just lemme get some sleep."

"Sorry, Little Sonny. We're goin' for a walk."

Devon slipped a skinny arm under his stockier cousin's body and tried to lift him out of the seat. Damn, the dude had gotten heavy, and with his body all limp it felt like lifting a waterbed mattress. And it really stank. The dude was sweaty and had barf all over his pants and shoes. He got Little Sonny's torso a few inches off the seat, then collapsed back.

Little Sonny seemed to be drifting constantly, perceptibly, away. Devon got his arms around his cousin's body and let his anger power him. He raised Little Sonny's torso up off the seat and then pushed with his own legs and pushed, and refused to let go the slumping body, until he got his cousin up on his feet.

"Little Sonny," he panted, "we're goin' now. Help me out now, man."

Little Sonny nodded faintly. Porky grimaced a little, but took up Little Sonny's left side. They started dragging him across the parking lot, and Little Sonny's feet made weak, tentative steps.

"We ain't gonna let ... Mimms kill you, cuz," Devon breathed in his ear. "He ain't gonna get the ... last laugh on old Little Sonny and Devon. No way. We gonna keep on fightin'. We gonna show that Mimms ... Rahis ... Sanalas ... they can't just go torturing and brutalizing and terrorizing. Doesn't matter who they are."

Little Sonny's head bobbed faintly, but his legs stopped moving altogether.

"Man, if you don't move them feet, we're gon leave you right in the middle of this parking lot and just drive right away," Porky threatened. "Leave you on the doorstep like the O.D. you are."

Little Sonny's feet shuffled vaguely.

"C'mon, man, walk! Walk!" Porky demanded.

They dragged Little Sonny into the waiting room and dropped him into a chair. Devon ran to the admitting nurse. "Nurse, this guy tried to kill himself with pills. We gotta get him to a doctor fast."

"What kind of pills?" she dully intoned.

"I don't know. Pain killers. He took 20 or 30."

"Please fill out these forms," she said, handing Devon a clipboard.

"I don't think you understand, lady! He's dyin'. My cousin is dyin'! Get him a damn doctor now, and I'll fill out the damn forms later!"

She looked at Devon with a frown, then turned to an orderly. "Get him in a chair and take him back."

They wheeled Little Sonny away, his eyes closed and his head bobbing, and Devon sat next to Porky and tried to relax. "Cuz, old Little Sonny hasn't been the same since that beating, man. I worry about him. He's gonna live this time, I think, but what if he didn't come over to Derek's house? What if he wrapped his car around a tree driving over? Or what if we hadn't been there?"

"Aww, that niggah's just weak-minded," Porky said. "He never wanted to kill himself. If he did, he wouldn't have come lookin' for us."

"Maybe he didn't mean to kill himself, but he coulda killed himself, and he could still if he keeps livin' on beer and pills," Devon said.

Devon filled out the forms while Porky went off and made some phone calls. After about two hours, the nurse told them they could come back and see Little Sonny.

He was sitting up in a bed in a tiny room without a TV, dressed in hospital blues. "Hey, cuz, I'm sorry about all that, man," he said. "I'm really sorry."

"No big deal, cuz, that's all right. How you doin'?"

"I'm okay. They pumped my stomach and gave me a shot of somethin' to counteract what I took. Man, did I puke all over my car?"

"You sure did, Little Sonny," Devon said, chuckling sadly. "You sure did."

"It's a lake in there, man," said Porky. "You know, that mother's gonna stink forever, Little Sonny. Once you puke in a car, it's over. You can't never get that smell out."

"Shit, now I got to get me another car. I can't go around in no stinkmobile."

"Aww, don't worry about that now," Devon said. "You just gotta get your head straight, man, and get your life straight."

"Yeah, man, I oughta get out of Clairton, away from those damn cops. Beat this bullshit rap they got on me. Keep workin' and stay straight." Then a look of panic crossed Little Sonny's face. "Oh, no. Oh no, oh no, oh no, oh no."

"What is it, cuz?" Devon asked.

"Nurse!" Little Sonny yelled. "Nurse! I'm shittin' on myself!"

Then a horrid stench rose out of the bed as Little Sonny began to squirm and shout, "Eww! Eww!" Devon and Porky turned their backs to the stink.

"Man, what the hell did you eat?" Porky asked.

"Nurse!" Devon cried. "Help! Little Sonny Brown needs help!"

A skinny little white nurse ran in. "Oh, Christ! What the hell have you done?"

"I shit all over myself." Little Sonny seemed near tears.

"I'll say you did. You'll have to wait a minute."

She ran off, but returned a minute later with a bed pan, rubber gloves, and two other nurses. Devon and Porky stepped out into the hall.

"It stinks out here, too," Devon said.

"I think he done stunk up the whole damn hospital," said Porky.

They could hear the nurses scolding Little Sonny. "Why didn't you call us so we could get you to a toilet? Don't you have the least bit of common decency? What on God's earth did you eat?"

Devon and Porky looked at each other and laughed, holding their sides, as the nurses marched out, emptied their bedpans in a nearby room - then marched back in for another round.

"I can't stop it," Little Sonny moaned. "My whole body's comin' out."

"Cuz, let's roll, let's go outside, man," said Porky. "I can't take this shit."

Chapter 8

Plea Bargain

Maybe a stomach pumping and a good shit was what Little Sonny needed. Get that poison out of there. He came out of the hospital in a quiet, thoughtful mood, and seemed to ease off the pills and the drinking. I didn't see much of him myself during that time, but Devon said he seemed resigned to slogging his way through the criminal case against him, holding on to his job as long as he could, sticking with his cantankerous girl for at least a little while, and hoping something good would emerge from the wreckage of his life.

On New Year's Day, 1995, Marie and Derek moved out of their rented place in McKeesport, the place where the night of terror had begun, and into a house in upper Duquesne. Though the place was modest to look at from the front, it was spacious and tasteful inside, with a large backyard. Best of all, Marie thought, it was in the better-off section of Duquesne, well up the hill from the ravaged, graffiti-strewn drug markets centered around Second and Priscilla.

For a few months, they lived in relative obscurity among their mostly-white neighbors. Then Derek set about turning that house into Duquesne's biggest tourist attraction. He installed colored lights and ornate, full-length mirrors he picked up secondhand, and generally gave the place the feel of a high class night club. He installed the obligatory high-voltage stereo system and a big-screen TV with a VCR and Nintendo. Add to that the five pet alligators, one huge turtle and a pit bull named Butch that Derek accumulated in a two-month quest for exotic pets.

Word quickly went around town that the Goodman crib was one crazy place. Derek's parties were crowded, loud, and rockin' affairs. On the street, they came to call Derek's place "Fantasy Island," and it quickly got a reputation as the address with the best house parties in Duquesne.

The cops, too, came to know Derek's new address. And it didn't take them long to realize that this Derek Goodman was the same one who'd been on TV criticizing the Clairton cops back in March and a few times since.

As Derek would soon find out, it was a bad time to be on the bad side of the Duquesne Police Department.

Duquesne is a tiny city of 8,000 built on the northern sides of a series of rugged hills rising out of the Monongahela River Valley. Long racially mixed - hell, I was born there - the races and classes maintained an amicable separation as long as the mills below were still lighting the sky on fire. Blacks lived below Second Street, whites lived above, but everybody worked in the same blast furnaces, shopped in the same little stores and even dated across racial lines.

But when the mills went dark in the '80s and many whites headed for the suburbs, the delicate racial balance started to shift. When whites moved out, blacks bought or rented their houses, including many above Second Street. The new proximity strained the town's traditional tolerance just as the lack of opportunity drove some Duquesne youth into the drug business. Suddenly "crime" became a code-word for "black," and by the mid-90's the town had elected an "anti-crime" mayor intent on driving out the renters and Section 8's, and bent on doubling the size of the police force.

Double it he did, by hiring inexperienced punks, Nazi wanna-bes, and cast-offs from other police departments - all white.

As a black family that dared to move on to a white street, had the audacity to have parties, and had a history of criticizing the police, the Goodmans came in for special attention. It started early in 1995, during one of Derek Sr.'s brief stays. One day the doorbell rang, and Derek Sr. answered it. A delivery man offered a package addressed to the previous owner of the home, and that old dope signed for it, maybe intending to forward it on, maybe intending to keep it. The delivery man pulled a gun.

"Hands up! Police! Derek Goodman is under arrest."

The package, it turned out, was full of cocaine. Though it hadn't been addressed to any of the Goodmans, and though none of them actually touched it, the police poured through the open door, tore up the house and found about an ounce of marijuana. They took not the old man, but Derek, Jr., down to county jail.

Marie put her house up as bail, and Derek was released. But the first strands in an entangling legal web were in place.

Meanwhile as relations between Little Sonny and his woman hit the skids, he started spending more of his time over at Fantasy Island.

In June he moved in.

It seemed a good move at first. Little Sonny cheered up visibly there, got to know people quickly, started shooting hoops down at the courts. When Derek picked up a sleek white '84 Trans Am, Devon swung down to help put in some new sounds, and the three cousins started hanging together again. That Trans Am became the cousins' official cruising mobile, and the three tooled all around the valley in it, blasting tapes by Duquesne D.J. Def Sef and packing that long back seat with sweet young ladies.

Though he'd cruise into the night and occasionally party into the morning, Little Sonny would always catch some z's, wake up to the alarm on his clock radio, shake off sleep and get off to work again. Every morning it was a risk, getting in his little red car and driving those Duquesne streets, with his license suspended as it was. But a man's got to work, and there was no bus service from Duquesne to tiny Pitcairn, where he earned his pay. So he drove carefully and slow, stopped at stop signs, used his turn signal, and avoided passing the police station down on Second Street at all costs.

But they say a cop only needs three blocks to bust even the most careful driver, and one evening on the way home he saw flashing lights in his rearview and heard the whoop of a siren. When he pulled over and rolled down his window, the fleshy, mustachioed face of Anthony Schaefer was a few feet from his.

Little Sonny already knew the guy by reputation. Schaefer was one of Duquesne's new recruits. He'd managed to get himself fired from the notoriously bad Brentwood Borough Police Department following accusations that he'd sold marijuana prior to becoming a cop, that he'd solicited sex from the subject of a drunk driving stop, and that he'd threatened to run over a pregnant woman who impeded his progress in a parking lot. Duquesne snapped the guy up.

And Schaefer quickly made an impression on Duquesne's black residents - sometimes literally. Within two years of his hire, Schaefer would be involved in at least 10 arrests in which excessive force was alleged, including a few which put the accused into the hospital. The young people came to call him "Mark Furman" after the cop from the O.J. Simpson trial who'd admitted to his pastime of going out and practicing his karate kicks on niggers and chicanos. Schaefer's legendary temper and notoriously foul mouth would get him special mention on the protesters' placards and civil rights lawsuits that would eventually result from the Duquesne Police Department's undeclared war on black Duquesne.

"Stay the fuck in the car!" Schaefer barked, though Little Sonny had made no move. "License and registration."

Little Sonny dug out the registration, feigned a search for a license. "Man, I must've forgot it at home. Can you give me a break, man? I'm just tryin' to get home from work."

"Work, my ass," said Officer Schaefer. "Stay right here."

Schaefer took his registration and went back to the cruiser, where his partner waited. Little Sonny wondered what, precisely, he'd been pulled over for. Driving while black, probably, he thought.

Schaefer approached again, and Little Sonny noticed that his partner was taking up a cover position behind the passenger door of the cruiser. "As if I'm some fuckin' violent fugitive," Little Sonny muttered.

"What'd you say, boy?" Schaefer demanded.

"Nothin'."

"Good. You Little Sonny Brown?"

"Yeah."

"Where do I know that name?"

"Dunno."

"I remember it now! You're the asshole who lied on Officer Mimms. You and your homeboys shot at Officer Mimms, fell off the curb and then accused Officer Mimms and those other officers of kicking your asses. You and that Derek Goodman up the hill are a bunch of fuckin' liars."

"I never fired on no one, and I never slipped on no damn curb," Little Sonny said.

"Well, you sure as hell did drive these streets with a suspended license," Schaefer said, with something like glee. "Here's a little something for your scrap book."

He handed Little Sonny a two-hundred forty dollar ticket.

A few days later Schaefer caught him again, driving the same route. It seemed Schaefer must've been waiting there just for him, because he let a half dozen cars pass and then swooped down on Little Sonny's little red hatchback.

"Aww, shit," Little Sonny moaned, punching the dash. He'd

worked all day to make an honest living and now this cop was going to take another $240 out of him, money he could by no means afford to pay. Was he going to do this every day now?

"I see you like paying my salary, boy," said Schaefer, his big, leering face in Little Sonny's window again. "Are you making so much at that job of yours that you can afford to pay $240 a day in tickets?"

"Man, I'm just tryin' to make an honest living," Little Sonny said. "Why don't you go bust some of those drug dealers or pimps who are workin' up on Priscilla?"

"You tellin' me how to do my job, boy?"

"No," Little Sonny muttered.

"Good!" Schaefer stood there and wrote up the ticket. He ripped it off the pad and held it out before Little Sonny like a bone before a dog.

"You want this?"

"Not really."

"You want me to rip it up?"

Little Sonny hesitated. It seemed a trap. But the answer was obvious. "Yeah."

"I'll tell you what. We've got a special deal going for whining shits like you. You go up to that house there, down the end of the street." Schaefer pointed. "Don't do it now. Do it in half an hour or so. You ask for Denny and then try to cop a bag of weed. You get the bag, you testify against Denny, and your ticket problems go away. Got it?"

So that was the deal. Little Sonny wondered if Schaefer wouldn't slap possession charges on him just to ensure cooperation through trial. He wouldn't put it past this guy. "Naw, man, I been a lot of things, but I ain't never been no snitch. You better find somebody else for that one."

"C'mon! The guy's white. It ain't snitchin' if the guy's white."

"Snitchin' is snitchin'."

"Have it your way." Schaefer dropped the ticket on to Little Sonny's lap. "If you change your mind, you know where to find me. Otherwise, see you tomorrow. And the next day. And the day after that."

That started a summer-long game of cat and mouse between the cops and Little Sonny. From that moment on every cop in town was on the lookout for that red hatchback, and every one of them knew that Little Sonny's license was suspended. Little Sonny eliminated all unnecessary driving, developed a host of alternative routes into and out of Duquesne, came and went at odd hours and sometimes got friends to drive him to work and other places.

Most of the time he made it through.

Sometimes they got him. Once Schaefer made a second offer, telling him he'd be free to drive all over Duquesne if he'd just fill out a little affidavit saying that Derek Goodman was a drug dealer. Little Sonny could barely keep himself from spitting in Schaefer's face.

"That's my cuz, cop," Little Sonny said. "Go to hell."

"Suits me." The ticket floated gently into Little Sonny's lap.

"Man, you try to do it right in this world, workin' and all, and all they do is throw shit up to keep you from makin' it," he complained to Devon over the phone. "In a good week I make $250. Then they stop me for five minutes and just like that it's all gone. It's like they want to drive me to drink. They want me to quit workin' and go on welfare or steal cars or sell crack. They can't accept the fact that a man can make mistakes, then come back and try to get legit."

If driving in Duquesne was hazardous, staying home could be worse. Derek and a few friends were working on remodeling his basement one afternoon when a timid knock tickled the front door. Derek ignored it. But it persisted, and he climbed the stairs and opened the door.

It was a homeboy they called Tae, a guy he barely knew. He'd heard the guy was a crackhead, and those dudes were always potential trouble. They'd do anything for a hit or a ten spot.

But he was a brother. Derek opened the door. "Yeah?"

"Hey, man, I was wonderin' if you got any stuff."

"Naw, I don't do that. Who the hell told you I do that?"

"I dunno. Just thought maybe you had some shit. Don't you got no shit?"

"Sorry." Derek shut the door. He watched through the peephole. The guy shook his head and looked around, paced a little, then turned and walked out of site. That was strange, and Derek felt a chill. He'd passed around a few bags in his youth - who hadn't? - but now he was clean and just trying to get his head together.

He wandered downstairs.

"Who was that?" asked Davey D., a wide-eyed, skeleton-thin freak who tended to hit the pipe but could lay tile with the best of them.

"Some dude tryin' to cop some shit," Derek said. "I wonder where he got the idea that I had stuff."

Just then the door upstairs shook under a pounding fist. "Aww, shit," Derek said.

The three guys who'd been helping him out dropped their tools and started toward the window well.

"Naw, stay put," Derek said. "You go takin' off it's just gonna look bad. Keep workin'. There ain't nothin' here."

Davey D. looked nervous. He straightened his dirty clothes and pulled his baseball cap down tight on his head. "You sure, Russ man?"

"Yeah."

Davey D. picked up another tile.

Derek climbed the stairs again, tried to calm his burning gut and opened the door. A paper and a black pistol barrel burst into his face and he fell back against the wall as four cops poured in, guns drawn, screaming, "Hands up!" and "Against the wall!" and "We got a warrant." A dog scurried in, baying and sniffing and waving its head from side to side.

One of the cops turned Derek around and slapped handcuffs on him, tight so they bit into the skin. "Well if it ain't the boy who likes to shoot at cops," the cop sneered, pushing him down on the ground. "Looks like we caught ourselves a cop killer."

The cop stood over Derek, gun held tight in both hands, while the other three fanned out. The cop who headed into the basement quickly yelled, "Backup, backup! Whole buncha niggers down here." Two others rushed to his aid while Derek's captor stayed in the hall.

"Think you're pretty smart, dontcha," the cop said, his arms stiff like he was holding a Colt .45 instead of a .38. "Think you can get on TV and play little black victim and that'll give you a free pass to do whatever the fuck you want. Think you can move in here and turn this neighborhood into a fuckin' jungle. Well this ain't Clairton, buddy. This is Duquesne, and this is Aryan Nation time."

Derek breathed deep but kept silent. Downstairs he heard the dog growling and metal hitting metal, and figured the cops were rooting through the toolboxes, throwing his stuff around, probably scuffing the newly laid tiles. Fuck. At least there were no drugs down there, he thought, no drugs in the house. He didn't even have a dime bag of weed, for God's sake.

A cop marched Derek's three friends up the stairs. "Man, he's got fuckin' alligators down there," the cop said. "They're in this big cage with sand all in it."

"It'd be a damn shame to have to shoot 'em," said another.

"I could use some new shoes, though. Baby needs a new pair of shoes!"

"Hey Derek," said one cop, leaning right into his face, "why don't you save us the trouble of tearing this place apart? Just tell us where the drugs are."

"There ain't no drugs."

"Don't play that game with me, Derek. You're a nigger. You've got friends over all the time. You've got some money. There's got to be drugs. Where the hell are they?"

"If there were drugs, I'd tell you," Derek said. "But there ain't no drugs."

"Suits me." The cop walked into the kitchen and started pulling out drawers and dumping the contents on the floor. Silverware clattered everywhere, and then he heard the whir of his refrigerator and the soft sound of food hitting the floor as the cop tossed everything out.

A few minutes later he stopped in front of Derek again. "This is a nice pad, sweetheart. Guess we'll have to tear it all apart, though. Shame. Unless you want to spare your poor mother the mess by telling us where it is."

"Where what is?" he spat. "I ain't got nothin'."

"Suits me."

One cop stood over Derek with his gun drawn while another sat down at the dining room table and opened up a laptop computer. Davey D. and the two other homeboys stood against one of the dining room walls, shuffling nervously and making quiet little remarks to each other. Davey seemed to have the jitters worse than the others, and kept looking over at Derek, trying to whisper something. Derek shook him off.

The other two cops took the dog upstairs, and Derek heard loud, thumping sounds and the pitter-patter of hound feet. It was a good thing the pit bull was outside, he thought. Things could've gotten ugly.

Soon the two cops brought the dog downstairs. All three seemed to plod and look at the ground. "If the nigger's got drugs, he sure knows how to hide 'em," one said. "Whaddaya know, Davey? You know where he hides his shit?"

Davey looked around. "Huh?"

"Whatsa matter, Davey? You stoned?" he said, getting up in the guy's face. "Derek baby get you high? You all fucked up?"

It struck Derek that Davey might be stoned - that would explain his restless shuffling and the hazy, bloodshot look on his face. But when did he smoke up? While Derek was answering the door for Tae?

"Naw, I'm fine," Davey muttered.

The cop with the laptop slammed it shut and got up. He'd been sitting on the blue windbreaker Davey had tossed on a chair when he'd come in. "Let's get out of here. We'll get this motherfucker another time. We'll trash the house every day if we have to."

"It's in my coat," said Davey, out of the blue.

"Huh?" the laptop cop said.

"You been sittin' on it. It's in my coat."

The cop picked up the windbreaker and pawed it. He felt something in one of the pockets and reached in, pulled out a tiny baggie with a few crack rocks in it. "Bingo," the cop said. "Derek's goin' for a ride."

"Ain't my coat," Derek said, silently cursing himself for letting this crackhead help him out, and cursing Davey D. for coming into his house holding drugs. He'd told Davey never to bring that shit in here, told him how the cops had a hard-on for him and would be looking for any excuse to bust him again. Still the nigger comes here holding. Shit.

"That's my coat," Davey confirmed.

"But where'd you get the shit, Davey?" the cop asked. "Here, right?"

"Nowheres."

"Who's Nowhere? Any of you boys know where I can find Nowhere?"

The cops chuckled. "Davey's coat, Derek's house, so I guess both of you niggers get free lodging for a while," one said.

"Get the fuck up, cop killer," one said. "Let's go for a ride."

The cops marched he and Davey out the door. If they want you, Derek thought, they can get you. And they sure as hell seemed hot for him.

* * *

By late-July, Derek was out on bail but facing charges of possession and possession with intent to deliver. Little Sonny was a basket case and buried in moving violations. Devon was trying to get on with life, and took solace in his reggae music and Rastafarian spirituality when things got him down.

I was waiting for something to happen. Anything. An FBI investigation had occurred, but I never saw anybody marched off in handcuffs. A grand jury had convened, but where was the verdict? We'd hired lawyers, but when I called them, they always had an excuse as to why they hadn't filed suit yet. And the Clairton cops who'd abused my son were back out on the beat.

I didn't often watch the news, but on July 28, 1995, I awoke on my couch to the jingle of the noon news. "Good afternoon, Pittsburgh. In today's lead story, Clairton Police Officer Clyde Mimms has pleaded guilty to charges of violating the civil rights of three young men, Devon Grey, Derek Goodman and Little Sonny Brown. Mimms appeared before federal Magistrate Judge John Price today and entered the plea, which followed a federal grand jury investigation in November. Sentencing is expected to occur within 90 days, and Mimms could face up to 30 years in prison and substantial fines."

I was up on my feet as the anchorwoman filled in the obligatory few sentences of background, saying the three men were charged with firing on Mimms as he drove down Route 837, and on and on. "Maniac Cop Mimms pleaded guilty!" I yelled, as Lillian and then Peeper hurried into the room. I told them what I'd just heard.

"Is he gonna go to jail, Dad?" Peeper asked.

"Well, we don't know yet," I said. "That's to be decided in a couple of weeks."

"He oughta go to jail, after beating up Devon like that," Peeper said. "If he wasn't a cop, he'd already be in jail."

He understood more about the world than a kid his age should, I thought.

Lillian turned away from the TV as they moved on from the Mimms case to a story about a lottery winner in Wilmerding or something. "I hope they get what they deserve," she said. "Does this mean they have to drop those charges against the boys?"

"I don't know," I said. "I doubt they have to drop them. But I wouldn't want to be that D.A., pursuing those charges when their main witness had just pleaded guilty to federal civil rights violations. They may have to bring Mimms in to testify in handcuffs."

Even as I said it, I knew this wasn't over. Mimms wouldn't just walk into a courtroom and plead guilty without getting something out of it, maybe a shortened sentence, maybe cushy time in some minimum security joint, something. The TV said he could face up to 30 years in prison, but I doubted Mimms would be walking out of jail in 2025.

And there was still the matter of the white cops. The news report said nothing about Rahis and Sanalas, nor was I sure whether the FBI had ever pursued charges against them. No, this thing was far from over.

Lillian went back to her business. Peeper started throwing around kung fu kicks, saying, "Take that, Mimms! How you like my moves, you big jerk?"

"What're you doing?" I asked him.

He stopped. "I'm pretending part of Mimms' sentence is 10 rounds in the ring with me."

Then the phone started ringing. First it was family, asking if I knew anything more than they'd said on the news. Nope, that was the first I'd heard anything about a guilty plea, I said. The FBI, the Department of Justice, they'd all failed to tell me. No one had even called me, nor the victims, I would later learn. I hadn't even known talks were going on. So much for victims' rights.

Reporters sneaked in between the family calls. "Mr. Grey, what do you think of Clairton Police Officer Clyde Mimms' guilty plea?" they asked, mostly.

"Well, I've said he's guilty all along," I said. "I'm glad he's finally come to agree. No one believed us. Now maybe the public will stop rushing to judgment. The maniac cop has been in denial for a year and a half. Now I guess he got over his denial and decided to tell the truth."

"What do you think his punishment should be?"

"Jail time. Lots of it. The man violated three young men's civil rights. Count 'em: one, two, three. He should lose some of his own rights for a while."

"Would you support a sentence which did not involve jail time?"

"Not involve jail time? For three counts of civil rights violation? Let me ask you this: What if your child was handcuffed, pummeled, kicked, beat with a shotgun, punched out, threatened with execution, kicked and punched some more and then charged with a crime for which there is no evidence. Would you want probation? If they don't jail that maniac, he's gonna keep on doing what he does, and sooner or later somebody's gonna be dead."

"Thank you, Mr. Grey."

And on and on. I did one interview for TV out in a windswept mall parking lot. Again, the media latched on to me, the biggest mouth and the easiest person to find, rather than going the extra step of locating and talking to the actual victims. I shrugged it off and spoke my mind, figuring that at the very least I was putting a little pressure on the Justice Department and the judge to deal sternly with Maniac Cop Mimms.

The case quickly dropped off the media's radar screen and we waited for the sentencing hearing. As it approached, another story broke that would eventually come to dominate the public discourse in Pittsburgh for much of the rest of the decade. On October 12, 1995, on a stretch of roadway in the white suburb of Brentwood, a cop took up pursuit of a 31-year-old black businessman who appeared to be tapping his brake lights and driving a Jaguar while black. Just inside the City of Pittsburgh limits, Brentwood Police Lieutenant Milton Mulholland pulled Jonny E. Gammage to the side of the road. In the minutes that followed, four other white, suburban cops arrived on the scene and Jonny Gammage lost his life.

It could have been just another black man killed "resisting arrest." But the next few days' investigation revealed that Gammage didn't have a criminal history, wasn't drunk or on drugs and carried no weapon more deadly than a cell phone. And the Jaguar was owned by

Gammage's cousin, a popular Pittsburgh Steeler lineman named Ray Seals. Seals had the money to hire good lawyers, pathologists and expert witnesses.

* * *

A week after Gammage's death, on a blustery October 19 afternoon, Devon, Little Sonny, Larry Vicious and I piled into my wife's Caddy and headed for Pittsburgh, back to that long, squat, stone Federal Courthouse. Derek had decided to stay home and catch the news reports; seemed whenever he got too close to a courthouse, somebody found an excuse to throw him in jail.

Down in front of the courthouse the first of the TV crews was setting up. Inside, the guards who manned the metal detectors seemed edgy. They made us take off our jackets, empty our pockets, walk back and forth through the metal detector, then scanned us up and down with their wands.

"Hey, we ain't the criminals on this one, guys," I said.

We rode the elevator up and huddled outside Federal Magistrate John Price's courtroom.

"What you think he's gonna get, Uncle Buster?" Little Sonny asked. "Ten years in?"

"Aww, they're gonna go easy on him," said Devon. "Cops don't do serious time."

"If he gets ten years in, I'll run naked down Grant Street," I said.

"Then they'll throw you right in with him," Little Sonny said.

"Hey, that's all I've ever been asking. Just a little time alone with Clyde Mimms. Make him beg for his civil rights. See how he likes it."

"Yeah, well, you can have it," Little Sonny said. "I want him inside, me outside. I figure if he gets serious time in, they gotta drop the bullshit they pinned on us. Ain't that right, Larry?"

"Well, it would certainly make it harder for them to get a conviction on you," said Vicious, but he didn't meet Little Sonny's eyes. I could tell he was just saying it to make Little Sonny happy.

We were still bullshitting when big pink Constance Cass lumbered by without even acknowledging us. She wouldn't have known the victims, having never interviewed them nor invited them to testify at the grand jury, and apparently having only seen doctored photos of the three, but she should've remembered me. Peggy Liu passed by shortly after, and even she didn't acknowledge us.

We heard a gavel and piled in. As we did, Maniac Cop Mimms and his lawyer turned around and stared, bug-eyed, as if they'd seen a ghost. I guess no one expected us to show up. The federal magistrate took one look at us and buried his nose in his papers, just like Clairton Magistrate Raymond Locke had done. Devon and Little Sonny took seats right in the front row on the defendant's side, where they could practically reach out and grab Maniac Cop Mimms' black sport coat. Larry Vicious and I ended up behind Mishelle Blunt and an old black lady I had pegged as Mimms' mammy. A fistful of reporters rounded out the audience.

"So you think they'll put that drug addict Mimms away for good, Larry?" I asked, loud enough for Blunt and Mimms' Mammy to hear. I saw them stiffen.

"We can only hope," Larry said, quietly.

I saw Little Sonny hissing, "Guilty!" and saw Mimms half turn his head and snarl. The judge seemed to hear it, and frowned. I didn't know why - Mimms had, after all, pleaded guilty. The man who'd called himself God was up front with a white lawyer, a young, thin guy with glasses, and the bailiff quickly swore him in as everyone took their seats.

"This is the time set for sentencing in the case of the United States versus Clyde Mimms, at Criminal Number 95-111," the judge announced.

The judge introduced the parties - Mimms, his lawyer Michael Cross, Cass and Liu. Then he ran through a ton of mumbo jumbo about sentencing guidelines, underlying offenses, offense levels, imprisonment, supervised release and electronic monitoring. I heard something about up to five years of probation, maximum fine of $100,000 plus restitution, but, the judge said, "No information regarding restitution has been received."

"Restitution means money to make up for our damages?" I asked Vicious.

"Yes," he said.

I thought about that for a second. Derek had dropped out of school because of this. Little Sonny had lost jobs and tried to kill himself. All three had hospital bills. I had some ideas about restitution. But the Justice Department had never brought restitution up to me, let alone to the victims.

The lawyers started arguing about whether Mimms would be allowed to continue to work as a police officer. Had I missed something? Was the part about jail over already?

"If that drunk wears a badge, it should say, 'civil rights violator,'" I said to Vicious.

Blunt and Mimms' mammy turned and glared, and I grinned politely back.

Officer Mimms had gone through counseling as part of his guilty plea agreement, Cross told the judge. "It was also the agreement between the parties that if the counseling had made a recommendation that Mr. Mimms take a certain leave of absence from his job to keep up with his counseling, that they would also do so. That is part of the plea agreement. The counseling people have not made such a recommendation."

"Your Honor, it's the government's position that, umm, as a minimum, the Defendant agreed as part of, umm, what he agreed to that he would take an unpaid leave of absence from the Clairton Police Department," Cass answered. Her voice crackled with nervousness, and I wondered if this was the first time she'd spoken in a courtroom. She looked even paler than usual, and scared.

The two argued on and on over whether Mimms should be allowed to continue to serve as a police officer while undergoing counseling. "This mean that alcoholic isn't goin' to jail?" I whispered to Vicious.

"I don't know, Leon," he muttered. He scribbled down some notes on a yellow legal pad.

The judge stopped the debate and rustled some papers up on his bench. He read silently and smacked his lips. "I am interpreting this to mean that in the event the Defendant were to enter an intensive counseling, perhaps an inpatient counseling program, that he would then be required to take a leave of absence," the judge said. "If he is to see a psychologist on occasion, I don't think it triggers this provision."

"What's that mean?" I whispered.

"It means that Mimms won't have to take a leave of absence from policing the entire time he's in counseling, just if he's an inpatient," said Vicious.

"What about jail time?"

"I don't know yet."

Cross spoke again. "I believe we are also in agreement that a term of incarceration is not necessary in this matter and, therefore, I leave the length of probation up to the Court, because that's what I would request."

Cross said the only two questions before the court were the length of Mimms' probation and the length of his home confinement. Then he argued that Mimms shouldn't have to wear one of those electronic ankle bracelets they have for monitoring people on probation.

"As we know, a City of Clairton police officer is going to be a busy person and they do have their problems out there with violence and drugs, and he is an active officer in that," said Cross. "So I would request that the Court consider, if actual monitoring equipment is necessary, or if it would not be more appropriate just to have a condition that if he is off duty, that when he gets home, if he is permitted, say, working nine to five for example, and he gets home by six, he call the probation officer when he is at home."

The judge let him say his piece, then announced that he'd already spoken with the probation office and the Clairton P.D. There were monitoring devices available that wouldn't interfere with Mimms' ability to chase bad guys, the judge said.

Price asked if Cass had anything else to offer.

She handed him a sheath of papers, and told him that they included his personnel records. "He joined the McKeesport Police Department in 1988, and he resigned in 1991, but he resigned as a condition that if he didn't resign, they were going to fire him," Cass said. "And of particular pertinence, Your Honor, I would like to point to then-police chief Daniel Beltree's statements made in connection with his decision that Mr. Mimms should be terminated, and in particular, he said based upon the prior instances, that what all these documents show is Officer Mimms has manifested a drinking problem, a tendency for violence, and a history of gun-related incidents."

She went on to say that in 1993, while off duty, Mimms had slugged somebody. He'd also had numerous incidents with an ex-wife, "one in which she was pretty beat up."

Cass finished up and asked if Liu could have a chance to speak on behalf of the Justice Department's Civil Rights Division. The judge nodded.

"Yes, Your Honor," said Liu. "The Government's position is that Clyde Mimms is a time bomb that's ready to go off, and we urge the Court to do everything within its power to prevent harm to the community or to Mr. Mimms himself."

Whoa. I sat up in my seat and Vicious stopped scribbling and looked up. Liu looked like a little puppet next to big Cass and in front of the judge's imposing black bench, but her delivery was firm and confident and her face was full of fire. Finally, I was hearing a little bit of truth.

"We ask the Court to consider three main points. First, Mr. Mimms' actions in this case were where he was an off duty police officer, that's true, but then through his actions in getting the individuals in this case arrested when they were already in police custody and subdued, that he went beyond what a normal citizen would do, and had access to a police shotgun, had access to the suspects after they were in custody, had access to them at the station, and took advantage of that access as a police officer to violate their civil rights and to assault them, and assault them in a manner which resulted in injury, substantial injury to them.

"So we ask the Court to take into consideration whether that is conduct that this community should approve of in allowing a police officer - and we say no in that circumstance because that is inappropriate behavior for a police officer acting under color of law to deprive citizens of their civil rights.

"The second thing we ask the Court to consider is the prior record of misconduct by Mr. Mimms. While he was a police officer employed by the McKeesport Police Department, he engaged in a series of assaults on individuals, which is well documented in the pre-sentence report.

"Again, we concede that a lot of these incidents occurred off duty, but just because a person is off duty doesn't mean that they are not also acting under color of law. Indeed, in at least one of the incidents Mr. Mimms did say in the process of assaulting someone with a firearm, 'I'm a police officer,' and the ability to invoke that color of law is what we're concerned about.

"If Mr. Mimms is allowed to remain a police officer, then he can always assert that authority, and that is an authority that we only give to people whom the public trusts, whom the public puts faith in, that this officer will protect and serve the community, not abuse it. So we ask the Court to take that into consideration.

"And the third point is the psychological report which documents Mr. Mimms' propensity toward violence, the fact he is not dealing with it, he is in constant denial he has a problem. He denies he has an alcohol problem. We all acknowledge he has an alcohol problem. He denies he has a tendency toward violence. The word "minimize" is used repeatedly through the psychological report characterizing the way Mr. Mimms regards his behavior. He doesn't think he has a problem, and until the message gets across to him, that this is not to be tolerated by anybody in our society, let alone a police officer, whom we give so much trust and authority to, Mr. Mimms will not begin to address his problems."

"All around us journalists scribbled furiously to keep up with Liu. Blunt and Mimms' mammy sat stone-faced. Cross turned red, and Maniac Cop Mimms stared dully in Liu's direction. I was electrified. Finally, somebody had stopped with the legal bullshit and had set out to tell it like it is.

On the bench, the judge frowned and shuffled his papers.

Liu urged that Mimms get maximum home confinement and lose his right to carry a gun or a badge for five years. "The Government is not saying we should lock him up and throw away the key. We are saying, he does have a problem, but we don't think the message will get across to him in any clear way unless he is asked not to be a police officer. He can certainly seek other employment. But as long as he is carrying a firearm and wearing that badge, I believe the community is at risk."

Cross stepped toward Liu. He seemed to be shaking. "I have just one question, and I forget the lady's name who just spoke to the Court, and I apologize, I just have one question for her. Have you ever talked to Mr. Mimms?"

"What does that matter?" I hissed to Vicious. As if talking to Maniac Cop Mimms would convince a person that he was really a good guy, just a little bit misunderstood, and once you got to know him, you'd understand how important it was to him to remain a cop, even if he did have this pesky habit of beating people.

The little lady didn't flinch. "Your Honor, I don't believe that this is a relevant question, and the Justice Department rules forbid us from speaking with people who are represented by counsel."

"That is fine. That's all I wanted to know," said Cross.

The judge said he'd reviewed the record, and so on and so forth. Then he said some things so unbelievable to me I lost track of what I was doing and where I was.

"It appears to me that permitting him to continue working as a police officer under appropriate restrictions would be both beneficial to the community as well as to the Defendant and permit him to continue to support his family," Price intoned. "I think having him terminate his employment as a police officer would be of no benefit to the community and certainly an extreme detriment to himself and his family. Realistically, he has a job now, odds of securing other employment are probably pretty slim. Barring his continued functioning as a police officer would be detrimental to the community."

I almost fell off my chair. Detrimental to the community? Detrimental to the community? This maniac had brutally beaten three men who had done nothing but dare to drive slowly on an icy road. He'd assaulted people, once with a firearm, in McKeesport and had been forced to resign. If it was detrimental to the community to lose Maniac Cop Mimms, then God help us all.

In spite of Liu's impassioned plea, this judge, like so many others involved in this case, had forgotten the victims. Somehow he seemed to have come to the conclusion that Mimms was the victim, and needed to be protected from further harm.

I felt a wave of nausea and a rush of fever heat. The federal government had pretended to be interested in getting justice for the crime perpetrated on my nephews, then had betrayed me. They weren't serious about prosecuting police officers who violated citizens' constitutional rights, who beat young men, who terrorized suspects, invented crimes and threatened people with execution. Instead, they were just confirming what I'd already feared: that cops are above the law. That badge is a license to beat and kill without fear of prosecution.

Gunn would later tell me that the (In)Justice Department didn't really want to prosecute the case because they had come to the conclusion that Devon, Derek and Little Sonny had fired shots at

Mimms. They reached that verdict without having ever investigated the alleged shooting, without any physical evidence, without a trial, based apparently on their ages and the color of their skin.

"An asset to the community?" I said to Vicious. "A cop that beats people and tries to kill people is an asset to the community? What a crock of shit. That community needs him like I need a hole in my damn head."

The judge announced his sentence. The crime Mimms plead guilty to, he said, was one charge of minor assault. Two years probation. One year on home detention, with an electronic monitoring device around his ankle. Substance abuse and mental health counseling. No carrying a firearm except when on duty.

Oh, and a special assessment fee of $25.

"Is there anything further?" the judge asked.

"Nothing, Your Honor," said Cross.

"No, Your Honor," said Cass.

"Okay, we will recess." The gavel went down.

And Little Sonny leapt up. "I was robbed! I was robbed!" he shouted, pointing at Mimms. "He beat me, kicked me, shotgunned me while I was handcuffed. Now he's gon get probation? Where's the justice? There's no justice in this court!"

I ran up and grabbed him as Mimms and Cross hurried out through a door on the other side of the court, with Cass hot on their heels. "You crazy? They'll throw you in jail for an outbreak like that in this court room," I said. I grabbed his arm and pulled him from one side while Devon pushed from the other.

He kept shouting as we dragged him past smiling Michele Blunt and Mimms' mom. A uniformed federal cop started moving toward us, but I shook my head and he held his ground.

When we got Little Sonny out the door, I turned to him. "What did you expect? This is how black people are treated in this country. Get used to it. No justice, no peace."

"Aww, fuck, Uncle Buster, he's done messed up my whole life," Little Sonny moaned, the sounds coming from some painful place deep inside. "Jobs. Girls. Everything's messed up. And now he ain't goin' to jail, and I probably am."

"This doesn't mean anything to you," said Vicious. "Your defense will stand on its own. They have no evidence to convict you on."

"Yeah, right, Larry. Like that's ever stopped them."

We got him over to the elevator and a crowd of reporters piled in with us. I ignored them, but they didn't seem to care, because Little Sonny kept ranting solid through. All they had to do was let him go and scribble in their little notebooks.

Devon just stood quiet, head bowed. He looked like somebody shot his puppy. Once in a while he'd shake his head.

"So you think that maniac cop got special treatment?" I quietly asked Vicious.

"Sure Mimms got preferential treatment," said Vicious. "He's a cop."

"And these guys are black, too," I said. "Them being black, and Mimms being black, pretty much nullifies any chance of him doing hard time. Black on black crime - who cares?"

The metal detector guys hustled us out of the courthouse. Out on the street the television cameras gathered around Little Sonny like anxious groupies around the latest pop star.

"How do you feel about the sentencing? "

"Man, you all were in the courtroom. You all heard the evidence. Do you feel that Maniac Cop Mimms should have gotten probation? You were there. Why don't you all do the right thing, and go up there and interview that judge and find out why he gave that civil rights violator probation?"

"Man, that guy fired on us. He beat us for no reason. Now he's gonna walk, and keep his badge and keep packin' a piece, and I'm going to trial and maybe jail? Can you explain that to me?" Tears started gathering in the corners of his eyes.

"Mr. Brown, do you have any message for Clyde Mimms now?" Little Sonny sniffled and thought for a second.

"I hope you're satisfied, Mimms," he yelled into the camera, teeth bared. "I have nightmares every night. I have a blood clot on my brain because of you. I lost jobs behind you, Mimms! I hope to hell you're satisfied."

Then Little Sonny turned, and we all turned to check out what he saw. Michele Blunt was a few yards away, walking down Grant Street all alone, her black dress and plaster-white skin making her look like a Holstein cow.

I don't know how she got there, but Little Sonny turned and

lunged after her, camera crews in tow. "She called me a nigger!" he screamed. "She spit in my face in that there station!"

Devon, Vicious and I grabbed Little Sonny, as a bunch of federal marshals who seemed to want to get on TV rushed at him, shouting,

"Back off! You're under arrest!"

"Fuck you!" Little Sonny yelled.

"Put your hands behind your back!" one of the marshals ordered. "You're under arrest."

"No he ain't," I said, getting between Little Sonny and the marshals. "No, we've got him under control, and we're taking him home. If that damn judge would have done the right thing, there wouldn't be any problem out here."

They stood there for a second and glanced at the rolling television cameras. They looked around for Blunt, but she was gone. "Well, all right, but get him the hell out of here," one of the marshals said.

We got back to the car and headed for the valley. All the way to Vicious's house, Little Sonny ranted and cried about the unfairness of it all, about how Mimms had screwed him, the judge had screwed him, the system was going to screw him. Vicious obligingly agreed, but I reminded him that it wasn't any judge's decision to let Mimms plea down to minor assault; it was the Justice Department's decision. "Bam-boozled, hood-wink is what Malcom X would call this shroud by the Department of Justice. Hell, this trail was nothing but a joke and a waste of tax payers money. It's painfully clear to me that Reno's Justice Department did not want to prosecute Maniac Cop Mimms. Hell, that fool (Clyde Mimms) pleaded guilty to multiple counts of human rights violations. His black, monkey ass should have been hauled off to a federal penitentiary kicking and screaming bloody murder. Can somebody please tell me, how in the hell can an indicted felon be allowed to carry a gun, remain a cop and not be fired? What kind of weird ass shit is that? Hey, so much for America defending black folk's civil rights. It's time to give a name to our pain! From this day on, our pain will be called the U.S. Department of (In)Justice," I said. Vicious agreed with that, too. I think he would have agreed if somebody said it was all the court reporter's fault. We dropped him off and rode on.

Devon turned to Little Sonny. "Hey, man, I told you they weren't gonna do nothing to Mimms. Cops can get away with beating people and killing people."

"Yeah, well, it shouldn't be that way," Little Sonny said. "I was just hoping that in this case, of all the cases, maybe we'd get some justice."

It was sad to see his bubble break. Since he'd been out of jail, I thought, Little Sonny had really tried to buy into the American myth that everybody has a shot if they work hard and keep their nose clean. It's a pretty myth. It's a shame when it gets ground up in that blender called the Justice System.

We stopped by Derek's house and picked him up, then headed for my place for a strategy session. Derek had just watched the coverage on the noon news. "Man, you were cryin' on TV," he said to Little Sonny, with a grin.

"Well that was the saddest fuckin' thing I've ever seen," Little Sonny said. "They might as well have given Mimms a medal for beatin' nigga's ass and told him to try for four or five civil rights violations next time 'round. Man, and to see that racist Blunt and Mimms' mammy all smilin' and shit - you'd have cried, too."

"That was a joke," Derek agreed. "He hung me over the side of that bridge and smashed me against the curb and beat me with those sack gloves and I'm gonna have to live with that for the rest of my life. And he gets probation."

That got Little Sonny riled again, and he quickly wound up to a fever pitch of ranting and crying. I tried to tune him out, to think instead about what the next step would be. I'd tried going legit, worked with the Federal Bureau of Investigation and the Injustice Department, and they'd failed me. They'd in fact made a mockery of the word "justice." There would be lawsuits, of course, and maybe the three cousins would get something, and maybe they'd get nothing. Who knew? Blacks alleging injuries at the hands of the police weren't known for getting runaway verdicts out of Allegheny County juries, but anything could happen.

Even if they did win, though, it would only be money. None of those three cops would serve jail time. None of them would even pay a dime - the City of Clairton or its insurance company would be on the hook. That wouldn't send any message to other cops who might be inclined to beat and terrorize people.

I thought again about the other option, the vigilante solution. I still had my guns, and my van would still make a mess out of the front door of that station. That would be a message signed with my own blood. That would tell the world that even when police brutality was accepted by the courts, it wouldn't be accepted by the community. Or at least by me.

"Hey, sit down, man," Devon said in back, as I rounded the bend on to the McKeesport-Duquesne Bridge. I am sitting, I thought.

"What the hell are you doing?" Devon asked.

Then there was a blast of cool air and in the rear view mirror I saw Little Sonny leap out of the back seat at 35 miles an hour.

"What's that fool doin'?" Derek cried as the car skidded to a stop. I craned my neck and saw Little Sonny starting up the fence separating the sidewalk from the ledge and the muddy, moody waters of the Monongahela River far below.

"He's gonna jump!" said Devon, and dashed out the door after him.

Little Sonny clambered up high enough to peer over the top of the fence and was about to yank himself up and over when Devon and Derek slammed against the fence. Each just managed to grab one of his feet. Both were yelling, "What're you doin', fool?" and "You crazy, man?" and "Get the hell down from there, you clown!" But Little Sonny pulled against them, jerking first one foot, then the other against their tenuous grip.

"I'm gonna jump!" he shouted. "They screwed me! I'm tired of being screwed by the system. Clyde Mimms should be in jail, but he ain't, and I didn't do anything and they're trying to put me in jail."

"Mimms ain't worth it," Derek said. "Get down off of that fence before the cops come, or they're gonna shoot you down."

"Let 'em. It's better than goin' to that damn kangaroo court again!"

Derek and Devon kept talking and pulling, as traffic backed up behind us. Some guy I recognized from Duquesne got out of his car and started yelling, "What are you doin' up there? Get down from there! What happened?" Somebody else barked, "Leave him alone! Let him be."

I didn't know what that was about.

Me, I joined the cacophony of voices, saying, don't let Maniac Cop Mimms and those cops have the last laugh on you, man, stick it out, this thing ain't over yet, and on and on and on. And a dry but wrenching sadness overcame me; they'd ruined this young man's life, damn it, and they weren't getting anything more than a little slap on the wrist.

If he jumps, they're dead, I vowed. As they fish Little Sonny out of the river, that Clairton station will be in flames. If those cops and this goddamned system takes his life, I'll take theirs.

"On three, yank him down," said Devon. "One, two, three!"

He and Derek yanked hard on Little Sonny's tiring legs, and he collapsed, his hands ripping on the twists at the top of the fence. He landed on his ass between them. "Aww, mother fucker!" he groaned, weeping, his head falling into his hands. "Why didn't you just let me go? There ain't nothin' in this world for me but trouble."

"You gotta live, man," Devon said, putting his arm around him and shaking him a little. "You can't go givin' up just because the system don't like you. That system don't mean nothin' anyway. You gotta make it through the hard times, 'cause you just don't know what better times are just 'round the corner."

Little Sonny shook his head and sobbed.

I was glad these three had each other. Because they didn't have much else going for them right now.

The guy from Duquesne sidled up to me. "That boy okay?"

"I don't know. I don't know. But we're gonna do what we can for him."

I walked from him toward the Clairton Three. Little Sonny dribbled blood and tears while his cousins on both sides of him said things like, "Man, you best not jump. We need a witness!" and "You can stop cryin' now - the TV cameras are gone." Little Sonny's sobs mixed with little ripples of laughter.

They were getting a little too comfortable on that bridge deck, like they were gonna spread out a blanket and have a picnic or something. "Let's get the hell off the road, before the cops come," I said.

The infamous Ravensburg Bridge is where three black motorists were attacked, fired on, beaten and threatened to be thrown over the bridge by Clairton's finest.

Route 837, a stretch of road that runs along the Monogahela River is where three black motorists had a dangerous encounter with a road raged, off duty cop who had one too many brews.

Arnold Staples investigating the beating of his son by Clairton cops, finds his son's blood smeared over the front door of the Clairton Police Station. Staples would also find pools of blood on the deck of the Ravensburg Bridge.

Arnold Staples (far right) joined by other protestors pulling down the American flag outside the County Courthouse in downtown Pittsburgh after a white police officer was acquitted by an all-white jury in the murder case of a black motorist.

Copyright Photo by Matt Freed/Pittsburgh Post-Gazette, 1999 All rights reserved, reprinted with permission.

Clairton's torture chamber, the brick station house on Ravensburg Road is where three black motorists were maliciously beaten, tortured, sodomized and had their civil rights violated by three sadistic Clairton Police Officers.

Clairton a.k.a. City of Prayer, is a small mill town along the Monogahela River whose city officals condone police brutality and it is also the home of an indicted felon who is employed as a police officer in the City of Prayer.

Chapter 9

The Sell Out

Devon didn't fall in with losers like Derek did or swallow handfuls of pills like Little Sonny, but I could see the stress of having a case hanging over him was taking its toll. He seemed listless then, and took what work came to him but didn't really go busting his butt. He was mostly hanging dry wall at the time, and there's always dry walling work to be had. But there are plenty of people who know that work, too. So if you don't go looking for jobs, it's not like they're going to come looking for you.

Devon let his child support payments slide, and pretty soon we were getting summons in the mail. I didn't pay too much attention, and apparently neither did he, because in January, when he went to Pittsburgh for a hearing, the judge told him he'd missed two previous engagements and tossed him in a downtown halfway house.

Failing to pay child support was serious in my book, but I couldn't but see a certain irony in the fact that Maniac Cop Mimms, Rahis and Sanalas were sitting in their home at night while Devon was locked up.

He called home daily. "Yeah, I'm doin' okay. They let you out during the day to look for work, but they keep pretty close track of you. It's not like you can go run around free and visit your friends or anything. And the food's all right. Every meal they've got a main course, something with potatoes or rice, and a vegetable. It ain't like mom's or anything, but it's okay. But then you've got chores, and you can't do what you want to. I'll be real glad to get out, Dad. Real glad."

"Well don't get too excited. Know what we got today?"

"What?"

"A notice of a pre-trial conference on the Mimms thing. March 6, 1996. Huh, that's the two year anniversary, isn't it?"

"March 6? Yeah, that is."

"Well, that's the pre-trial. From what the lawyer says, they might go straight into trial after that. Or they might not."

"So I might go straight from here to a real prison, huh?"

"You didn't commit a crime, did you?"

"No."

"Then you shouldn't be going to no prison."

Of course I knew it wasn't that simple. If the world made any sense, if the so-called justice system was anything but a kangaroo court, then the D.A. wouldn't even be bringing charges. I mean, their whole case was based on tall tales told by Maniac Cop Clyde Mimms, a man who'd pleaded guilty to violating the civil rights of the accused during the arrest. Their so-called confession was a piece of paper that didn't make any sense, signed by a young man who'd been beaten into a stupor.

Maniac Cop Mimms' punishment wasn't much of one, unfortunately. Friends of mine reported seeing him all over the tri-state area during his so-called house arrest. What a joke. If Maniac Cop Mimms was on house arrest, I was on kidney dialysis.

Regardless of all of that, the D.A. and cops would be gunning for convictions, hoping that by putting these guys in jail they could screw up the civil suit. A mostly-white jury was pretty much a certainty, and if they decided to convict three innocent black men, well, it wouldn't be the first time.

Then there was the problem of lawyers. The ones we had acted like a bunch of assholes without an ounce of real compassion for Devon, Derek and Little Sonny. I've seen public defenders show more compassion toward their scuzbag clients than our attorneys showed to their innocent, badly wronged, paying clients. Since the preliminary hearing they'd done nothing but ask for extension after extension after extension and send us bill after bill. For months Jipenstein didn't return my phone calls. His secretary set up meetings and then canceled them at the last minute. When I finally did catch him on the phone, Jipenstein told me he was going to turn the case over to his partner, Attorney Richard "Fat Boy" Reinhardt.

"I didn't hire Richard 'Fat Boy' Reinhardt," I said. "I don't know Richard 'Fat Boy' Reinhardt. I hired you."

"Look, Leon, he's my partner. It's the same as having me work the case. Attorney Reinhardt is an experienced, well-reputed public defender. He even works out of the public defender's office. As a matter of fact, he's probably better qualified than I am to handle the case."

I thought about this for a few days. This lawyer had taken our case, then told me he'd rather not handle the civil suit. Now he wanted to dump the criminal defense off on this guy I'd never heard of. Obviously Jipenstein valued his cozy relationships with Mon Valley cops and mayors more than his duty to his clients. After a few days, I talked with Devon, and we fired him.

We checked in with Vicious, who recommended Melvin Mason, a union attorney who did mostly civil work, but also defense. We hired him, and he filed a civil suit against Mimms, Rahis, Sanalas, Abbet, the Clairton P.D. and Mayor Lou Costello on Nov. 7, 1995.

I don't know whether the two were related, but it didn't take long after for the D.A. and judge to schedule that March 6, 1996 pre-trial in the criminal case.

That morning the three accused, Mason and Vicious, Arnella Brown, my eldest son Curtis and I piled into a conference room in our lawyer's office. Devon had cut off his dreadlocks for the occasion. I was pleased, but I have to admit he looked a little naked without them. Derek's lawyer, Richard "Fat Boy" Reinhardt, wasn't there. He'd phoned ahead and said he couldn't make it.

When everyone else was seated around an oval-shaped table, Mason stood at one end with both hands rooted into the table, like a general about to hand out the marching orders. It struck me as a ridiculous pose for the tall, balding, Charlie Chaplin-like joker. By that I mean he blinked like Charlie Chaplin, deliberately and constantly. I think all that blinking made him seem sympathetic, as if he was shocked by what you were saying and was just able to hold back tears. But it also made him seem goofy.

"Thanks for coming down," he said. He surveyed the black faces around the table, blinked three times and swallowed, as if resolving to go through with his plan despite being badly outnumbered. "Ahem. Before we go in there today, I need to know one thing: Who had the gun?"

Everyone stared at him. Had he failed to pay attention up to this point, or was this some lawyer trick? "Nobody had a gun," Devon said. "The cops must've planted a gun in the car, because nobody had any gun."

Mason looked down at the table, then back up. "They're going to produce a statement by Derek saying that Little Sonny had a gun. If we are compelled to admit that someone had a gun ... would that someone be Little Sonny?"

"I didn't write any confession," Derek said. "That's not even my writing. I signed a piece of paper saying I was advised of my Miranda rights."

"Well, there was a confession on the other side of that paper, and they're going to say you wrote it," Mason said.

Derek shook his head. "Well, what am I supposed to say?"

"Just tell the truth," Mason said. "I can't tell you what to say."

"OK, man, I got you. Tell the truth."

"Truth is they tortured him so bad he'd have said anything to make it stop," said Little Sonny, shaking his head slowly. "The fact is, I didn't have no gun. Nobody had a damn gun."

"They're going to produce a weapon and they may well have fingerprint evidence," Mason said. "What if Derek's prints are on the gun?"

"What if they aren't?" I said. "They've had every chance to produce fingerprints, but they haven't. I don't think they have any."

"But what if they do?" Mason asked.

"Look, if you're trying to separate these three guys, just stop," I said. "I know you want to get Devon off and Larry Vicious wants to get Little Sonny off and that Richard "Fat Boy" Reinhardt or whoever he is probably wants to get Derek off. But these guys aren't just friends or acquaintances. They're cousins. They're family. They should stand or fall together."

"Tell 'em, Uncle Buster," said Little Sonny.

"The state charged all three with this crime," I said. "They charged all three. Let them try all three. No one is going to be cut out of this. No one is going to take the fall for this rap."

"That's right," said Devon.

Mason looked at Vicious. "All right, no gun," he said. "I guess we can sink or swim with that. My only word of caution is that juries don't usually believe that cops plant guns on people or in their cars, and that, in essence, is what we're saying."

"We're not saying anything like that," I said. "We're saying, 'Hey, D.A., you've got a gun, but there's no fingerprints on it. You've got a confession, but it doesn't make sense and was signed behind torture. You go ahead and prove your case, because we aren't gonna do it for you.'"

"Didn't you tell me they got the burden of proof, Larry?" Little Sonny piped up.

Larry Vicious laughed heartily. "Hard to argue with that. Where'd you guys get your law degrees?"

"Community college," I said.

We talked a little more, then headed over to court, where Judge David Gibson would hear pre-trial motions before jury selection began. There we met Richard "Fat Boy" Reinhardt, a fat guy in a rumpled shirt and wrinkled khaki slacks. I'd seen him on TV before, crying when he'd lost the case of a man who raped his five year old stepdaughter. I think he was wearing the same slacks when they put him on TV for that. He had a general air of sloppiness to him, and he greeted us only briefly and suspiciously before buttonholing Derek and going off whispering to him.

Derek came back shaking his head and frowning.

"What was that all about?" I asked him, quietly.

"Aww, nothin', Uncle Buster. That wasn't about nothin'."

"I don't know why you hired that damn Jipenstein and this partner of his, when I fired him. What in the hell is wrong with you? What kind of fool are you? He's going to sell you out, just watch what I tell you."

Derek just shook his head and scrunched up his mouth. I could tell there was something he wanted to tell me. But for some reason, he couldn't.

Reinhardt grabbed the other two lawyers. "The judge has asked us to conference in his chambers." He looked over at us, and his eyes seemed like olives in his doughy face. "We'll only be a few minutes."

The three lawyers disappeared into the back. A younger white guy who I figured was an Assistant D.A. followed. That made me nervous. These people who we hired to defend us somehow found it necessary to meet with the judge and prosecutor behind closed doors and out of earshot.

We waited quietly in the hall. After a few minutes Vicious hurried out and asked, "Which of you guys has a criminal record?"

Derek had a juvenile sheet, but nothing as an adult. Devon had nothing but failure to pay child support. Little Sonny was the only one with a real rap sheet.

"You know I've got a record, Larry, because you represented me,"

Little Sonny said. "I got a record for stealing cars. I did some time behind that."

"That's right. Stealing cars. Thanks. We'll be out shortly."

But they stayed in there quite a while longer. When they finally did come out, each one ran to his respective client.

"They're going to drop charges against Devon for lack of evidence," Mason murmured to Devon and me, panting a little and blinking like crazy and grinning and shaking his own hand.

"Well they'd better drop charges against all three, because there isn't any more evidence against any of the others than there is against Devon," I said.

"I can't guarantee what they'll do with the others. Devon is my client, and all I can be sure of is that he's not going to jail for this."

Over to my left, Reinhardt held Derek by the elbow and leaned close, but I could just make out what he was saying. "You're going to be fine. I'm going to put you on the stand. There's three questions I'm going to ask you. The answers are, no, no, and yes. Then you're off the hook."

Derek nodded.

A few feet away, Little Sonny asked Vicious what was going to happen.

"I don't think there's any real evidence against you," Vicious said. "That statement Derek signed will never hold up, umm, at trial. But I'm not sure we should, ahh, take the risk."

"Whatcha mean, Larry?"

"Well, the district attorney is willing to plea bargain this down to disorderly conduct. You'd spend 30 days in jail, that's it. Then this whole thing would be over."

"Thirty days in jail? For disorderly conduct? How can you do disorderly conduct in a moving car? Piss on that. Let's go to trial."

Vicious seemed to be hurt behind it. His little eyes narrowed and his moustache twitched, like he'd been slapped.

"You're taking a big risk. You're looking at five years in the hoosegow if they get a conviction."

Hoosegow? I sidled up, just as Arnella and Derek got there.

"Look, the D.A. might even be willing to work it so you do your time in a halfway house, not county jail," Vicious argued, as he looked about, twitching. "I really think you should take it, Little

Sonny."

Then we were all yelling.

"My baby ain't going back to jail!" Arnella shouted.

"He didn't have no gun," Little Derek roared.

"Man, you must be crazy!" Little Sonny burst out. "I am not going to jail for you or no one else! I'm innocent! I didn't fire any gun at that maniac cop. I told you two years ago, I was asleep. Man, Devon and Derek said the car backfired, why can't you believe that? What in the hell do I have to do?"

"Look, Little Sonny, as your lawyer, it is my duty to tell you what the D.A. is willing to do. And as your lawyer, it is my duty to advise you that going to trial is a terrible risk. You could get years in jail, even if you are innocent. I have to recommend that you strongly consider the D.A.'s offer."

"You want somebody to go to jail for something they didn't do, then you go," Little Sonny said.

Just then Judge David Gibson strolled out, somebody yelled, "All rise," and we had to stand in silent reverence. A broad, bald man with syrupy, angry eyes much like Maniac Cop Mimms', Gibson called the court to order. The lawyers approached the bench and started tossing around their lawyer words - nol pros, exculpatory, nullity, adjudication. They seemed to be talking mostly about Little Sonny and Derek, but it was hard to tell, because they rarely said names. It was mostly, "my client did this" and "your client should do that" and "Mr. Reinhardt's client will have to do the other."

I tried to pay attention, but it was hard. Gibson seemed to be mediating some dispute between Reinhardt and the D.A., and doing it in a condescending manner that the attorneys seemed to eat up. "You said it better than I could, Your Honor!" they crowed. "That's why you're the judge and I'm just a lawyer!" they trumpeted, with a self-deprecating laugh. I supposed the winner was the one who jammed his head the furthest up the judge's rear end. It all just made me nauseous.

Finally they came to some kind of agreement, and Reinhardt called Derek to the stand. I wasn't sure what this meant. There was no jury, just a judge, a bunch of lawyers and the family. But the way the lawyers were biting their lips and rubbing their hands together, it seemed this was important.

Derek seemed to shake as they swore him in, and he looked sidelong at me, then Devon, and then, longest, at Little Sonny.

"Mr. Goodman, there was a handgun found at the scene of this incident back on May 6, 1994," said Reinhardt. "Did you ever possess that handgun?"

"March 6," the D.A. corrected.

"March 6, 1994. Did you ever possess that handgun?"

"No," Derek said.

"Was it ever in your possession?"

"No."

The third question was almost whispered. Reinhardt was right beside the witness stand, practically leaning into it, and I could barely hear what he said. What I did make out, I could hardly believe.

"Is that the handgun that you identified on at least two occasions as being in the possession of Mr. Brown?"

"Yes, because, oh, yes - "

Reinhardt elbowed Derek in the side and interrupted. "I believes that's - "

"I'm satisfied," the D.A. blurted.

Derek tried again to say something, but the judge turned and cut him off. "You know you're still at risk for another nine hours?"
"He hasn't been hit with a subpoena yet, Your Honor," Reinhardt answered for him. "Maybe I can get him out of here before they can subpoena him to be here tomorrow." He motioned for Derek to come out of the box.

I turned to Arnella, and saw tears in her eyes. "I don't like this shit," she sobbed. "I just know they're trying to put my baby in jail!" The D.A. then told the judge that in light of the testimony he'd just heard, he wanted to drop the charges against Derek and Devon.

Judge Gibson turned to Little Sonny, and then in that movement, I knew what he reminded me of: an iguana. With his big forehead and heavy-lidded eyes, his slow, deliberate way of moving, he seemed perfect for the part of sticking out a long, sticky tongue and snagging flies. Then in my mind's eye, I saw his big body in a pink dress, spinning daintily on the heel of one red shoe. I was sure at that moment that this lizard who dressed in black robes and pretended he was the emperor of all that he saw, this leaden puppet of the racist test tube politicians who run this county, this deluded pretender, was just a little girl inside.

He looked Little Sonny in the eyes, and Little Sonny's eyes bulged, just like that fly's might in the moment it realizes that the big tongue is coming for it, but it's too late to buzz away. "Mr. Goodman, do you feel like you got a bull's eye on you?"

"That's Mr. Brown," the D.A. corrected.

Gibson nodded. "'Cause you sure are getting targeted."

Little Sonny snickered pathetically, and Devon shook his head sadly and let out a little snort. Richard "Fat Boy" Reinhardt started to laugh, and the jollity spread through the courtroom. Everyone seemed to think Gibson was just a barrel of laughs! Vicious was practically doubled over. I didn't see the humor in any of this, but maybe that's just me.

Arnella got up next to me, and the tears were actually rolling off her face. She hurried out of the courtroom.

They mumbo jumboed a while about the terms of Devon's and Derek's dismissals, then decided they'd postpone the trial, which would now be called the Commonwealth of Pennsylvania vs. Little Sonny Brown.

My son was off the hook, but my blood simmered as I realized what they were doing. The D.A. had decided he couldn't get all three. If he pursued the charges against them all, Derek would take the Fifth. Then the D.A. couldn't get him to testify to the false "confession" he gave his torturers. Maniac Cop Mimms' guilty plea on the civil rights charges would destroy his credibility. It would be Devon's word versus Mishelle Blunt's - a coin toss.

Instead he'd drop the charges against Derek and Devon, meaning neither could plead the Fifth. He'd try to force one or both to testify against Little Sonny, playing two cousins against the third. All he needed to do was get one conviction, one pound of flesh to save the face of the Commonwealth - and as an added bonus, it would likely mess up the civil case. It was divide and conquer at its finest, and our attorneys were playing right along.

The gavel came down, and Derek rushed up to me. "My lawyer told me to say yes," he pleaded. "I tried to explain that I only said those things to stop them from beating me, but everybody cut me off!"

"I know, I know," I said, trying to maneuver him out of the way so I could get to those stinking lawyers. "I saw it all, Derek."

I got out of the row of seats, but Mason and Reinhardt were already out the door. By the time I got out the door, they were literally running down the hall, so fast their feet were smoking.

"Hey, Mason, you owe me an explanation!" I yelled after him. "What in the hell is going on? You guys trying to sell us out?"

"I'll call you, Leon," he said, disappearing into the jaws of a closing elevator.

Behind me, Little Sonny was screaming, and I turned to help drag him out of the courtroom. "I'm going to jail! I'm going to jail!" he cried, and the way he was thrashing around, I was sure if we didn't get him out of there, he'd take a swing at somebody.

"I'm gettin' locked up!" he yelled.

"You are if you keep yelling in courtrooms," I said, dragging him out the door and down the hall toward the men's room.

"Man, they screwed me! You heard what that judge said about a bull's eye. A bull's eye! I'm being targeted, Uncle Buster, even though you said we all stand together. What's with that?"

"I don't know, Little Sonny," I said. "Looks to me like those damn lawyers are cahootsing to mess up this case."

Outside, Arnella was bawling and blubbering at the same time, as Curtis tried to comfort her. "What are they trying to do to my baby? They're trying to send my baby back to jail for a crime he didn't commit," she wailed. "And Larry didn't do a thing, just sat there. Just sat there! I don't believe what I heard."

I had a hard time believing it, too. Richard "Fat Boy" Reinhardt as good as put a gun in Little Sonny's hand.

Little Sonny was still yelling, and the cops were eyeing him and shuffling around nervously, so I dragged him toward the bathroom. Derek trailed us. "I was scared, Uncle Bus," he said. "That Gibson frightened me. I thought he was going to throw me in jail, Uncle Buster."

"Yeah, I know, Derek. I saw what was going on."

I finally got Little Sonny through the men's room door. He stopped fighting me and collapsed, crying, against the mirror.

"Man, I'm goin' back to jail, and I didn't even do nothin'. I was asleep in the back of the car, man! I only woke up just in time to get framed and get my ass beat."

Vicious came in and put a hand on his shoulder, but Little Sonny shrugged it off.

"You have nothing to worry about, Little Sonny," Vicious said. "There's no evidence, and you aren't going to jail."

He spun, and his face was streaked. "Then why didn't they drop the charges against me, like they did my cousins?" He stepped forward and I thought he was going to choke Vicious. "How come that judge said I got a bull's eye on me?"

"Oh, that's just Judge Gibson," Vicious said, stepping back.

"That was Gibson speakin' the truth," I said. "'Cause when Larry came out and asked who had a criminal record, that was because they were in there deciding who was going to take the fall for this. They were in there cahootsing. This way those white lawyers get their clients off, the D.A. gets a prosecution, Little Sonny goes to jail, and the civil cases get all jacked up because of your conviction."

"You don't know what you're talking about!" Vicious yelled, now backing toward the door.

"I don't look like Ray Charles. I can see, man."

"This whole thing was engineered by Richard "Fat Boy" Reinhardt," Vicious said. "He and the D.A. were talking about whether Derek would plead the Fifth, what he would testify to. They negotiated it right down to how Reinhardt worded the question about the gun. I didn't have anything to do with it!"

"Exactly. You didn't object, you didn't ask to question Derek about the circumstances of his statement. You did nothing."

I turned to Little Sonny. "Man, you should fire this fool and get a new liar - I mean, lawyer."

Vicious shook his head and seemed to be searching for words. "You're impossible!" he finally gasped, then turned and hurried away.

* * *

I stewed for a few days, just thinking things through. The civil cases were filed. All three cousins were trying to take Clairton for millions, and it didn't look too good for the city. After all, they'd hired Mimms, a cop with a history of violence; Maniac Cop Mimms had used a police shotgun to beat three men, and had continued the beating at the station; and fellow officers Rahis and Sanalas had not only failed to stop him, but had, in various ways, participated.

Big verdicts were possible. But no Allegheny County jury would give them a penny if they thought one of them had fired on an off-duty police officer. A Detroit or New York jury, maybe, or one picked from South Central Los Angeles. But not here.

So the D.A., and maybe the judge, had one simple mission: get one conviction, any conviction, and save Clairton millions. Sell Out Reinhardt and Mason, either knowingly or unwittingly, were playing along. And Larry Vicious was either along for the ride, or just out of his league.

Devon was apparently thinking along the same lines. "I don't trust any of them, including that Mason," he told me, a few days after the trial.

"Well you've got a problem then, because he's still your attorney for the civil case."

"Can't I get a different attorney?"

"You can always do that. You just have to write up a letter saying you no longer want his services, deliver it by hand so he can't say he didn't get it, and he's fired."

He thought about it a little, then said, "Let's write up that letter."

Meanwhile I got word that Vicious was still pushing Little Sonny to take the plea bargain. But Little Sonny was adamant: He didn't do a crime, he wouldn't do time.

Vicious wasn't done screwing up the case. He would get another chance just five months later, when Gibson scheduled Little Sonny's trial for August 7 and 8, 1996. I was working nights at the time and tired of the whole sham and I didn't attend. What I missed had little to do with justice.

On August 7, Mimms repeated the same old lies, alleging that he was fired on after he tried to pass the black Camaro on icy Route 837. When Vicious cross-examined him, he admitted that he swung a shotgun at the men and "may have hit Goodman with my fist."

Devon later took the stand, wearing one of the "Maniac Cops Mimms, Rahis and Sanalas" T-shirts we'd made up for the preliminary hearing, so long ago. The DA argued that it would prejudice the jury, but Gibson overruled him, saying the shirt was protected under the First Amendment. It seemed a surprising finding for Judge Dave "my-courtroom-is-my-castle" Gibson. The D.A. didn't keep Devon on the stand long.

On August 8, the prosecution called their star witness: Derek Goodman. After softening him up with about a hundred meaningless background questions, the D.A., Bobbi Jo Vallie, sprung the trap that Derek's own lawyer had carefully set March 6, 1996. She had Derek read his testimony from the preliminary hearing, the same testimony that put a gun in Little Sonny's hand.

"Were you ever asked about identifying it as being in Mr. Brown's possession?" Vallie asked.

"The reason why I said yes-"

"Wait, Mr. Goodman. You need to listen to my question. Did you, under oath, state that Mr. Brown was in possession of the weapon on that evening, on March 6, 1994?" she insisted, moving in closer.

Gibson leaned over Derek like a big black thundercloud with an angry white head.

"Well, saying you ain't really letting me answer the whole question," Derek said, squirming in the leather seat.

"Can you answer my question?" Vallie demanded.

"Mr. Goodman," Gibson boomed, "did you or did you not say that Mr. Brown was in possession of the gun? It's a simple question, yes or no."

"I said on here says yes," Derek said, pointing to the transcript.

"So you did testify under oath that day that Mr. Brown was in possession of the gun?" Vallie blurted.

"Yes." Derek's shoulders sagged.

She then made him admit that he understood what it meant to testify under oath, that he knew it was against the law to lie. She then turned the beaten witness over to Vicious.

Vicious walked him through the same B.S. about whose Camaro it was and what he remembered about Mimms and on and on. Then he sprung his own pathetic trap.

"Now, when the district attorney asked you about the questions you answered on March 6th of 1996 in this courtroom, and she asked you concerning the oath you took about lying, did you lie in this courtroom on that date concerning the possession of someone having a handgun?"

Before Derek could speak, Bobbi Jo Vallie jumped up. "Your Honor, can we approach?"

The two lawyers and the judge huddled before the bench. Vallie and Vicious snapped at each other as big Dave's face got redder and redder. Then Dave bellowed, "We're going to find out!" and waved them away.

Vicious asked Derek why he answered yes when asked if the gun was Little Sonny's.

"Because my attorney told me before I even came up to the podium, he told me he wanted me to say yes to these three questions," Derek said.

Gibson glowered and leaned over him again. "Now, Mr. Goodman, I'm going to ask you the question. On March 6, 1994, did Mr. Brown possess a firearm, yes or no?"

"No."

Gibson immediately ordered the jury taken out.

"Mr. Goodman, I'm going to advise you that you now have a right to a lawyer, because I am going to direct that the sheriff place you under arrest and I'm going to direct that the district attorney's office charge you with the crime of perjury," Big Dave boomed. He then had Derek taken out in handcuffs, and declared a mistrial.

Gibson then turned his red face and white-hot eyes on Vicious. "Mr. Vicious, I suggest that you never repeat that performance in my courtroom again. You knew what that witness was going to say. You put him up there so he could commit perjury. I'm not a happy camper."

Vicious said nothing.

Derek spent two days in the county jail while Marie arranged for bail yet again.

"Intimidation is what I called it, a judge out of control. Derek was terrified of big Dave, of the way he leaned over and asked questions as if he was the prosecutor's assistant, of his explosive temper. He didn't know what to do if and when he was called to testify at Little Sonny's next trial. "Gibson's out to get me," Derek told me.

"They're all out to get me, Uncle Bus. He doesn't want me to tell the truth. If I tell the truth, he throws me in jail."Derek, I know Dave doesn't like you, but you've got to tell the truth. Tell the court that your liar told you to say yes to the question." I had begun to use the word liar for lawyer all the time. "He tricked you. Derek, I was sitting in that courtroom. I heard and saw what happened. Those three liars sold you guys out. Derek, if the truth is that Little Sonny never had a gun in his possession, then that's what you have to tell the court. Don't be afraid of Dave. He's jut a weak white man who likes to beat up on niggaz who can't fight back. I'll be in the courtroom with you, and God is on our side. Before this is all over, the truth will come out. So don't worry, Derek."

He smiled sadly and nodded his head. It was easy for me to say, I knew. I wasn't facing perjury charges. Liars weren't conspiring to get me to say things that would send my cousin to jail and ruin my civil case. Poor troubled Derek, whose life had been on a downward spiral ever since he hit the turbulence of Maniac Cop Mimms, had all that hanging over his head.

The Dave Gibson Show wasn't over yet. Just a month later the case took an even stranger turn when Gibson convened a hearing on the perjury charges.

Vallie and Assistant D.A. Zolinas walked into Big Dave's courtroom a few minutes late, and the judge grumpily called the hearing on Commonwealth vs. Derek Goodman to order.

"Are you ready to proceed?" Gibson asked.

"Uh, your honor, upon review of the case, we have no evidence upon which to proceed against Mr. Goodman," Zolinas said.

Gibson's eyes narrowed and a redness spread over his face. He started to shake, like Mt. St. Helens. Then he rose out of his chair.

"You better go out and get some evidence! I want him found guilty!"

Then Gibson launched into a tirade about Zolinas being late for the hearing, and how lawyers were constantly arriving late to his courtroom. He was pacing behind the bench, bounding from side to side, when with no warning he grabbed the top of his long, black robe, ripped it from his from body, and threw it right on poor Zolinas' head.

Thank God he was wearing a shirt, tie and slacks underneath that robe.

Then Gibson stormed out the back door of the courtroom, and everybody in there kind of looked at one another, thinking, maybe, "Was that for real?" Zolinas gingerly took the robe off his head. But there wasn't even time enough to crack a joke before Big Dave burst back in, with a sheriff's deputy in tow.

"Arrest that man for contempt of court!" he shouted, pointing at Zolinas.

The deputy shrugged and walked up to the assistant D.A. The family members, lawyers and spectators watched in stunned silence as the deputy led Zolinas out.

"I've had it up to here with Mr. Zolinas!" Gibson bellowed as they left. "He doesn't show up. He doesn't call! He just wasn't here." Gibson then put his thumb to his nose and wiggled his fingers. "Mr. Zolinas went like this to me!"

The courtroom was in shock. This well-known judge was undergoing a complete meltdown, right here in front of everyone. Now he hurled his bulk about the dais at the front of the courtroom and launched into a rant about the declining manners and lax dress codes of lawyers these days. "They come in here with dungarees, cowboy boots, no socks, no ties. There is a professional code of conduct. It has to stop! If that means putting lawyers in jail, that's what I'm going to do."

Zolinas' boss, Claire Kopelic, rushed in to argue that Zolinas shouldn't be jailed.

"I don't care!" Gibson fumed.

Zolinas spent an hour in jail. The perjury charges against Derek were eventually dropped. Gibson's blow-up became a two-day news story, in part because the judge was also handling the highest profile case of alleged police misconduct Allegheny County had yet seen - the case of the death of Jonny E. Gammage. But Little Sonny, Derek and Devon were left with the fact that their own lawyers had laid a trap for them that could be sprung at any time - and that time would come as sure as Little Sonny's retrial.

I didn't understand how these lawyers could live with themselves, taking peoples' money and then screwing them and their relatives. Oh, they made up excuses left and right, saying they were doing the best they could and that they'd have to take their lawyer licenses off their walls if they didn't do this and didn't do that. But I could tell they knew what they were doing, and they knew it wasn't right.

A few months later, Lillian and I were waiting in line at the food court at the Ross Park Mall, and out of the corner of my eye I saw a chubby geek in a rumpled shirt and some familiar-looking khaki pants. I turned, and sure enough it was Richard "Fat Boy" "Sell Out"

Reinhardt, licking an ice cream. As soon as he saw me he stopped licking, his jaw dropped, and he turned and took off. His feet were smoking as he rushed out of the mall..

What a way to live - in fear of the relatives of your clients.

We hired attorney Timmy McMurphy, an ace cop buster and one of Pittsburgh's most activist attorneys, to take over the civil suit. I told Lillian I'd try to stop obsessing about the case and move on with life. But the world seemed to be catching up with me.

* * *

Late that March of 1996, the American Civil Liberties Union and McMurphy filed a lawsuit against the Pittsburgh Police Department, detailing 68 cases of abuse and alleging a systematic pattern of brutality, cover-up, and unresponsiveness to complaints.

The victims were of every race and age, income group and profession, even clergy. By and large, they weren't criminals, and weren't engaging in crimes when the cops blew up at them. These were normal people unlucky enough to get in the way of a bad cop on a bad day. The cases were gleaned from hundreds of reports of beating and intimidation the Pittsburgh ACLU had received over the years.

While the suit was celebrated in the streets of many Pittsburgh neighborhoods, the police unions and Pittsburgh Mayor Tom Murphy mocked it and promised a long fight in the courts. Not only would the mayor refuse to pay the monetary damages called for, but he summarily rejected the reforms in police hiring, training and discipline the suit demanded.

Little did Murphy know that within a year he'd be signing a paper agreeing to most of the very same reforms demanded by the ACLU, because even as the civil rights group was lining up its plaintiffs, a parallel investigation by the U.S. Department of Justice was getting in gear. In late February 1997 the Justice Department came to Murphy with a choice: sign on to a series of reforms to how you investigate and punish instances of brutality, or prepare to defend yourself against a suit by the federal government.

Murphy initially railed against the feds, saying his 6-year-old son knew more about running a police department than they did. A few days later, he grudgingly signed a consent decree with the Justice Department that would alter the rules governing the Pittsburgh Police Department forever.

The Pittsburgh cops would be in for other changes, too. For as long as anybody could remember, allegations of police brutality were investigated by cops. A victim who wanted to report a beating had to find the courage to walk into the cop-heavy Public Safety Building, tell the story to a uniformed officer, then go through other interviews by cops to get the matter looked at. Not surprisingly, only a few hundred a year bothered to go through the process, and almost none ever got any satisfaction.

But starting in 1996, a bunch of activists began demanding that a panel of civilians receive the complaints and investigate the cops. The mayor said it wasn't needed. The president of the police union said it would shackle the boys in blue and cause anarchy. City Council narrowly voted it down.

But there were other means. Starting early in 1997, a group called Citizens for Police Accountability began petitioning for a ballot referendum on civilian review of police misconduct. They got enough signatures to put the matter on the May ballot, survived court challenges by the Fraternal Order of Police, and began a door-to-door campaign to get out the vote.

On May 20, it passed convincingly, 58 percent to 42 percent. Conservative, mostly-white Pittsburgh had agreed that police should be judged by civilians, and not the other way around. The vote would have been unthinkable before the consent decree, the ACLU suit, and the case of the Clairton Three.

But it would have been especially unthinkable before Jonny Gammage. The name of Jonny Gammage, the cousin of Pittsburgh Steeler Ray Seals who was killed by five suburban cops in a routine traffic stop just within the city limits in October, 1995, became shorthand for police brutality, and for the pathetically sorry system designed to punish it.

The D.A. decided to try only three of the five cops present for Gammage's death. The first two cops tried, Milton Mulholland and Michael Albert, had their case end in a mistrial. Next up for trial was Brentwood Officer John Vojtas.

Vojtas was considered the best shot the D.A. had of a conviction.

The guy had a record of beating women - one of his ex's even killed herself with his service revolver, or so he claimed. Plus he was the one who first hit Gammage with a flashlight, the one who apparently pushed him up against his cousin's Jaguar.

And the trial, everybody was saying, went well for the D.A., smoother than the mistrial of Money and Albert. Still, I wasn't convinced that you could convict a white cop of beating or killing a black man in Southwestern Pennsylvania.

I happened to be in Pittsburgh on the gray November day that the Vojtas verdict came down. A little before one o'clock my son and I arrived at Tim McMurphy's office for Devon's deposition in the civil case against Clyde Mimms.

McMurphy sat us down at the table in his conference room and started telling Devon what to expect. The guy was a mid-sized Irish-looking guy with a thick mustache and glasses, and this day he was dressed in a light blue shirt and an unassuming tie. He seemed okay to me then, not so full of himself as, say, Mason, and not afraid of rocking the boat like Jipenstein.

When they were done, we headed for the elevator on our way to the building next door, where Clairton's attorney had her office and where the deposition would be held. I figured I'd come along for moral support.

"Would it be all right for me to go into the deposition with Devon?" I asked McMurphy, as the elevator plunged down.

He turned and looked at me, and his eyes seemed to start doing calisthenics in his head. "Umm, ahh, I don't think it would be a good idea," he said.

"What are you saying? I can't go in there?"

"Well, I just, ahh, don't think it's a good idea."

"Why don't you just tell me, yes or no? Can I go into this deposition?"

"I don't think you should."

I shrugged as we got off the elevator. We walked about 50 feet from the door of the Allegheny Building to the Frick Building. It struck me how close the supposed good guy McMurphy's office was to the headquarters of the bad guys who represented bad cops and out-of-control police forces. That bothered me. They should be all the way across town from each other, not right next door.

We waited for an elevator in the Frick Building lobby, and who should walk up and stand beside us but James Ecker, one of Vojtas's attorneys. He was a short guy, looked to be in his sixties, with a long face and the expression of a boxer trapped in the corner of the ring but determined to punch his way out. To me, he seemed like pure evil, a soul in need of an exorcist.

Elevator doors opened, and Devon, McMurphy and Ecker walked in. Though there was plenty of room, I said I'd take the next one.

"Whatever," said McMurphy.

The elevator door stayed open, and Ecker gave me a curious look.

"What's wrong with that guy?" he asked McMurphy.

Timmy just shrugged.

I took another elevator up and stepped out into the lavish lobby of Clairton's lawyers. It looked like defending maniac cops paid pretty well. McMurphy told the receptionist he had a deposition scheduled, and I guessed this was goodbye. I took Devon aside.

"Go in there, tell the truth. Don't get nervous. Don't let them intimidate you. Don't let McMurphy intimidate you. Because you've been through a deposition before, with the McKeesport police problems, so it's not like you've never been to one. You know how they act."

"Okay. No problem, Dad."

Timmy walked over.

"If you don't want me in there, I'm going to run across the street and see what's happening with that Vojtas trial," I said.

McMurphy nodded, and he and Devon headed back into the depths of this huge law office.

I went out and crossed Grant Street to the County Courthouse. On the steps I ran into two local civil rights activists, guys I know as Wayne and C.J. Wayne had a big cardboard sign handing around his neck, with a few dozen "Justice for Jonny Gammage" pins stuck in it. The words circled the face of a young black businessman with serious, but compassionate, eyes. Unfortunately, the young man was dead.

They asked me what brought me down here, because they hadn't seen much of me during their long months of protest. I told them about the deposition. While I was updating them on the Clairton three, activist Wilson Flowers joined us on the stairs. Flowers said he was originally from Clairton.

"Everybody down there knows the cops are out of control," he said. "Buster, it's a damn shame the people of Clairton didn't get involved in your case. They might've made a difference, got some reforms going in that department, if they'd just have opened their mouths."

"Well, the people in the Mon Valley are a little different from the ones in Pittsburgh," I said.

"Man, if that had happened to my kids, I'd have killed those cops," C.J. said.

"Well, C.J., I was close. I was close, but no cigar. I was stopped."

"Well, no one would have stopped me."

"Yeah, whatever you say, C.J."

That ticked me off a little. This guy was casting aspersions at my manhood, when he hadn't walked in my shoes. I thought about taking it further, but in the end decided just to let it slide. We were all on the same side.

Things got a little chilly out there, and I'd just had my head shaved, and I hadn't worn a hat. So I told Wilson, "Let's go see what's happening with this verdict."

He nodded and we went upstairs. C.J. and Wayne stayed on the courthouse steps. Up on the third floor, where Judge Gibson had temporarily set up shop, the hall was packed with people. There were news media, curious county workers, police, and a dozen or so activists, led by Mary Jones and Etta James. Everyone was mingling and talking while, presumably, the jury deliberated.

Over in the corner, a TV crew was interviewing Marshall "Smokey" Hynes, the head of the Pittsburgh police union. Though Vojtas and the others were suburban police, and therefore not in his union, Hynes took it upon himself to defend any cop anywhere for anything.

I don't know exactly what Hynes said that pissed Wilson off, but as soon as the camera stopped, old Wilson was in Smokey's face. "You think it's all right for a police officer to kill a black man, don't you?" he asked.

Hynes backed up a step and was silent for a second. Then it seemed like a dam burst. "I didn't say that! I didn't say that! And neither you nor no one is going to put any words in my mouth! I did not say that." Now he was chest-to-chest with little Wilson, pushing him back on his heels, a torrent of words.

Flowers held up his hands to try to push Smokey off of him. "Well, you think it's all right for a police officer to kill a black man and not go to jail for it," he said.

"I didn't say it was all right. It was a horrible thing that happened to that man, Jonny Gammage. I did not suggest, nor am I suggesting that it's all right for a police officer to kill someone the way that man was killed."

"Well, then, do you think Vojtas should go to jail?"

"I didn't say that, either. You're trying to trap me! You're trying to trap me."

I tapped Wilson on the shoulder. "Come on, Will. It's not worth it. You're going to wind up on the white man's slave ship." That's what I call the jail.

Flowers took a step back but still glared at Hynes.

I ain't going to jail today," I said.

Hynes turned and walked away.

"Wilson, you see how the man reacted," I said. "He knows what happened. I wonder how many niggaz he beat and killed when he was a regular police officer. Because it was a touchy situation. It was a touchy subject that you asked him about. It ignited a fuse in him. Apparently he's got some guilt. Maybe he beat and killed some niggaz back in his day."

May nodded.

"They're all a bunch of cowards. These police officers are all a bunch of cowards," I said.

Two cops must have heard, because they looked over at me. They were maybe six feet away, and weren't wearing any uniforms, but I could tell they were police. I can tell a police officer just from the way they look. I used to see horns on their heads. I don't see horns anymore. But I can still tell, just by their demeanor.

One of them turned to face me and said, "Why don't you tell Smokey to his face that he's a coward?"

"Hey, I'll tell Smokey to his face that he's a coward, I'll tell his mammy that he's a coward, and I'll tell you that he's a coward."

"Well, why don't you tell Smokey to his face that he's a coward?"

"Where is Smokey? Smokey's gone. You go get Smokey, and I'll tell Smokey that he's nothing but a coward."

As we went back and forth, two McKeesport cops came around the bend. I recognized one as the guy who tried to run me down when I lived there.

"You're afraid to tell Smokey that to his face," the cop said again.

Now I was facing four cops, and others seemed to be getting interested.

"Well, you go get Smokey. I'm right here. I'm not going anywhere."

"I should go get my brother and turn this damn place out," said Wilson.

"It's not even worth it," I said.

Gradually the cops drifted away, but they kept looking sullenly back my way. "Man, are they touchy," I said to Wilson. "Everybody's touchy up here. You've got to watch what you say, you know. If you say something, you've got to be ready, because with all of these people around, you don't know who's friend or foe up here."

"Sure got that right," Wilson said.

"Let's go before we end up on the white man's slave ship."

We went over to the media mob, and I tapped Lynn Hayes Pitts on the shoulder. She was a black TV reporter I'd known for a long time. I even knew some of her family. "Hey, how you doing?"

"Hey!" she said. "How's your sons?" Everybody thinks the "Clairton three" are all my sons.

"They're okay." I told her I was in town for Devon's deposition.

"How's your dad doing?" I asked.

"He's recovering from that heart surgery he had."

"Well when you see him, tell him I said hi."

"What was that all about?" she asked.

"Oh, it was just some cops showing their support for killer cop Vojtas. You know how they go."

"Uh huh." She gestured toward the courtroom, down the hall. "Well, what do you think's going to happen?"

"Well, the experience I had with them - "

"Yeah, I know."

"The experience that I had with the police, a black man, a white cop - he's gonna walk."

"I don't know, Leon. I think it's going to be another mistrial, a hung jury."

"No. A white cop killing a black man, an all-white jury - he ain't gonna get no time, and not even one juror is going to vote to convict. He's going to be acquitted. I'll bet you anything."

"You've got a bet." We shook hands.

It couldn't have been more than a minute later that cupped her hand up to her ear, apparently listening to some message coming through her earpiece.

"Not guilty? What the hell?" she said.

"Looks like I won the bet."

Loud cheers went up. The cops, sheriffs deputies, city and county employees all started smiling, shaking hands, hugging, cheering. The photographers and cameramen started jockeying for position and frantically preparing their equipment. The reporters all whipped out their cell phones and started dialing like crazy. The protesters stood silently, looking like they were in shock. Some clutched each other for support.

Then Lynn Hayes Pitts stuck a microphone in my face and her cameraman whirled on me. "How do you feel about the verdict?"

"Well, I'm not shocked about it. We're living in Pittsburgh. What do you expect? Do you expect a jury to convict this man? I don't think so. Not in Pittsburgh. It's not going to happen."

She frowned and found someone else to interview. I guess my reaction was too complicated for the TV news. To really explain what I thought, I would have to get into the racist nature of this city, its worship for authority figures, and my own experiences with a system that protects its enforcers.

I found Wilson Flowers. He was like in a daze. "Do you believe that?" he told C.J. in a slow monotone. "They acquitted that guy."

"Aww, c'mon! Where do you think you are?" C.J. said. "We're not living in America. We're living in Snakesburgh, Pa."

Then all hell broke loose as a phalanx of sheriff's deputies, Vojtas and Ecker stampeded out the courtroom door. The media surged forward, the protesters charged, the scattered cops moved to shield their just-acquitted brother. It was pandemonium, like a fire in a concert hall.

"Officer Vojtas, Officer Vojtas! Do you have anything to say?"

"You'll get yours yet, killer cop!"

"You the man, John!"

The cops pushed through the mob and into a stairwell, silent, steel-eyed, snarling at the cameramen, scribblers and black people who tried to hem them in. C.J. and I took one look at that mess and ran for another stairwell. We'd head 'em off at the pass.

We pounded down three flights of steps and out the front door of the courthouse, then ran around a corner and caught up with the mob as it exited through one of the big archways out of the courtyard. Vojtas and Ecker were still at the center of the mob, surrounded by a dozen sheriff's deputies, then about 10 or 15 black protesters, then a thinning media mob - a few cameramen, some pad-toting writers. Swirls of black and white, like a Ho-Ho. We crashed right into it.

The next few seconds runs in super-slow-mo in my memory. This swarm of people surged down the wide sidewalk of Forbes Avenue, some yelling, "Killer cop! Killer cop!" Up ahead, at the corner of Forbes and Grant, a huge young black guy stood, his arms and legs spread wide like he could just envelope all of us. He was shouting, "How does it feel to kill a black man, you no-good bastard? How does it feel? You should be in jail. Killer cop! Killer cop!" And this pack of wolves was headed right for him.

Then, right next to me, a cameraman crashed to the concrete. The cops and protesters and other media stomped all over him. I mean, that poor joker was trampled. Somehow he created a hole in the protective shell around Vojtas, and into that gap I pushed.

Suddenly it seemed like the whole world was just him and me. In the next second I called him mother fucker, killer cop, murderer, everything I could think of. Then I gathered a big wad of spit in my mouth, and launched it all over him. I spat on the guy.

Vojtas is a huge man, a bodybuilder, with a round, muscled face. Just by looking at him you can tell he understands violence. He looked at me then. His eyes were watery, bloodshot eyes. Like when people get drunk, they get that glassy, red eye. He looked at me like it was nothing, like, piss on you, I got away with this shit. There ain't nothing you nor nobody else can do about it.

Then the sheriff's deputies managed to shove me out of there, and a second later this crowd smashed into that big black boy on the corner and just bowled him over. It was 30, maybe 35 against one. He was no match. We burst across Grant Street, stopping traffic, then to the doors of the Frick Building. At the doors, four cops spun around and formed a wall, Vojtas and Ecker disappeared into an elevator, and the hunt was over.

The protesters and media wandered back across Grant Street to the courthouse. It was a weird scene. This black woman in a long fur coat just started screaming and crying. She was screaming like it was her child who had died. You could hear this agonizing scream echoing all the way up and down Grant Street.

Over next to me someone asked C.J. about justice, and he told them that justice was buried with Jonny Gammage. That started him up and pretty soon the little knot of 15 or so protesters started screaming and hollering, "No justice, no peace!"

A short black guy ran down off the steps to the flagpole, grabbed the rope, and started pulling that flag down. Seeing him there, I had a moment of clarity. That flag represented liberty, freedom and justice for everybody. But the principles behind that flag had failed. Then I knew how those demonstrators must have felt in the Vietnam era. That flag is flying falsely over this land. That flag is nothing but a farce, or maybe even worse, a con.

I rushed down, with C.J. right beside me, and grabbed that rope. Those jokers didn't know how to take down a flag, but I'd been a Marine. I'd sworn to protect that flag, and I knew how to take it up and down a pole.

Out of the corner of my eye I spotted a cop watching me from up the street. He started coming my way, and straight away the little guy let the rope go and ran back up on the steps.

C.J. and I struggled with the cord as the flag whipped in the wind, and I saw Wayne standing up on the steps with his sign on. "Come on, Wayne! Help us pull this goddamn thing down! What're you standing up there for?" I yelled.

He threw down that sign, sent all of its Justice for Jonny buttons clattering to the concrete. He ran down and started pulling it with us. Two cops from inside the building came out, screaming, "Leave that flag alone! That flag doesn't belong to you!"

"Yes it does! I'm a taxpayer. I'm a Vietnam veteran. I have a right to pull my flag down. That's my flag! I paid for that flag."

"You didn't pay for this flag!"

They ran down the stairs, as the cop from down the street came at us from the left and a whole slew of cops from across the street ran to the defense of the flag. C.J. ran up on the steps. Wayne took off. So I was the only one pulling the damn flag when the cops converged on me.

"What're you doing?" a white cop screamed.

"I'm pulling the flag down!"

"I suggest you leave that flag alone, or you're going to jail."

"I ain't going to jail. They ought to put Vojtas's ass in jail. That's the one they need to put in jail."

That cop started screaming at me that it wasn't my flag, that the county had paid for that flag, not me, and I had no right taking it down. I screamed back that it was my flag as much as it was anybody else's. He talked tough, but for some reason the guy wouldn't get into my face.

Somebody pushed two lady cops in front, one black and one white. The guy behind them kept yelling at me, but I wasn't paying attention to him any more. He was a lost cause, irrelevant. But this black woman in blue, she seemed the saddest thing in the world right then and there.

"Why don't you take that uniform and that badge off and come and join us?" I asked her. "Because what happened to Jonny Gammage could happen to one of your kids. Come over and join us. I dare you to take that uniform off and throw that badge down right now."

She looked at me like I was nuts. She just stood there.

Then Etta James and the lady in the fur coat, the one whose screams tore up Grant Street, came up behind me and tapped me on the shoulder. "Hey, it's not even worth it," Etta said. "You don't have to go to jail."

They pulled me back to the stairs, and the cops yanked that flag back up that pole. I'd had it all the way down on the ground, I saw, and people had stepped all over it. Technically, they were supposed to burn it, I realized. That's what they'd taught me in the Marines, anyway; if the flag touches the ground, burn it. These cops didn't seem to know that, or they were ignoring it.

I sat on those courthouse steps, feeling like a virgin getting raped. The full weight of the past year hit me: Maniac Cop Mimms' pathetic probationary sentence, the continued prosecution of Little Sonny, and now the Vojtas verdict dislodged whatever loyalty or patriotism I had for this country. I'd now seen two miscarriages of justice, two legal atrocities, two human rights disgraces that should have been reported by Amnesty International. I'd seen America stripped down to her snarling, brutish, petty, white skin. Timothy McVeigh, the Unabomber, Saddam Hussein and Moammar Khadaffi - America's enemies - could be my friends now. The American dream had turned to nightmare.

* * *

The next weekend La Rue and I drove into Pittsburgh for that city's biggest protest since the '60s. I brought a sign nearly the size of a billboard and a rented bullhorn, and was determined to exercise my First Amendment right to get loud, get in the face of the cops, and get free therapy on the streets of the big town.

In McKeesport, I'd stood almost alone against the police, and that made it easy for them to retaliate against me. In Pittsburgh, though, I'd be one of thousands. Let's see them try to frame us all up, put us all in jail, or run us all down in their cruisers.

I went down to the march more because I felt for the Gammage family than anything else. His mother and ex-cop dad had lost a 31-year-old son, and it reminded me that I could have very easily lost my son. I brought a huge cardboard sign - I mean, this thing was about 12 feet wide - with the words "CIVIL RIGHTS VIOLATORS, CRIMINAL COPS" in bold letters, then the names of the five police involved in Gammage's death and the three who'd violated my son's civil rights.

John Vojtas. Milton Mulholland. Michael Albert. Sean Patterson. Keith Henderson. John Rahis. Edward Sanalas. Maniac Cop Clyde Mimms.

Vojtas has since been promoted to sergeant. Money and Albert's trial ended in a mistrial, and Money retired to work as a part-time janitor. Rahis left policing and was working for a cable TV company, last I heard. The others are still on the beat.

Jonny Gammage died at the hands of Brentwood Borough cops, on a dark and isolated stretch of Route 51. I wanted the protesters to know that just 13 miles south of Brentwood on that same Route 51 was the City of Clairton, another town stained with the blood of victims of police brutality.

La Rue and I walked up Grant Street and found a crowd of about 2,000, about half black and half white, milling around the City-County Building and Courthouse. As we approached I put the bullhorn to my lips and said, "No Justice, No Peace! No Justice, No Peace!"

"Shush!" some lady said, rushing toward me. "This is a silent protest."

I joined the crowd, which was apparently trying to encircle the edifices of power. "What's this about a silent protest?" I asked the man next to me. "I figure we've been silent long enough."

"It's Tim Stevens' idea," he said. Stevens was the president of the Pittsburgh branch of the NAACP, a man who could get an audience with any white politician or businessman in the city.

"Personally, I don't think we should be quiet either," the man said. "Like you said, we've been quiet too long. But leave it to Tim Stevens to invent a silent protest."

We walked around and around those buildings as TV cameras rolled and cops watched attentively just a stone's throw away. I guess my shoulders started to sag, because La Rue tapped me on the shoulder and asked, "What's wrong with you? You don't seem to be too enthusiastic."

"I don't care much for silent marches, and I don't care for Tim Stevens. He's a joke. I bet a bunch of white guys bankrolls his damn NAACP."

Eventually the marching stopped, and everyone gathered in front of the City-County Building for a bunch of speeches about the Jonny Gammage incident.

A couple of guys in the back kept yelling, "How many brothers gonna die, before we get a plan?" But the politicians, activists and mourners who spoke from the steps of the building didn't propose a plan. They seemed to know there was a problem, but didn't approach having a coordinated plan.

When the speechifying ended, everybody started milling around congratulating each other, and eventually a white writer wandered up to me. "Who's Maniac Cop Clyde Mimms?" he asked.

I asked him who he was. He said he was a writer for a socialist newspaper, The Militant.

I told him that back on March 6, 1994, Maniac Cop Clyde Mimms, John Rahis and Edward Sanalas beat and tortured my son and my two nephews. I told him the story quickly, just hitting the highlights, because he kept looking off to the side, as if he had somewhere else to be, and fast. "Mimms pleaded guilty to civil rights violations, and got a year probation," I said. "Rahis and Sanalas weren't even tried. Rahis got a new job, but Sanalas and Mimms are still on the beat."

That's amazing," he said, shaking his head. "I've never heard about that before. Was it in the papers?"

"And on the TV and radio," I told him, wondering if he read the papers. Maybe just the business section. "You want a story? Here's one. The biggest offenders of human rights in America are the cops." I pointed at a black cop who was standing across Grant street staring at us.

The writer left, but that black cop kept giving me dirty looks. I stared right back, but the whole scene made me a little uncomfortable. After a little while, La Rue and I split. Neither of us had any illusions that protests like that one would put criminal cops in jail.

Over the next few months I went to every protest I could. I went for the therapy, more than anything else, because it was obvious none of this was going to change the world. The well-meaning folks leading Pittsburgh's rallies weren't talking about a revolution. They didn't even dare block traffic, for fear that the cops wouldn't grant them a parade permit next time around. Nobody sent stink bombs to the mayor or judge, like we did back in the early '80s when U.S. Steel closed the mills. Nobody put dead fish in safety deposit boxes at the banks that underwrote the police state, another thing we did back then. I think two people were arrested during years of protests behind Gammage's death.

In a struggle, people are supposed to go to jail, I would tell them. People are supposed to put their lives on the line. These cops aren't law abiding. Why should the protesters be law abiding?

But I remember one protest where a little white college girl was bouncing around trying to convince people to block traffic on Grant Street, to bring the lawyers and bankers and judges to a halt. Man, the rest of those protesters looked at her like she was Timothy McVeigh.

Not that stopping traffic would have ended police brutality any more than stink bombs and dead fish had kept the steel mills open. The whites with money understood one thing and one thing only, near as I could tell, and that was property damage. When black people and poor people burned things down, then, sometimes, things changed. Most often what they torched was their own neighborhood groceries, laundromats, even homes, and that was a pity. But fire seemed to capture the rich white imagination like nothing else.

Rodney King's abusers, we all knew, were convicted in federal court, thanks to brothers in the streets rioting, looting and burning. And the cops knew we knew that, because every time one of the Gammage trials neared its end, the cruisers ran up and down the borders between white and black Pittsburgh in packs, like sharks.

There would be no burning in Pittsburgh. There would be no convictions of the cops who squeezed the life out of Jonny Gammage either. But there was a camaraderie out there on the streets. There was the beginning of an understanding of the problem. And even though those marches were about justice for Jonny Gammage rather than police brutality in general, maybe they had something to do with the passage of civilian review of the police at the ballot box. I don't know.

Chapter 10

Verdict

If you ask me, the trial of the century was played out over four days beginning on Aug. 18, 1997, out of reach of cameras, in a sanitized courtroom, far from the scene of one of western Pennsylvania's worst-ever human rights atrocities. It didn't involve a perjuring president, a celebrity like O.J. Simpson, nor a cousin of a professional football player, just a poor black man framed by the system. It didn't even get much media coverage - certainly not as much as it deserved. But more than any other legal proceeding I know of, it got to the bottom of a police atrocity, putting it on the record and in the light of day for everyone to see.

Three years, five months, 13 days and about 992 lies after the assault on Devon, Little Sonny and Derek, the Commonwealth of Pennsylvania finally got around to putting Little Sonny Brown on trial for allegedly firing on Clyde Mimms, a man who had earned the new middle name "Maniac Cop." Though their key witnesses included convicted civil rights violator Mimms and two other cops implicated in the beatings, Rahis and Sanalas, the District Attorney's office had the nerve to put Little Sonny on trial.

To me, the number one outrage of the trial was that it was allowed to occur in the first place. All three officers should have been arrested for civil rights violations and that should have been that. Derek, Little Sonny and Devon should have been witnesses in the prosecution of the officers, not vice versa. How many criminals have been let off the hook just because cops have forgotten to read them their Miranda rights? I wondered in the days leading up to Little Sonny's trial. Shouldn't the same happen when the police violate the defendant's civil rights by beating, kicking, threatening and urinating on them?

It took until almost the eve of trial, but Little Sonny had finally realized that he shouldn't bet his future on Larry Vicious. None other than Judge "Big Dave" Gibson told Little Sonny to get a new liar, saying Vicious would just land him in jail. Little Sonny went shopping around and settled on Wendy Wright, a tall, young, blonde defense attorney whose good looks, people said, hid a ferocious competitiveness that roared forth at trial. She was one of those attorneys who's always around the courthouse trying cases, rather than back in some law office on the phone working out plea bargains, or lurking in hospital halls looking for new clients.

That Tuesday morning, the family gathered outside Big Dave's courtroom as we'd done all too many times before. At least this would be the last time, we figured. We had a good attorney working for us; there would be no more delays, no more mistrials, no more shady back-room deals, no more bullshit.

Little Sonny stomped about, one minute cursing the justice system to his brother or Devon or Derek, the next minute passionately necking with his girlfriend in the stairwell, like some rock star or a soldier going off to war. Devon and Derek were concerned, but stayed low key; neither wanted to make any trouble there, in the courthouse, with sheriffs everywhere poised to arrest and jail any defendant, witness, or even lawyer who challenged Big Dave's domain. Arnella, Little Sonny's mom, was a ball of nerves, flying from stormy rage to weepy dejection at her son's troubles. Me, I was tired and grumpy from working all night and then coming straight down to the courthouse, but my head was clear. I knew things were pretty much out of my hands, but I understood what was at stake, and knew I had to be there by the family's side.

"I don't know if this will help," I told Wendy Wright, as soon as she came on the scene. "But I taped the preliminary hearing before Judge Raley. Maybe you can compare what these jokers say today with what they said three years ago."

"Thanks, Leon," she said. "I'll listen to it tonight."

She seemed a little tired, a little harried to me, and I wondered if she was up to the task.

My doubts were soon dispelled when trial finally started in mid-afternoon. The judge had the bailiff march the jury in - 10 whites and two blacks, plus one white and one black alternate. When it came time for her opening statement, all that tension I saw seemed to melt away. Wendy stood behind the defendant's table and rolled the dice without a second thought.

"Sonny Brown is not the type of guy who you would want to date your daughter," she told the jury. "But he works. He has always worked."

She ran through a litany of jobs Little Sonny had, drawing a picture of a man who had his ups and downs, but kept plugging away, trying to live right. This was no welfare cheat, no drug dealer, no bum. He'd had his problems, but he was trying to do right.
Little Sonny Brown is a lot like you and me, she was telling that jury. He works for his pay.

She reminded the jury that they must consider her client innocent until and unless the prosecution could prove otherwise. "My client's liberties are at stake here. You're going to hear some biased testimony from biased police officers who are involved in this case. I'm going to tell you why it's biased."

Just then I noticed that juror number one, a white guy, was dropping off to sleep. He was the jury foreman, the one who I knew would eventually be entrusted with guiding the jury's deliberations and reading the verdict. It was stifling hot in that courtroom, and I guess it must have gotten to him. His chin hit his chest and bounced up, then fell down again and stayed there. He must've nodded right through the guilty-until-proven-innocent part. A deputy walked over and gently shook him awake.

Wendy told the jury she would put Little Sonny Brown on the stand and let him tell the world why the police testimony in the case could be biased. "His testimony will shock you," she warned.

So there it was; she would ask the jury to take the word of this black man with a history of car theft over the testimony of a bunch of cops. To me, it seemed liberating to hear it. The time for deal-making was over. Wendy would go right after the rogue cops of Clairton, boldly saying what no other lawyer had the guts to say - that a black man's testimony was just as good as anyone else's, and maybe better. Out in the hallway after the opening statements, not everyone was as inspired as I was.

"Man, that one guy was catchin' z's," Little Sonny said, fidgeting against the wall. "My freedom is on the line, and the dude is takin' a nap."

"Whole lotta whites on that jury, Little Sonny," said Derek.

"I know. What ever happened to 'jury of my peers?'" Little Sonny said. "Those aren't my peers. If it was my peers, it'd be all African

Americans. Or at least six and six. White people are never going to believe me over those cops."

"They say whites will believe one cop over 50 civilian witnesses," said Larry Vicious, who was hanging around for no reason I could discern. It wasn't like he was Little Sonny's lawyer anymore. He'd been fired. "Your case might be different, but that's the conventional wisdom."

"I wouldn't bet against you just yet, Little Sonny," said Devon. "The truth has a way of comin' out."

Just then Mimms, Sanalas and Rahis came strutting out of the courtroom, talking and slapping each others' backs. "We got them now!" Rahis said. We all fell silent, and Mimms saw us gathered over by the stairwell.

He turned, his aquiline nose and glassy eyes still giving his face equal parts arrogance and brutishness, and walked our way.

He was about five feet from us when he pointed a finger straight at Little Sonny's face and said, "You're going to jail."

Little Sonny lunged at him, shouting, "You should be in jail, maniac cop! You should be in goddamn jail." Devon and Larry Vicious held him back, or he would have lit right into Mimms in the middle of the courthouse. The maniac cop in his dark suit turned and walked away. He and his henchmen yucked it up as they strolled to the elevator.

"Don't worry," I told my son and nephews. "Those who laugh first are going to be crying later. Once the truth comes out, they're done."

When trial resumed, Assistant District Attorney Ken Uhrig called Mimms to testify.

"Let the lies begin," I whispered to Arnella, as Mimms climbed to the stand. "Put his right hand on the Bible and the first words that come out of his mouth are lies. What a sinner. Something bad is going to happen to him down the road, you just watch. He will never prosper. He's going to always have bad luck. You can't just put your hand on a Bible and lie again and again and again. Unless you're an atheist, I guess. Maybe Maniac Cop Mimms is an atheist. Arnella, that Maniac Cop is in trouble with God, so we don't have anything to worry about here. God will take care of Little Sonny and he will deal with Maniac Cop Mimms accordingly. Just wait and see. He called himself God, and now he's in trouble with the real God, Jesus' father. Wait and see. He's done."

Driving down an icy, winding road with his piece and his pregnant girlfriend by his side, Mimms claimed, he was fired on as he tried to pass a black Camaro. The shots came from near the top part of an open driver's side door, Mimms said.

"I had my service revolver, I just stuck it out of the window and shot once, just to let them know I had a weapon so they could stop shooting back my way," Mimms said.

He chased them deep into Clairton, where, he said, another shoot out took place. He emptied his revolver at the black Camaro, Mimms said. Then the two cars parted ways, Maniac Cop Mimms heading toward the police station.

There he found reinforcements in the persons of Rahis and Sanalas, and almost immediately spotted the Camaro, creeping past the station toward the Ravensburg Bridge. In two cars, the three surrounded the car on the bridge, barked orders to get out, then approached on foot.

"I tried the passenger side door and it came open," Mimms said. "When it came open I just saw someone moving around inside."

Incredible! I thought. The man claims he's been shot at from inside a black Camaro, so he goes and pulls over the first black Camaro he sees and yanks open the door. Either he was drunk or had a death wish, I couldn't be sure which.

"I knew I had just gotten shot at from inside the car," Mimms said. "I didn't know if they were reaching for the gun again or not, so I just put the shotgun in and started swinging it."

Mimms said he didn't see a gun at that time, just kept swinging that shotgun, holding it by the wooden stock, flailing away with the barrel. Then he got the front seat passenger out of the car - that would be Derek - and punched him.

I felt myself getting drowsy as Maniac Cop Mimms piled lie upon lie in his dull monotone voice, as the temperature rose and as a sorry excuse for an air conditioner whirred and sputtered somewhere near the front of the courtroom. Even Big Dave, up on the bench in his black-robed glory, started complaining about the heat. Jurors were starting to nod again. If I were on trial, I would sure want the jury to stay awake for every scintilla of testimony, especially the parts about how my accuser swung a shotgun at me and beat people.

The assistant D.A. finally finished up and Wendy got her turn. She honed right in on the controversial parts of Mimms' testimony - the fact that he'd been drinking, that he kept his gun on the front seat of Mishelle Blunt's car, that his attempt to pass occurred on an icy road in a no-passing zone, that he emptied his revolver in the middle of a populated area of Clairton, that there were bullet holes in the front of the Camaro which he could not or would not explain. In the span of a few minutes, Wendy turned Mimms from a victim into a raving maniac. I saw jurors start to perk up.

Then Wendy maneuvered Mimms out on to the bridge, and started on the beatings.

"Were you ever trained to take a loaded shotgun and wave it around inside the car to hit whomever you could in the head?" she asked.

Mimms coughed. "No. At the time that happened I was angry, upset."

She reminded Mimms that in his statement to the FBI he confirmed hitting Derek and Devon with the shotgun, and admitted to punching Derek several times, and beating Devon while he was handcuffed. Mimms leaned forward in the leather witness chair and gripped the armrests like a big cat wishing it could pounce, and denied remembering any of it. The A.D.A. and Gibson were both fidgeting like mad. "Maniac Cop" Mimms squirmed like a worm on a fishhook.

"Do you recall holding Mr. Goodman over the Ravensburg Bridge and threatening to drop him off the bridge?" she asked.

Cough, cough. "No," Mimms said, dully.

"Your honor, may we approach?" the A.D.A. shouted.

The lawyers gathered in front of the bench and argued in low tones for a few minutes before Gibson waved them quiet and called it quits for the day. We all sat while the jury filed out, then rose and walked through the molasses heat to the courtroom exit.

The second day of trial Mimms returned to the stand, and Wendy started back right where she left off - quizzing the maniac cop on the beatings. This time, though, each time she headed in the direction of the beatings the A.D.A. shouted "Objection!" Then the two lawyers would march up to the judge's bench and hiss at each other a while.

Little Sonny would shake while they were up there, knowing his fate hung on the outcome of these discussions he couldn't hear, then settle down when they got back to business. It seemed that morning they spent as much time arguing with each other up by the judge's bench as they did questioning Mimms.

When Wendy tried to ask Mimms about the civil rights charges brought against him, Uhrig jumped up. "Objection, your honor, completely irrelevant!" he shouted. Instead, Wendy had to ask Mimms what he pled guilty to in federal court.

"Something called the color code, I believe," Mimms said.

Wendy tried to get more out of him, but he just kept repeating that code phrase, "color code." What the hell does that mean? Nobody knows what the color code is. The jury would recognize the words "civil rights charges," but color code? Still, that was about as close to the truth as Big Dave would let Wendy go.

Other than that, Big Dave didn't really reign Wendy in. And slowly she started driving a wedge between the cops who had, just yesterday, been backslapping and proclaiming victory.

"Are you aware that Officer Rahis has testified or made reports that you jumped on - that Mr. Grey fell to the ground while handcuffed behind his back?" she asked him.

Cough. "Yes, I am aware he made that statement."

"And that you jumped on Mr. Grey and punched him three or four times?"

"Yes, I'm aware of that."

"Kicked him three or four times?"

Mimms coughed. "Yes, I'm aware he said that."

"Is that true?"

"No, it's not."

"Do you have any reason why Officer Rahis would make that charge against you if it wasn't true?"

"No I don't."

Maniac Cop Mimms took to coughing after just about every question, like he was dying from tuberculosis right there on the stand. He'd put his hand up to his mouth, look down, and utter a little huh-huh! I figured it was either a nervous tick or a way of buying time while he thought about how best to dodge the question.

It didn't seem to break Wendy's momentum, though. She moved

in like a shark. Having succeeded at getting Mimms mad at Rahis for ratting on him, she got Mimms to accuse Rahis of repeatedly kicking one of the young men who was trying to tie their shoes. I knew that was Devon, though Mimms seemed to think it was Little Sonny.

"Are you aware Officer Rahis says that at that point where you accuse him of kicking Little Sonny in the head you are punching Little Sonny, giving him uppercuts as he's cowering against the wall, and that you stopped once Little Sonny's in a ball?"

The A.D.A. jumped up. "May we approach?"

They had a short discussion with the judge. "Objection noted and denied," Big Dave said.

"That judge doesn't like Little Sonny," Arnella said, next to me. "He wants to see my baby go to jail. He's the one said there's a bull's eye on my baby's back."

"He denied the objection," I said.

"He didn't want to, though," she said. "He wants Little Sonny back in jail. Little Sonny done his crime, and he done his time. Since then he's held jobs. He's tryin'. Why would anybody want to send him back to jail?"

"Some people want us all in jail," I said, hoping to end the conversation.

But Arnella kept talking and talking, the same stuff, about how her baby shouldn't have to go to jail and why are they targeting him and he was asleep when this damn car chase occurred and on and on. Finally Gibson's aide, a tall, white woman with short hair and a Germanic face that brought to mind Nazi stormtroopers, rushed over to us and bent down in my face.

"The testimony is graphic, but you shouldn't be talking in front of the jury, because they might hear you. If you continue to talk, I'm going to have to ask you to leave," she said.

I just stared at her. She couldn't have known what it felt like to hear details of the beating of my son and nephews in this sanitized courtroom atmosphere. She couldn't know how much it agitated me to know that the real criminals, Mimms, Rahis and Sanalas, were free and essentially unpunished, while one of the victims was on trial fighting for his very freedom. And then to be told to be quiet. I should have been screaming at the top of my lungs.

She hurried away, looking back over her shoulder a few times as she retreated. I sat there a minute, then moved to the back of the courtroom, away from Arnella.

Wendy kept pounding away, bringing out details of the beatings, slamming Mimms for violations of a half dozen Clairton regulations, getting him to admit to taking a beer out of the Clairton police station refrigerator, bring up the civil rights charges. The A.D.A. objected to just about every question, and sometimes Big Dave sustained the objections, and sometimes he denied them. It didn't seem to matter one way or the other to Wendy; by the time the objection was lodged, the question had already reached the ears of the jury, who seemed wide awake this time around.

When she was done with him, Mimms was a shaking, coughing, shifty-eyed wreck. He stumbled from the stand like a quarterback who'd just been sacked. He sat down next to Abbet, just behind the table where Rahis and the prosecutor had set up shop.

The prosecutor called for Mishelle Blunt, and the bailiff went out in the hall to get her. She swept in, all dressed in black, her black bangs slapping against her pasty white face as she walked, and handed her purse to Mimms as she stormed the witness stand. This was the woman who'd spat at the young men and called them niggers. Not niggaz, like black people call each other, but "niggers," with that ugly "r" sound.

I didn't feel like sticking around for her lies. One more lie and I would lose my fucking mind, right there in the back of the courtroom. I left the courtroom and found Devon in the hall, sitting with his back to the wall. As a potential witness, he wasn't allowed in the courtroom during testimony. I told him about Mimms' lies and the white lady who gave us our warning.

As we sat and talked, refugees from the courtroom came out and updated us on the trial. Someone told us Blunt said she never saw the driver's side door of the Camaro open, contradicting a key piece of Mimms' testimony. "I wanted to go home. That was my full intention that evening, to get home," Blunt kept saying.

Next Jefferson Borough cop Rich Gadget claimed that Derek told him he could find a handgun under the rear driver's side seat of the Camaro, and sure enough, there it was. "It was loaded," Gadget claimed. He couldn't remember if an empty clip was found, whether Mimms seemed drunk, or whether Derek looked bloodied. He said he couldn't find any empty shell casings in the car.

Meanwhile Rahis, who had long before left his law enforcement job for a career in telecommunications, reluctantly ratted out Mimms. Wright questioned him relentlessly on the discrepancies between the various reports he wrote on the Ravensburg Bridge massacre. He'd left all mention of injuries or excessive use of force out of his original report, he admitted, and only documented the incident when ordered to by Borough Manager Wendy Thomas and Public Safety Director William Abbet - the same Abbet who obstructed justice, in my opinion, when he told Maniac Cop Mimms to say the three cousins fell on the ice.

Rahis tried to hold his ground with Wendy, saying he didn't see what Mimms was doing on the bridge. "I'm on the opposite side of the car" from Mimms, he kept saying. But he couldn't deny the blood - blood that ended up all over his hands, blood that he described to the courtroom as "warm and fresh," blood that he had to wash off with sanitary napkins the Jefferson Borough cops carried in their car. "I don't want anybody's blood on my hands," Rahis said.

Rahis said he took a shotgun away from Mimms after he threatened to kill the three young men. But in front of the station, he did nothing when he saw Mimms attack Devon, hitting the already bloodied captive repeatedly.

Though he ratted on Mimms, Rahis covered his own ass. "Did you ever kick any of the other boys when they were in their cell?" Wendy asked.

"No," he said.

"Did you ever go in and ask someone to take their shoes off and then kicked them in the cell?"

"No."

Though he was the official investigating officer, Rahis admitted he never smelled the gun to see if it had been recently fired, never felt it to see if it was warm; never returned to the scene of the shooting to search for evidence; never performed gunpowder residue tests on the hands of the three cousins, nor Mimms.

While I was in the hallway with Devon, Larry Vicious rushed out of the courtroom all excited, like a rat in a wood pile. "Wendy Wright tore Mimms and Rahis new assholes! She ate them up!" he crowed, as if he'd played some kind of role in it all.

I wondered to myself why he never did the same. It was the first time anybody had ever really cross-examined the cops, that much was true. The male lawyers had always seemed afraid to ask the tough questions. Given the opportunity at the preliminary hearing, Vicious and Jipenstein had wanted to know what kind of cars the cops drove, how old they were, what kind of toothpaste they used - everything but what happened that night, everything but how they beat three young men on a frozen bridge. They'd wanted to make big speeches for the cameras and scribes. But they'd danced around the truth - that the cops went nuts.

One witness nobody called, not even Wendy, was Steve Timmons. Timmons had said he saw Clyde Mimms drinking at the WeeBee Back Saloon just a short time before the Clairton cop shot at the Camaro, but neither Jipenstein, Vicious, Mason, nor anybody else bothered to track him down, in spite of the fact that I had his car license plate number. Timmons could have torpedoed Mimms' credibility once and for all, maybe even put an end to the case against Little Sonny, Derek and Devon three years earlier, at the preliminary hearing. But nobody had the gumption to find him or the balls to subpoena him.

Other than Timmons, the whole cast of characters wandered in and out of that courtroom, the cops who beat and lied, the lawyers who cahootsed and covered-up, the witnesses who'd stayed silent for years, and the reporters who'd swallowed the campaign of lies and deception officials of the police state had perpetrated against three innocent men. While I was pacing around one of those reporters, Jan Nelson of the Pittsburgh Post-Gazette - I commonly refer to it as the Pittsburgh Punk-Gazette - came up and tapped me on the shoulder.

"They're in there lying," she said. "They're a bunch of liars, Mr. Grey. They've been lying for four years."

"Make it five."

"Umm, Mr. Grey, I want to apologize for the articles I wrote early in the case," she said.

"Ain't no need to apologize. The damage is already done," I said, and walked away. I knew even as she apologized that she wouldn't write the truth of the beatings for the next day's paper - and she didn't.

During one of the breaks, a reporter named William Duke from the rag paper McKeesport Daily News - I refer to it as the McKeesport National Enquirer, for Narrow Minds - tried to interview Little Sonny.

"Man, why should I talk to you?" Little Sonny snapped. "For all these years all you done was accuse me of shooting at that fuckin' maniac in there. Your paper never mentioned the fact that the cops kicked our asses. Get the fuck out of my my face before I kick your ass."

"Your paper lied for three-and-a-half years about this case," I told him.

Devon joined in. "You never once reported the truth of what happened. Anything the cops said you put in there like it was Gospel, and anything we said you put was 'alleged' even after that Mimms pleaded guilty. You'll do the same thing in tomorrow's paper."

"Hey, that was another reporter. I wasn't even with the paper then," the guy said. But they just kept on him until he threw up his hands and walked away.

So happened Nelson was walking by. "Don't worry about it. I get the same treatment," she told him.

After a while Arnella came out, her face looking drawn and twisted, her eyes moist. "I know those jurors are gonna believe those cops and their lies," she said, "and if they do, my baby's gonna go to jail. And what's that lawyer's plan for beating this thing? Put Little Sonny on the stand. You just know that district attorney's gonna tear into him and get him all tongue-tied and make him look like another guilty Negro to that white jury."

I couldn't say much to that. Now that she put it that way, it was hard to imagine that jury believing that Little Sonny snoozed through a car chase and shoot-out, and disbelieving a cop and his girlfriend. Even if Wendy did convince the jury that the cops beat the piss out of Little Sonny, Derek and Devon, the judge might tell them to ignore that and concentrate on whether Little Sonny fired on Mimms. It seemed like a tough sell.

But I couldn't say that to Arnella.

"The truth has a way of coming out," I said instead, though I wasn't all that convinced of it anymore. "Hey, let's get out of this stinky courthouse for a bit."

We walked down the courthouse's winding stairs. It's a strange place, the Allegheny County Courthouse, an old stone building turned brown by a century of soot and dirty rain. If you come in the front door, a wide marble plaza opens up to you, with a huge central staircase that eventually splits and winds to the third floor. But the hallways that circle out from that majestic centerpiece are a dreary yellow, lit with flickering and buzzing fluorescent bulbs, crowded with cops, bureaucrats, and pacing, nervous defendants and suspects, and littered in every corner with cigarette butts, right under the "No Smoking Under Penalty of Law" signs.

We got out of there and settled on an empty bench in the courthouse courtyard. It was another sunny day, but not as hot, and people were sitting on park benches out there, eating lunch or smoking cigarettes, or just getting a little bit of air before going back to cramped cubicles or sweltering courtrooms. Across the way there was a little portico where the politicians parked their shiny taxpayer-funded cars. The August sun and the fact that I hadn't slept much in a few days made it all seem unreal, like a poorly produced movie.

We didn't say much for a few minutes. I didn't know what to say to Arnella. Her son was on the auction block, waiting for a bunch of white people to decide whether to send him to the slave ship with no sails, prison. I didn't much want to remind her of the trial, but nor did I want to make small talk that would trivialize her worries. So I just watched the people go by.

Then out of the courthouse strode the maniac cop himself, with his partner-in-lies Mishelle Blunt right beside him, and all my wrath welled up again. This was the Fife who threatened to kill my son and was trying to jail my nephew. This was the pled-guilty civil rights violator who played God and got a slap-on-the-wrist sentence. This guy thought he was the Almighty three and a half years back, surrounded by white cop friends, maliciously beating handcuffed young men with a shotgun.

Then I realized everyone was looking at me, Arnella and the smokers and the lunchers and cops. The thoughts that boiled in my brain and breast were pouring out my mouth. Then it was like I was outside myself, watching myself from above. "That guy is a civil rights violator!" I heard myself yell. "He beats kids! I wonder what that Maniac Cop Clyde Mimms would do against someone who's not handcuffed and is his own size and age."

I could see Mimms' eyes light up, but he wouldn't look up from the ground, and said nothing as he scurried by.

"Civil rights violator!" I yelled again. "Fucking maniac cop! Human rights violator!" At the moment, those were the worst things I could think of to shout.

But even as I cursed him, I realized Mimms was also a victim. He was a victim of a system that used him to shield two white cops who were just as guilty. The U.S. (In)Justice Department had tried him and him alone, making it a black-on-black case. If you want to blame someone, blame a nigger, is how the U.S. (In)Justice Department apparently saw it. By doing so they cleverly sidestepped the issue of whether it was a hate crime, and deflected media attention. This was just some niggers beating up on each other - nothing to get excited about.

* * *

Thursday the prosecution opened with their riskiest gambit yet: Derek. I suppose the prosecutor must have thought that the usual rule - one cop's testimony outweighs 50 civilians - didn't apply when the cops were ratting each other out for beating handcuffed suspects. So they'd have to try to turn cousin against cousin to move the jury. And who better to put on the stand than Derek, who'd signed, under torture, the back side of a paper on which the cops wrote a contrived confession, and who'd already been jailed once for refusing to say what Judge "Big Dave" Gibson wanted him to say?

Derek took the stand in a blue sweatshirt, looking every bit like every white's stereotype of a ghetto gangbanger. His lawyer, Chuck Newton, came before the court and argued that Derek should be allowed to plead the Fifth Amendment, but Big Dave shot him down. Derek had no Fifth Amendment rights, Gibson said, because he isn't charged with any crime. He would have to testify, or face contempt of court charges.

Chuck Newton walked away from the bench shaking his head. I caught up to him at the back of the courtroom. "Someone should 302 that Big Dave," I told him, "put him in an institution. He's crazy. He's done lost his mind."

Newton looked at me, his eyes drooped in resignation, and just shook his head.

The prosecutor started with the usual routine, name rank and serial number, then led Derek back to the scene of the incident. Then he whipped out a copy of the so-called confession, and asked Derek if he signed it.

Derek paused and squirmed in his seat. He looked up at Gibson, the black thundercloud with the round pink head. The judge was leaning from his bench over the witness stand, leaning so far I thought he might tip over and fall on poor little Derek. I saw my nephew gulp.

"I just wanted them to quit hitting me," he said.

It wasn't what the A.D.A. wanted to hear. He led Derek back through the incident, asking him the same simple questions, trying to train him, it seemed, to give the desired answer and only the desired answer to each question. Derek looked up at Gibson after each question, as if trying to read from the judge's pink face what answer would get him thrown in jail and what answer wouldn't.

Big Dave glowered, but Derek stuck to the truth. Little Sonny didn't fire any gun, he said; Little Sonny was asleep in back the whole time. Derek didn't write the so-called confession; Rahis did, then he and Mimms tricked Derek into signing it.

The A.D.A. seemed flustered, then read over a part of the confession that referred to a "Toby."

"Isn't Toby the nickname you use for your cousin, Devon Grey?" the A.D.A. asked.

"Toby? No."

"You don't call him Toby?"

Genuine puzzlement crossed Derek's face. I felt it too. Since the day he was born, I'd never heard Devon called Toby.

"No," Derek said slowly, glancing up at Big Dave. "We sometimes call him Von, but not Toby."

I don't know if the jury caught it, but to me that exchange was as good as setting fire to that confession. "Mickey Mouse" Rahis had referred to Devon as "Toby," something he probably remembered from watching the miniseries Roots or something, a name perhaps he thought all black people should go by, but not a name that Derek or Little Sonny would ever tack on to Devon.

Derek wasn't out of the woods yet. Assistant District Attorney Uhrig was joined by Big Dave, who relentlessly interrogated Derek as if he was a second prosecutor. Even when Wendy took over the witness and started tossing him softball questions and asking him about the beatings, Gibson was there, hovering over him, peppering him with hostile inquiries and smart remarks. Derek handled much of it with one word - "Huh?" Gibson didn't seem to like it, but he couldn't call it perjury.

Finally they got done toying with Derek and let him off the stand, and the assembled relatives and friends of Little Sonny Brown sighed with relief. Derek wouldn't win any awards for poise and elocution, but he hadn't contradicted himself, hadn't perjured himself, and hadn't played into the prosecution's divide and conquer strategy.

Gibson seemed deflated and called a recess.

As Little Sonny thanked Derek for testifying, Vicious pulled me aside.

"Leon, there's something you should know about," Vicious said. "Little Sonny is very scared of going back to jail, and Arnella's even more terrified than he is. There's a chance he might crack and do something unpredictable. I'm afraid Arnella might be trying to get that boy to say that Devon or Derek fired a gun at that Mimms. She might think Derek and your boy are off the hook because it's been more than two years."

"They aren't off the hook if Little Sonny fingers them for a felony," I said.

"Right. As you heard Ms. Wright point out, the statute of limitations for a felony is five years," Vicious said. "If he pointed the finger at Devon or Derek, the prosecution would still have almost two years to file charges."

I could see it happening. Little Sonny was obviously scared of going to jail behind this crap, and might look for any way out, even one that would screw his cousins. It would be the ultimate flip side of the A.D.A.'s divide-and-conquer tactics: Having failed to turn Derek and Devon against Little Sonny, he would watch as Little Sonny implicated one or both of his cousins. The A.D.A. probably wouldn't care if it was true or false, as long as he got his conviction.

I walked over to Little Sonny and pulled him aside.

"Little Sonny, I know you're scared and everything, but did you tell Wendy Wright or Larry Vicious that you were going to say that Devon or Derek fired a gun that night?"

He looked at me long and hard. "No way, Uncle Bus. There wasn't no gun that night. I'm sticking to the truth."

"O.K., I just wanted to check. Because I know you don't want to do time behind this shit, and I just want to make sure nobody does anything stupid. The truth is going to set you free. I just want you to know, nobody's off the hook here yet. They can still charge Derek and Devon with a felony, up until five years after the incident."

I could see his face darkening, the muscles around his eyes tensing. "Uncle Bus, man, if you think I'm gonna pin it on Devon or Derek after all we been through together, you don't know me, man. I ain't a rat. No way I'm going to rat out my cousins, who didn't do nothing neither." He was talking loudly now, playing to the nearby audience. "Man, Uncle Bus, I'm surprised you'd even ask that. I'm going to sink or swim with the truth, and that's all there is to it."

"O.K., man, I'm with you," I said, and walked away. I'd done what I had to do. I went back to where I'd been and leaned up against a wall, alone.

It couldn't have been more than a few minutes before Arnella was in my face, arms failing, finger pointing, shouting you better mind your own business and not mess with my son's case and all you ever cared about was your own son's freedom and don't you ever, ever speak to my son again and on and on.

I told her I just wanted to make sure the truth came out.

"That D.A. don't want no truth," Arnella yelled. The assorted cops and lawyers and witnesses and families all looked at her. "He wants my baby in jail."

"I know. And the only way he gets what he wants is if somebody lies."

"Somebody's already lying! Them cops are lying. How come it's only my boy who has to tell the truth?"

She went on for a little bit, then stormed off. The pressure was getting to her, just as it was getting to Little Sonny. Day Three of a trial that should have never occurred can do that to a soul, I guess, especially when the real criminals were sitting with the prosecutor.

When we got back in, the prosecutor called Dr. Damian Delellis from the Allegheny County crime lab. Delellis testified he had 23 years experience in the field, and he had an air of credibility about him. I could tell this guy wasn't just a hired gun who'd play ball for the prosecution.

He knew his stuff, too. Delellis explained to the jury the difference between a .22, a .25 and a .357. He told them the history of the Phoenix Arms Co., maker of the weapon allegedly found in the Camaro. Under questioning from Uhrig, he talked about the weaknesses of gunshot residue testing, which Rahis and friends had somehow neglected to perform.

"If a person has active use of the hands, a person washes his hands, then this residue has very little adhesive qualities to it," Delellis said. "It can come off quite easily, so the longer you wait between the time of the shooting and the time the hands are swabbed, the less likely you will have positive results from the gunshot residue."

Uhrig had Delellis admit that an altercation, or contact with ice, would shake loose some of any gunshot residue that might be on someone's hands. I figured he was trying to get the cops off the hook for not doing that test. To me, it just made the cops look dumber. I mean, if it's so important to perform this residue test right away, why didn't they do that, rather than putting the cousins through a reign of terror without any evidence whatsoever?

Then it was Wendy's turn. She pointed to the Phoenix .25 pea shooter on the witness stand in front of him, asked Delellis if he'd examined and test-fired it. He said he had.

"You have no idea if this weapon was fired that night?" she asked.

"Oh, no. I have no idea if it was fired."

"So you have no idea if this was ever fired or not, this gun."

"That's right."

I could barely keep from laughing. The case against Little Sonny Brown got more farcical with every twist and turn. The cops turn out to be criminals. The gun may never have been fired.

Wendy didn't let up, now asking Delellis whether it's common for police agencies to collect the shell casings and bullet fragments from the scenes of shootings. Uhrig leapt up to object, but Big Dave shot him down.

"We do get cartridge cases and bullets collected at various crime scenes, including drive-bys," Delellis said. "They generally are submitted to the laboratory by police agencies."

Wendy was using the prosecution's own witness to shred the

prosecution's case. Uhrig tapped his fingers nervously on the wooden tabletop he shared with telecommunications professional John Rahis. Arnella, sitting across the room, stared blankly. The jurors seemed in various states of consciousness, some attentive, with quizzical looks on their faces, others heavy-lidded and apparently about to nod off. I wondered how much of this was really sinking into the minds of these 12 people who would decide Little Sonny's fate, none of whom had lived with the intricacies of this case for the last three-and-a-half years, like I had.

Late that afternoon, Wendy called Little Sonny Brown to the stand. He got up slowly from the defendant's seat and walked to the witness stand. There was no swagger in his step, and he looked as serious as I'd ever seen him as he swore to tell the truth. I hoped what I saw was a determination to tell it like it was, in plain and simple terms, and cut through the lies and obfuscation the cops had spread for three and a half years.

It was a risky step, putting Little Sonny on the stand. Most defendants take the fifth, and sit silently throughout trial rather than risk getting crossed up by a sly prosecutor. In this case, it was a sly, white prosecutor, a black defendant, and a mostly-white jury. Add to that the fact that Little Sonny wasn't an angel, with a record marked by guilty pleas to charges of car theft years before. But Wendy wasted no time turning Little Sonny's minuses into pluses.

"Why did you plead guilty to those crimes?" she asked.

"Because I committed those crimes."

"Why didn't you plead guilty to firing shots at Officer Mimms?"

"Because I'm innocent and I didn't fire any shots at that man," Little Sonny said with icy determination.

Wendy led him through the events of the fateful day, when Little Sonny worked a double shift, and the following evening, up to the time the three cousins got in the car. About as soon as he got into the back seat of that Camaro, Little Sonny said, he fell asleep.

When Little Sonny woke up, the car was on the Ravensburg bridge, and within seconds Mimms was at the door, beating Derek with the shotgun. Wendy guided him through the terrifying events that followed, from Mimms beating him on the bridge to the torture at the station. From pain and shock to terror to rage his emotions went, Little Sonny testified, and when a cop took his handcuffs off, he lost control.

"I know that was a dumb mistake for me to do, but I went after Mimms, I hit him in the balls," Little Sonny testified.

"So why did you attack Mimms?" Wendy asked.

"I was tired of getting my ass whipped. I said, what the hell."

For that he was beaten mercilessly by Mimms and the two other officers, Little Sonny said, shot with a 25,000 volt stun gun and urinated on. As he knelt on the floor, paralyzed by the stun gun, Little Sonny told the mesmerized jury, the cops mashed their stinking penises against his face.

The cops grabbed at his pants and threatened to fuck him if he didn't admit to being a bitch, Little Sonny told the jury. When he was finally hauled off and tossed in a woman's cell, Mimms licked his chops and said, "Yeah, you're my bitch."

It was graphic testimony, and the jury was obviously shocked. The black male juror watched Little Sonny for a while, then turned to Maniac Cop Mimms, and stared with disgust and hatred. I could guess the questions running through his head: How could you do that to another brother? What convinced you that the blue of your sorry ass City of Clairton Police uniform canceled out the black hue of your skin, or the red of your blood that you share with every other human being? What kind of a monster are you?

Then I saw juror 11, a white lady, grimace in horror. Slowly a glassy sheen obscured her eyes, and then fat tears started flowing down her face. As Little Sonny described the relentless torture, the salty drops followed each other down her face. I was amazed. This white woman was moved to tears by the sufferings of a young black man she'd never known prior to seeing him on trial, who'd admitted to stealing cars, who was accused of firing on a cop and his pregnant girlfriend.

The older black woman a few seats away looked stunned, but wasn't weeping like the white lady. When I saw that white lady crying, and that black woman wasn't crying, I thought that was really something. It was the first time in three-and-a-half years that I'd seen any real outpouring of sympathy for the victims of the beatings. Raymond Locke hadn't shown any. Mayor Lou Costello and his puppets on the Clairton City Council certainly shed no tears. Constance Cass of the U.S. (In)Justice Department sure didn't, either, and the liars we'd hired saw us as just another paycheck. The media were just a pack of piranhas hungry for a story. What made it more surprising was that the jury was mostly white. It wasn't often I saw evidence that white people saw black people as human beings. But here it was.

Then there was Gibson. Big Dave sat on his throne, squirming, bouncing up and down, looking back and forth from Little Sonny to Wendy to the jury to Uhrig. Beneath his eyes the prosecution's case was melting like late-spring snow under the searing heat of Little Sonny's tale of police brutality and subsequent cover-up, and it seemed to me he was looking for a way to stop it. But there was none. He'd already ruled that evidence of the beatings was admissible, because it reflects on the credibility of the cops. Now Wendy had put the cops on trial, where they belonged. Still, the only one faced with years behind bars was Little Sonny Brown, I reminded myself.

When she was done, Wendy entered into evidence a series of blown-up photos taken of Derek, Devon and Little Sonny at the hospital the morning after their meeting with a maniac. Without speaking, Wendy carried the photos to the jury box and showed them around. Some jurors stared with glazed, glassy eyes and couldn't seem to look away. Others looked wide-eyed and then, wincing, turned away, as if they themselves had been struck. Some faces tightened into frowns, others went slack-jawed with shock.

There was stunned silence in the courtroom. After a few seconds that seemed much longer, Gibson broke it. "I have to apologize for all the noise that comes in here from the street," he said to the shocked jury. Noise from the street has obviously been the furthest thing from their minds during the hours of blistering testimony.

But Gibson went on, telling him that his court was one of the worst located rooms in the entire Courthouse. He complained and complained, Gibson said, but couldn't get moved from this wretched room. "The architect who put this courtroom here should be fired or jailed," he said.

I couldn't tell if he was joking or insane. The jury, the attorneys, the gathered cops and even Little Sonny looked about in embarrassment as Big Dave railed against the designer of his courtroom. "What the hell is he talking about?" somebody in a seat near me muttered.

Gibson looked exhausted, and recessed the trial for the day.

Maniac Cop Mimms wandered out looking like a whipped dog.

Little Sonny stormed out, geeked up like he was just made king of the world, obviously relieved to have finally got his story off his chest. Arnella came out with tears in her eyes. And the reporters were hopping around like they were about to have orgasms.

"Uncle Bus, did he really tell them about what they did, with peeing on him and all?" Derek asked. He'd waited outside during Little Sonny's testimony.

"He told them everything, pee and all," I said.

His head fell back and he laughed out loud. It was the purest, freest laugh I'd heard out of his mouth in a long, long time.

* * *

The next morning we met in the Courthouse again. I was wiped out from working nights and spending my days watching the farce of the century, but this was expected to be verdict day, and that kept me going. Mimms wasn't there, I noticed, though he had been every other day.

Uhrig took over, and set to trying to trip Little Sonny up, searching for little discrepancies in his testimony here, there, wherever he could find them. Little Sonny wasn't about to take any shit, though. He sparred with Uhrig on question after question. He was asleep during the car chase, he told the jury. He never fired on Mimms. There was no gun in the car. And that was that.

The prosecutor didn't touch the matter of the beatings on the bridge or in the station. He wasn't about to make the mistake of reminding the jury of those events, I figured, or giving Little Sonny another opportunity to recite the graphic details.

When he was done Wendy made her closing arguments, tearing the scabs off the wounds she'd spent three days inflicting on the prosecution's case. There was no proper investigation of the alleged shooting, she reminded the jury. Rahis had never so much as searched the scene of the shooting for bullets or other clues. No gunshot residue tests were performed on the three cousins. Tests on the supposed gun couldn't even conclude whether it had ever been fired. The only witnesses to the alleged shooting were a crazed off-duty cop who'd been drinking, and his girlfriend. And then there were the beatings.

The prosecutor got the last word, and spent his half hour trying to sweep all that under the rug. Mimms and Blunt said it happened, he told the jury. "The evidence is entirely consistent with Ms. Blunt's testimony and with Clyde Mimms' testimony," he said. A gun was found in the car, Uhrig said, and the "suggestion" that the gun was planted "would have to be supported by a shred of evidence. ... But there is none."

This time, Uhrig couldn't get around the brutal beating the three cousins took. He admitted to the jury that Mimms went "ballistic" on the cousins. "Think of a man and a woman that are driving along on a road and they are shot at," he told them. "I'm not asking you to excuse him for that. I'm just asking you to understand."

The way Uhrig had it, Mimms' raging assault on the three handcuffed prisoners with fists and boots and a shotgun was a temper tantrum - regrettable, but understandable. Kind of like when you lose control and slap your kid or something. I wondered if behind the blank faces of the jurors this had struck a chord.

Then there was the so-called confession of Derek Goodman. "Goodman is all over the board," Uhrig said. "There are things he says which are consistent with the evidence in this case, and there are things which are not."

So what should the jury believe? They should believe Derek's alleged statements on that terror-filled night on the Ravensburg Bridge and in the station, Uhrig suggested. "Even if he was being struck, what he said was the truth," Uhrig said.

He closed by pointing out that Derek and Little Sonny had prior brushes with the law. Once a crook, always a crook, seemed to be the implication. I wondered why he didn't go into Mimms' extensive record of run-ins with the cops. I guess in the eyes of this prosecutor and this judge and this system, the reckless actions of a gun-happy cop aren't relevant. Youthful crimes like receiving stolen property are.

Gibson took over, charging the jury to put bias or sympathy aside and weigh the evidence. "You should abhor what happened that night. You should be morally outraged that police officers would engage in that kind of behavior," Big Dave told the jury. "You may be outraged, and you should be." But that outrage shouldn't cause them to excuse the behavior of the defendant, Little Sonny Brown, if they believe he is guilty, he said.

It sounded like a last minute plea for conviction by the judge, and I was seized with doubt about the outcome. To me, it seemed cut and dried. But as the mostly-white jury filed out, I realized what was crystal to me might be mud to them. The jurors had probably never been beaten by cops. They'd almost certainly never stood trial for shooting at one. It's unlikely they'd had their homes searched without a warrant, had their houses burned down under mysterious circumstances, or had to leap out of the way as a cop car tried to run them down. Maybe I was crazy to think they'd believe a young black man with a record over a cop and his girlfriend.

The bailiff led the jury out. Before the rest of us could rise, the judge asked, "May I see those pictures?" and pointed to the blown-up photos of the cousins' battered faces on the exhibit table. Wendy carried them to the bench.

Big Dave paged through them, studying each carefully. I was almost certain he'd seen them before, and wondered if he was just putting on an act for the audience.

"These pictures are criminal," Gibson finally intoned. "Mimms is an asshole. He went out of his way to try to kill these guys."

He leaned out over the bench and looked down at the court reporter. "I don't care if you put that down or not," he said, then rose and walked out.

As the newspaper reporters rushed up to see the pictures, the rest of the assembled audience staggered out into the hall, not exactly sure what to think of the drama that had just unfolded.

While the jury deliberated, we escorted Wendy across Grant Street to her office. I tried to count how many times I'd been down here among Grant Street's lawyers and bankers and homeless since this nightmare began. First to meet with the FBI; later for hearings in the criminal case, the grand jury testimony, the so-called sentencing of Clyde Mimms, Devon's deposition in the civil trial the day one of Gammage's assailants was let off the hook, and now for this trial. These Clairton cops, in one night of handiwork, had given a small army of lawyers, judges, investigators and reporters an excuse to keep drawing a paycheck. I wondered how much the taxpayers had forked over thanks to the actions of these bumbling, brutal Barnie Fifes.

At Wendy's office, we all sat down in her little conference room. She gave me back the tape of the preliminary hearing, saying it had helped her fine-tune her cross-examination of Mimms.

"I find it hard to believe you got much out of it," I said. "Jipenstein and Vicious hardly asked Mimms anything but little softball questions. They pussy-footed around like those cops were their dinner guests, and they didn't want to offend them."

"That's right," said Devon. "Wendy here is the only lawyer on this case who showed any kind of balls. Little Sonny, you got yourself one damn good lawyer."

"She's got more balls than any of those male attorneys we had to fire, Jipenstein and Mason, sell-out Reinhardt and Vicious," I said, as Wendy leaned against the wall and smiled. "She be bad. She got more balls than all of those fuckers put together."

"Yeah," Little Sonny said, looking out the window. That was all he said. Mentally, it was like he wasn't there. He seemed disconnected, with a vacant look on his face, like you see on the faces of defendants on TV when they know their fate is in somebody else's hands. It struck me that he must be going through a lot, not knowing whether by the end of the day he'd be free of the albatross he'd carried for more than three years, or in jail.

"Hey, Little Sonny, you're gonna be all right. Don't worry. It's gonna to turn out just fine," I said. But the words rang hollow, even to me.

After a while talking to Wendy and Little Sonny, I started disconnecting from reality myself, I was so exhausted. I realized I wasn't much use hanging around Wendy's office, and said goodbye. "Little Sonny, you call me either way. You go to jail, call me. You don't go to jail, call me," I told him.

"Okay, Uncle Buster," he said. "Hey, thanks for being there."

I gave him a hearty handshake and pulled him to me, then hugged him. Little Sonny had his little foibles, but he'd stuck with the truth. Under enormous pressure, and against the advice of so-called lawyers, he'd held his ground for more than three years and refused a plea bargain. You had to respect him for that.

When Devon and I got home, around noon, there were no messages on the answering machine. Exhaustion from working nights and going to trial every day was coursing like waves through my body, and the world was all funny, like I had a fever or something. I hit the bed, and about two seconds later I was out cold.

* * *

"Not guilty! Dad! Dad! Dad! Wake up!"

I shook the dust off my shaved head and sat up. My first thought was, "I knew O.J. was innocent." Then I remembered that was years ago, when under almost identical circumstances, Devon had awakened me in the middle of an afternoon to tell me The Juice was found not guilty of the murder of his wife. This was deja vu all over again.

Devon's voice echoed through the house like a psalm. "Little Sonny was found not guilty! I told Little Sonny, you told Little Sonny, that they didn't have a case against us. Turns out we were right."

Derek had just called with the news. The jury had deliberated all afternoon, then returned to Big Dave's chambers at about 5 p.m. with a not guilty verdict. And it was good. Little Sonny Joe Brown was a free man.

It was a landmark victory in Allegheny County. A black man had faced a cadre of cops determined to jail him, and had come out on top, in spite of a system set up to screw him. Little Sonny stuck to the truth, his family stuck by him, and Wendy Wright tore at the curtain of lies the cops threw up, and that was what it took to whip all the judges, prosecutors and cops arrayed against them. Though the mainstream media would largely miss the point, the case would not be lost on others whose loved ones were brutalized by the police, I predicted. It would give them the inspiration to fight on.

I was still trying to get my bearings when Peeper walked into the bedroom. Those three hours of shut-eye after four days of round-the-clock action were some of the deepest hours of sleep I'd had in a long time, and I was having a hard time shaking them off.

"Dad, did you think Little Sonny was going to be convicted?" he asked.

The question brought so many ugly thoughts into my head; thoughts about how people are brainwashed into always believing the cops, about how lawyers try to screw their clients, about how white jurors often bring deep-rooted racism into the courtroom and convict black defendants whether the evidence is there or not. I thought about Big Dave Gibson, the politically connected judge who had to be removed from the Jonny Gammage case by a higher court, and who had leaned over Derek not like a judge, not even like a prosecutor, but like an interrogator in some Third World prison.

I didn't know how much of this I wanted to saddle Peeper with at his young age. He goes to a school system that is mostly white, but has managed to get good grades and make plenty of friends. Already he'd run into teachers who had told him his thoughts were wrong, when really they just came from a different perspective. He was bound to run up against that color barrier soon enough, I figured, like I had when I tried to rent that house from the old white lady in Duquesne. Maybe I shouldn't hasten it.

"Did you, Dad?" he asked.

"Peeper, I prayed for the best and prepared for the worst. This time, I guess we got the best."

* * *

It was a cool afternoon in late October 1998, and things seemed right with the world. Devon had been home from Renewal Inc., a halfway house, for two weeks, following a three-month incarceration for failure to pay child support. His kids were happy their daddy was home, especially little Shatia, now age seven. He'd enrolled in a trade school to learn to fix airplanes, and was due to begin classes Jan. 5. Plus the City of Clairton had finally caved in and settled his civil suit stemming from the beatings, so he had a little cash with which to try to plan a future.

He's a good kid with a heart of gold. Smart, too. Now and then he gets derailed. He went and had kids too early, if you ask me, and there were a few years there after the beatings during which he seemed directionless. But that cool October day, he seemed to be back on track. The rain was gone, the sun was peeking through, and a rainbow shined brightly over the Grey family.

Still, in a world where you can get beat and prosecuted for being the wrong color in the wrong place at the wrong time, the gray clouds of uncertainty are never too far off.

That morning Lillian and I decided to go out to States Tires and

Wheels in McKeesport. It was a trip both of us hated to make. We dread going back to that corruption-infested town. Lil had been there only once since we moved out of town - for her brother-in-law Charles' funeral in the spring of 1998. My kids don't go there, because their experiences with the police there still weigh heavy on their minds.

I'm the exception. Every week I go down into McKeesport to visit my 78-year-old mother who is in a nursing home, suffering from Alzheimer's. Other than that, I try not do buy anything there or spend any significant time there. But it was the only place I could get a good deal on the set of four new Vogue tires I wanted for my wife's Cadillac Eldorado. I couldn't pass up the deal.

Lillian and I were headed for the garage door when Devon called out from the living room, "Hey, pops, can I tag along?"

"Sure you can, Chrome Dome. We don't mind if you tag along. Get your coat and let's rooooollllll, Chrome."

It was the first time in a long time I'd called him by his old nickname, Chrome Dome. Devon wasn't bald - far from it, though his dreadlocks were shorter now than they had been years before. He got the nickname as a kid, when he climbed up to the very top of the highest tree in our back yard, couldn't figure out how to get down, and ended up tumbling straight down through the branches and landing on his head. He could have broken his neck or back, but amazingly, he wasn't hurt - not even a headache. I chainsawed that tree to the ground that day, and the name Chrome Dome was born.

So Chrome, Lil and I piled into the Eldorado, and I was thinking how appropriate that old nickname was. Here it was four-and-a-half years after he'd been beaten nearly to death, and after investigations, court hearings, wrist-slap punishments or no punishments at all for the real criminals, Derek's troubles and Little Sonny's suicide attempts, and now his child support problems, Devon was still his cheery old self. Life smacked him on his hard head over and over again, but he kept bouncing back. He was home, the trouble was over, and we were one big happy family again.

He seemed to sense what I was thinking, and put his hand on my shoulder from behind. "Hey, Dad, it was no joke being locked up," he said. "I hope to God I can stay out of that kind of mess from now on."

"You know what, Chrome, I can sympathize with you. You're

home now, so don't worry about anything."

But as we headed into the Valley, I started to get nervous. This was where the bad times started: the persecution, the harassment, the attempted assassinations, the final act of setting our house aflame. I'll remember that all my life. We would only be at States Tires for 15 or 20 minutes, I reasoned. What could go wrong? part of me thought. But anything can go wrong any time in a police state. You're never safe.

I could see it in my wife's eyes, too. "Babe, why do we have to go to McKeesport for tires?" she asked the second time I looked over at her.

"Well, it's like this: I'm getting a deal. It's a chance to save some money. Everything is going to be all right. Don't you worry."

As we got closer I started to get flashbacks of the Fifes holding me at gunpoint, pushing my wife out the door and charging into my home without a search warrant, violating my Fourth Amendment rights. Almost as if they were right in front of me I saw them trampling through my house, terrifying my one- and two-year-old grandbabies, pawing over my property with their blood-soaked hands, picking up Peeper's puppy and slamming him down to the ground. All in an illegal hunt for my son, Devon, who had done nothing. They hadn't been able to get me, so they were going after my children.

Then I was returning from vacation, knowing full well my house had been burned in my absence, with Lil in tears beside me. The only question in my mind on that ride home from Port Clinton was whether the house would be salvageable, or whether we'd have to move.

Then I was driving past Froggy DeMarco's house, crouched low in the car, seeing his plump body and the glint of cold steel at his side. And then I was jogging across the street, and just noticing, out the corner of my eye, a speeding police cruiser barreling down on me.

When people ask me about my ordeals with the Fifes, I tell them, if only I'd had the weapons I have now, things would be different. I wouldn't be walking this earth, for one thing. I would be six feet under ground, as would some of the Fifes. The McKeesport Fifes are the reason I went out and bought my AK-47, Mr. Justice, and some of his boys. I figured I had to protect my family and myself, because no one else was going to do it. The boys in blue, supposedly there to "protect and serve," had proved to me they were nothing better than an occupying army of thugs. I'd had to go out and buy weapons of mass destruction to defend my rights and the rights of my loved ones not from criminals, but from cops.

Devon broke the brooding silence, reaching over from the back and popping a reggae tape in the cassette player. He's loved his reggae for a long time, and my wife and I have learned to deal with it. We let him have his way with the tape player, even though we really can't stand the stuff. With the music jacked up almost all the way, and the dark cloud of our memories of McKeesport hanging over us, we didn't talk much the rest of the way to States Tires.

We pulled in, and the tire guys took our car immediately. Devon waited out in the parking lot, watching the cars drive up and down the boulevard, while Lil and I sat quietly in the waiting area.

Suddenly the front door swung open and a tall white guy sauntered into the tire joint. To everybody else, he might have looked like a normal man, but to me he had all the revolting ugliness of Godzilla. I studied him carefully, confirming he was the cold-blooded, lizard-like creature I remembered.

My eyes must have been burning holes in his back, because he turned around and looked me right in the face. There he was, crew-cut, peanut-headed, the very same bastard who'd tried to run me down with his police cruiser that morning years ago in McKeesport. He was also one of the small army of Fifes who'd arrested Curtis for a trumped-up crime years back, I remembered. I didn't blink or look away from his arrogant eyes. He turned away.

It's times like this I'm glad I don't carry a gun. It took everything I had to restrain me from jumping on the Fife, and if I'd been packing a gun, the temptation might have been too much.

"It's him, Lil, it's him!" I said.

"What are you talking about, Buster?"

"It's that no-good mother fucker who tried to run me over."

"Settle down, babe," said Lil, putting a firm hand on my arm. "I don't want you to get into any trouble here in McKeesport. You know what can happen once you get into their custody. Please don't start any trouble."

"I'm under control, Lil," I hissed. "He tried to kill me, and arrested Curtis for something he never did. He's the one needs to be worried about being under control."

Years had passed since I'd last had eye contact with Godzilla. I could see that he recognized me, though, and he shook a little as he turned back to the sales clerk and hurried through his conversation, which was about tires for his 4-by-4. He left without buying anything, and though he never looked in our direction, I could see his eyes were full of fear.

As he walked past, I jumped up. Lil tried to hold my arm, but I turned and said, "I'm O.K.," and followed the Fife out. Devon was just outside the door, and I pulled up next to him as Godzilla got in his vehicle and drove off.

"Hey, Chrome, you know who that fucker is?" I asked.

"Sure do. Back in the day, my boys told me he sold drugs big time. At least that was the talk in the hood."

"I can believe that. You know, he tried to run me over with his police cruiser and arrested Curtis twice for the same trumped-up bullshit. He's a no-good mother fucker and I don't care who knows it."

Then I remembered the other place I'd seen him: in the County Courthouse the day I took Devon into Pittsburgh for his deposition, the day Brentwood Police Officer John Vojtas was acquitted of the murder of black motorist Jonny Gammage. Godzilla was out in the hall that day, slapping backs and celebrating with all the other thugs. I'd had my sunglasses on that day, and hadn't made the connection, but now it was clear as a photograph.

"I guess that bastard is still on the police force," I said.

"You can call it what you want to, Dad, there is no justice when a cop breaks the law," Devon said. "You saw what happened to Maniac Cop Clyde Mimms - nothing. He wasn't arrested, he didn't have to post bail, he didn't go to jail or even pay a fine or get fired."

"Devon, you remember that case a few months ago where that guy was jailed for two-to-seven years for cruelty to a dog, and those animal rights protesters were all around the courthouse with signs? Meanwhile when humans are abused, the perpetrators get probation, if even that. What a fucking joke, right, Devon? That Fife is really no different than Mimms or Vojtas, but all three are still on the beat."

"It seems unjust, doesn't it," he said.

I started shaking as the store employees finished putting the tires on my wife's Cadillac. This was the same town where that Fife had tried to kill me years ago. It was time to get the hell out of the 'Port. I looked at Devon and gestured with my head toward the inside. We walked in to where Lil was sitting nervously.

"Are you O.K.?" she asked.

"Yeah, I just want to get the hell out before Godzilla comes back with his boys to kick my ass," I said. Her face darkened and she grit her teeth. I could tell she was angry. "I'm just joking, babe, don't take it so seriously. Just joking. Just joking."

"You shouldn't joke like that. You know how these people are over here," she said in a loud whisper. "You should try to forget that mess with them and go on with your life."

"Maybe you can forget, but I can't. I'll never forget how they wronged us and one day I'm going to tell my story. You wait and see. I'm going to tell the world how we were persecuted like Jews by the Gestapo in McKeesport."

We sat quiet, on edge and brooding, while the tire professionals finished their work. It seemed a long time before the sales clerk called me up and gave me the bill for $800. I pulled out my checkbook and wrote a check for that amount. He took the check, wrote up the receipt, folded it and handed it to me. I thanked him and headed for the door, Devon and Lillian right behind me.

As I reached for the door knob, my check fell out of the folded receipt. The clerk had apparently handed it right back to me with the receipt. Shocked, I picked it up and said, "Hey, man, don't you want your money?"

He smiled, and said, "Yes, sir. Thank you, sir."

I walked back over and gave it to him again. Lil laughed for the first time since we left home, and all the tension that lingered from the encounter with Godzilla washed away.

We climbed back into the Eldorado, complete with four new radials.

"Hey, babe, that was a nice thing you did back there," she said.

"Yeah, I could have kept the check. But it wasn't the right thing to do. I wouldn't want someone to keep my check. Hey, Lil, it's written in the Bible somewhere that what goes around comes around. And I do believe it works both ways. Maniac Cop Mimms and that Godzilla back there and the rest of their boys are going to have to answer to God. They escaped man's justice, but they won't escape

God's. Anyway, you wouldn't know what to do with $800 if it fell out of the sky and hit you on your head."

Devon and I laughed.

"Hey, ya'all, let's set a course for home and get the hell out of this town."

"Word up with that, Pops," said Devon.

The End

Chapter 11

No Justice, No Peace, No Wall

Staples' List: Police Brutality Victims

In our nation's capital there is no wall commemorating the names of countless men, women and children killed and brutalized by the "official violence" of the police. There are also no national statistics on the number of police brutality victims. It has been the federal government's responsibility to collect national data on excessive use of force by the police, but Congress has failed in its duty to provide funding.

Some observers estimate that a person is killed every day in America by a police officer. If a "wall of justice" were built in our nation's capital, it would stretch for miles and miles with the names of Asians, African Americans, Europeans and Latinos killed and brutalized unjustly by the police.

Incidents of police brutality are systematic. Some law enforcement agencies would have you believe they are isolated incidents; They are not. It's very unlikely that a rogue cop will be held accountable for committing illicit, criminal and murderous acts on a person of color.

The overwhelming number of police brutality victims are African Americans and Latinos. America has adopted a policy of brutality against its minorities. This policy is advertised through media shows that show a constant stream of black-and brown-skinned criminals, and encouraged by a criminal justice system that has failed to hold rogue cops accountable.

We the people must stand up against this politically sanctioned injustice and build a national movement to stop police brutality. It's time to break the silence and stop cop violence before more innocent lives are stolen.

Staples' list is a catalog of 40 police atrocities committed in the United States by police officers. The list is by no means exhaustive. It was winnowed from thousands of reported cases. It is a testament to the murderous mandate of the police, and to the official oppression of African Americans, Latinos, other people of color, and sometimes whites. The list is a cross-section of the growing mountain of crimes against humanity.

1) **Margrett Mitchell**
    54 years old
    May 17, 1999
    Los Angeles, Calif.

    Mitchell, a five-foot tall, 100 lb. black homeless woman was gunned down in broad daylight by a white Los Angeles police officer. She was shot once in the back at close range. No charges have been filed against the officer responsible for the shooting death of Margrett Mitchell.

    Since the beginning of 1999, five African American women have been gunned down and killed on the streets of Los Angeles by the police.

2) **Amadou Diallo**
    22 years old
    February 5, 1999
    New York, NY

    This unarmed West African immigrant was gunned down outside his apartment. A police source close to the case told reporters that Diallo reached into his pocket and the officers, all white, thought he was going for a gun. In total the police fired 41 shots, striking Diallo 19 times. Diallo died on the scene. Four white New York police officers have been indicted by a grand jury for the murder of Amadou Diallo.

3) **Franklyn Reid**
    27 years old
    Dec. 29, 1998
    New Milford, Ct.

    Following a foot chase, New Milford police officer Scott B. Smith, also 27, shot a kneeling Reid in the back. Smith indicated in an affidavit he thought Reid was reaching for a weapon. As of this writing, Smith is suspended with pay awaiting trial on a murder charge.

4) **Tyisha Miller**
   19 years old
   Dec. 28, 1998
   Riverside, Calif.

   Around 2:00 a.m., Miller pulled into a gas station to fix a flat tire on her car. She called a family member, then returned to her car and fell asleep behind the wheel, with a .38 caliber pistol on her lap. When the family arrived, Miller was locked in the idling car, unconscious and foaming at the mouth. They called 9-1-1, and police arrived. An officer broke a window with a baton, heard a "boom," dropped to the ground and fired off nine shots from his 40 mm Glock pistol. Fellow officers began firing. News reports say the four officers fired 24 rounds into the vehicle, of which 12 riddled Miller's body, including her head. Witnesses say at least 40 shots were fired and 27 hit Miller.

   As of this writing, the officers are suspended with pay pending the results of an investigation.

   African Americans have long complained that police stop them for "driving while black." In Riverside, residents grimly joke that Miller was killed for "sleeping while black."

5) **Deron S. Grimmitt Sr.**
   32 years old
   Dec. 21, 1998
   Pittsburgh, Pa.

   Police pursued Grimmitt following an alleged traffic violation. Pittsburgh Police Officer Jeffrey Cooperstein, who was on foot, shot Grimmitt in the head as his car approached. As of this writing, Cooperstein has been charged with murder, but not yet tried.

6) **12,000 men, women and children**
   All ages

Sept. 5, 1998
New York, N.Y.

At about 4:03 p.m., New York riot police attacked a group of about 12,000 unarmed participants in the peaceful Million Youth March. About 3,000 police and a helicopter moved on the crowd after Khalid Abdul-Muhammad delivered a blistering speech against police, Jews and the city's mayor.

7) **Shaun Murphy**
10 years old
Sept. 5, 1998
McKees Rocks, Pa.

Murphy was among several boys age 9, 10 and 11 jailed for smearing mud on to another child. Murphy and friends were held in a cell in the McKees Rocks police station for 30 minutes. Murphy's mother filed a complaint through the ACLU against the McKees Rocks police department.

8) **Evan Gross**
28 years old
Dec. 26, 1997
Carnegie, Pa.

Mr. Gross, a white motorist, led state police on a high speed chase through two counties before stopping on an on-ramp. A videotape of the stop revealed that Gross offered no resistance as he got out of his vehicle. Troopers swarmed over him, punching him, spraying him with pepper spray, and slamming his head into the asphalt before handcuffing him and mashing his face against the hood of his car. In an unusual move, the Allegheny County District Attorney convened a grand jury to investigate the incident. At least three of the six officers at the scene are not expected to be indicted.

The officer who activated a cruiser's overhead lights and triggered the videotaping of the beating has been labeled a "rat" by his fellow officers.

9) **Craig Brodrick**
30 years old
Doug Brodrick
27 years old
Sept. 20, 1997
Boise, Idaho

These two white brothers died in a shoot out with police in hail of bullets after a routine traffic stop on a downtown street. Coroner's autopsies showed that Doug sustained seven gunshot wounds at close range, and his brother Craig took at least 12. Because all of the shots were fired at close range and because the incident was one of seven police-related shootings in Boise in 18 months, it attracted national attention. A forensic expert labeled the killing an execution. "Something is wrong," said famed attorney F. Lee Bailey. No charges have been filed against the police.

10) **Abner Louima**
30 years old
Aug. 9, 1997
New York, N.Y.

Louima was picked up by New York City police outside a Brooklyn night club and arrested for disorderly conduct. A Haitian immigrant, Louima was reportedly beaten and sodomized with a stick, said to be a plunger handle, in a Brooklyn police station bathroom. Five white police officers were charged in what prosecutors say was a racially motivated attack. Louima suffered damage to his colon.

On Aug. 29, 1997, 7,000 angry but peaceful protesters marched on City Hall, demanding justice for Louima and attention to rising police brutality by Mayor Rudolph Giuliani. The crowd waved signs demanding, "Giuliani Must Go," and calling him "Brutaliani."

Officer Justin Volpe pleaded guilty to charges centered around his repeatedly shoving a wooden stick into Louima's rectum. Volpe is serving a live sentence for his crimes.

11) **Sixty-three Pittsburgh residents**
Ages: Various
March 27, 1997
Pittsburgh, Pa.

Alleging physical and verbal abuse, false arrests and unlawful searches, 63 Pittsburgh residents from a variety of backgrounds filed a landmark class action suit against the city and police department.

The suit, compiled by the local chapters of the American Civil Liberties Union and the National Association for the Advancement of Colored People, accuses city officials of deliberate indifference to a long-term pattern of police brutality in the so-called City of Champions.

Pittsburgh Mayor Tom Murphy has repeatedly denied widespread problems in the 1,100-officer police bureau.

12) **Larry Powell**
26 years old
July 26, 1996
Pittsburgh, Pa.

Powell, a former U.S. Marine and Desert Storm veteran, got into a confrontation in a bar with three black Housing Authority of Pittsburgh police officers. A waitress told them to take it outside, and they did. Moments later shots were fired and Powell lay dead in a pool of blood from three gunshot wounds to the head. An inquest was conducted, but none of the officers were charged.

13) **Jerry Jackson**
23 years old
Dec. 27, 1995
Atlanta, Ga.

Jackson was shot three times by plainclothes police officers, who mistakenly believed the Moto Cycles shop he was working in was being robbed. The first shot struck him while he was in the shop. He tried to crawl away from police, but collapsed on a sidewalk outside. According to witnesses, he pleaded, "Please don't shoot me anymore," but police fired on him, hitting him twice. Jackson died on the way to a hospital. Witnesses have described the police action as an execution. "It was cold-blooded murder, murder is what it was," said Brenda Jackson, mother of the deceased.

14) **Gary Klein**
Age: Not available
Darlene Klein
Age: Not available
Nov. 22, 1995
Westmoreland County, Pa.

The Kleins were conducting a birthday party for their young daughter when their neighbor Allegheny County Sheriff Eugene L. Coon fired several shots from a .30-06 rifle over the heads of the elementary school students gathered there. The Kleins testified that they feared for their lives when one of the rounds from Coon's high-powered rifle struck a tree several feet above their heads.

Coon was found guilty of disorderly conduct and harassment, and sentenced to six months house arrest. He was ordered to attend Alcoholics Anonymous meetings. Coon did not run for what would have been an eighth four-year term as sheriff.

15) **Joseph N. Cooper, Jr.**
21 years old
Nov. 11, 1995
Washington, D.C.

Cooper, a black man, was shot and killed near Robert Kennedy Memorial Stadium by a white off-duty police officer. Cooper was unarmed. No charges were filed against the officer.

16) **Jonny E. Gammage**
31 years old
Oct. 12, 1995
Pittsburgh, Pa.

Gammage, an unarmed black motorist from Syracuse, N.Y., died in a struggle with five white suburban police officers after he was pulled over for tapping his brakes in a white neighborhood. Gammage was beaten with a flashlight and a nightstick and died from asphyxiation due to compression of the chest and neck. Gammage's death was ruled a homicide by the coroner's office. Three of the five white police officers were charged with homicide; one was acquitted, and charges against the other two were dropped after several mistrials. The Gammage family won a $1.5 million liability settlement from the suburban municipalities.

17) **Maria Rivas**
    25 years old
    Sept. 17, 1995
    Manhattan, NY

A Latino, Rivas was killed by a stray bullet fired by a drunk off-duty police officer who was harassing customers in a restaurant in Washington Heights.

18) **Ernest Sayon**
    24 years old
    April 29, 1995
    Staten Island, N.Y.

Witnesses allege that Sayon was beaten and placed in a choke hold by arresting officers. Sayon's death in police custody was found to be caused by asphyxiation from compression of the chest and neck while his wrists were handcuffed behind his back. Months later, a grand jury voted not to file charges against the arresting officers.

19) **Jerry Jackson**
    Age: Not available
    April 6, 1995
    Pittsburgh, Pa.

Pittsburgh Housing Authority police officer John Charmo was pursuing Jackson for a traffic violation. Charmo alleged that Jackson entered the Armstrong Tunnel, did a 180-degree turn, and tried to ram

Charmo's police vehicle head-on. Jackson was shot 25 times and killed. No officers were charged in his death. In January 1999, a video tape of the scene of the killing was uncovered, and a second coroner's inquest was conducted. The results have not been released as of this writing.

20) **Yong Xin Huang**
16 years old
March 24, 1995
Brooklyn, NY
This Chinese 9th grader was shot in the head and killed by a police officer who first threw the teenager into a glass door. Yong was an honor student.

21) **Ha Vu**
24 years old
Cuong Vu
17 years old
Ronald Williams
25 years old
March 4, 1995
New Orleans, La.
Black New Orleans cop Antoinette Frank and an accomplice burst through the front door of a Vietnamese restaurant in New Orleans and shot and killed fellow Officer Ronald Williams at point blank range. They proceeded to attempt to rob the restaurant, shooting Ha Vu and Cuong Vu execution style in the process.

Frank's arrest made her the fourth New Orleans cop arrested for murder in a year's time. Since October 1994, 31 New Orleans officers have been arrested for crimes including rape, homicide and drug trafficking.

Frank was convicted on three counts of first degree murder and sentenced to death by lethal injection, becoming one of 42 women on America's death rows.

"The only organized crime in New Orleans," said Mary E. Howell, a Louisiana civil rights attorney, "is the police department.

22) **Anthony Baez**
   29 years old
   Dec. 22, 1994
   Bronx, NY

This Puerto Rican man was killed in a choke hold by police after his football accidentally struck a parked police cruiser.

23) **Orlando Sullivan**
   18 years old
   Oct. 19, 1994
   Lexington, Ky.

Five armed, white police officers arrived at Sullivan's home with an arrest warrant, charging him with assault. As Sullivan stepped into his living room, a revolver carried by one of the cops discharged, killing him. Police claimed it was an accident. Hundreds of blacks took to the streets, overturning police cars and throwing rocks at whites.

24) **Kim Groves**
   32 years old
   Oct. 19, 1994
   New Orleans, La.

Groves was gunned down in front of her home one day after filing a complaint accusing New Orleans police Officer Len Davis of a brutal assault on a teenager. Davis was convicted for conspiracy, civil rights violations, and the premeditated killing of a federal witness. He faces the death penalty.

25) **Nicholas Heyward, Jr.**
   13 years old
   September 29, 1994
   Brooklyn, NY

This black child was shot and killed by a housing authority cop while playing with a toy gun with friends. The housing cop was not charged.

26) **Edward Mallet**
    25 years old
    Aug. 25, 1994
    Phoenix, Ariz.

Mallet, a black, double-amputee motorist with two artificial legs, died in a struggle with Phoenix police. Police said Mallet took a boxing stance and shouted profanities after his car was stopped. The police said it took pepper spray, a neck hold and several officers to subdue Mallet. Mallet died from the effects of a choke hold. His death was ruled an accident by the coroner. An investigation failed to find any criminal wrongdoing by police. Mallet's parents sued the Phoenix police and were awarded $45 million.

27) **Anthony Walton**
    Age: Not available
    Aug. 12, 1994
    McKeesport, Pa.

During a high-speed chase through the City of McKeesport, Walton, an unarmed white motorist, was shot two times in the chest by an off-duty McKeesport police officer, after the officer walked out of a bar. The officer was charged with involuntary manslaughter and later acquitted in a court of law.

28) **Maneia Bey**
    23 years old
    November 1993
    Pittsburgh, Pa.

Bei was shot 16 times - 13 in the back - and killed after he fled officers who were investigating reports of drug dealing in the East Liberty neighborhood. The officers, who said Bey opened fire first, were quickly cleared of any criminal wrongdoing, a result which led to a lengthy and ultimately successful citizens movement to establish a civilian police review board in Pittsburgh. The police and the Bey family have a history of conflict going back at least 35 years.

29) **Archie Elliott**
    24 years old
    June 18, 1993
    Prince Georges County, Md.

Elliott was arrested by Prince Georges County police for DUI. Elliott was handcuffed with his hands behind his back and placed in the rear of a police car. En route to the station, Elliott was shot 14 times. Police said that Elliott was reaching for a gun - while his hands were cuffed behind his back. No police officer was ever charged for any crime in relation to Elliott's death.

30) **Anthony Agurs**
    15 years old
    March 15, 1993
    Pittsburgh, Pa.

Agurs was riding a bike when he was run over and killed by Officer Bernard Hont, who was driving a city police car. Hont was charged with homicide and later acquitted. Hont was a ten-year veteran of the Pittsburgh police force. Agurs' parents sued the City of Pittsburgh for the wrongful death of their son.

31) **Michael Bryant**
    22 years old
    March 10, 1993
    Los Angeles, Calif.

While in police custody, Bryant was shot with an electric stun gun after falling into a swimming pool face down with his hands and ankles bound together from behind. He died. A coroner found the cause of death to be acute cocaine intoxication and asphyxiation due to restraint.

32) **Malice Green**
    35 years old
    Nov. 5, 1992
    Detroit, Mich.

Green died in a routine traffic stop. The unemployed black steelworker had an encounter with two white Detroit police officers. He died from 14 blows to the skull from a flashlight. Detroit Mayor Coleman Young would later call the two officers, Walter Budzyn and Larry Nevers, murderers. Budzyn and Nevers were tried and convicted on second-degree murder charges, and sentenced to 18 years in prison.

33) **Randy Weaver**
    45 years old
    Vicki Weaver
    42 years old
    Aug. 21, 1992
    Ruby Ridge, Idaho

Vicki Weaver, her son Samuel and the family dog were killed in a shoot out with FBI agents when bureau agents recklessly attacked the Weavers' cabin. The standoff at the Weavers' cabin began after federal agents tried to arrest Randy Weaver for failing to appear in court to face charges of selling two illegal sawed-off shotguns. The Weavers are alleged to be white separatists.

A Senate subcommittee concluded that the FBI and its sharpshooters used rules of engagement that violated the Constitution, and that some agents had violated orders. A sharpshooter who killed Vicki Weaver was charged with manslaughter. Randy Weaver sued the U.S. Government and won a multi-million dollar settlement for the murder of his wife and son and other rights violations by the FBI.

34) **Terrence Bull**
    14 years old
    January 1992
    Duquesne, Pa.

Bull was arrested by the Duquesne Police and put in the city lockup. While in his cell, the teen was reportedly beaten with a telephone book and repeatedly called "nigger" by police. Chief Francis Long was apparently violently retaliating against the teenager for getting into a fist fight with Long's son. Long was fined $50 for a misdemeanor offense, and resigned from the Duquesne police force one year after the assault on the teen.

35) **Rodney King**
  25 years old
  March 3, 1991
  Los Angeles, Calif.

King, a speeding black motorist, was beaten after a routine traffic stop. The infamous King beating was videotaped by an amateur videographer and has become the most infamous single act of police brutality in history. Preisdent Bush called the footage "revolting." King was chased and stopped by the Los Angeles Police Department. Once he stopped and left his vehicle, he was hit twice with a Taser stun gun, hit with night sticks, kicked and punched while he lay on the ground surrounded by a small army of cops. A police helicopter circled above.

On April 29, 1992, a suburban jury acquitted four LAPD cops in the case, sparking a widespread rebellion.

When the rebellion ended, 53 people lay dead, 2,300 were injured and rioters had damaged $1 billion in property. After the riots, officers Stacey Coon and William Powell were convicted on federal civil rights charges and jailed. King would later sue the city of Los Angeles and win a multi-million dollar settlement.

36) **Carl Masi**
  45 years old
  March 19, 1990
  Pittsburgh, Pa.

Greyhound bus driver Carl Masi was on a picket line in a labor dispute with his employer. Allegheny County Sheriff's deputies Theodore Huges and Jeffrey Sheldon are alleged to have attacked Masi and beaten him on the head with night sticks. Masi sued the county and got a $112,000 settlement.

37) **Walter "Squeaker" Collins**
   38 years old
   June 6, 1985
   McKeesport, Pa.
   Collins was found hung by the neck with a belt in a holding cell in the McKeesport police station. Prior to his death, Collins was reportedly wearing suspenders to hold up his trousers. The coroner's office examined the body, but did not conduct an inquest. Family and friends suspect that Collins was a victim of foul play. The alleged perpetrator is still on the McKeesport police force.

38) **Samuel Waite**
   34 years old
   April 4, 1984
   McKeesport, Pa.
   Waite was found dead in a holding cell in the McKeesport police station, hung by the neck. The coroner's office examined the body, but did not conduct an inquest.

39) **Andrew Wilson**
   35 years old
   Feb. 14, 1982
   Chicago, Ill.
   At a Chicago police station, Wilson was subjected to an electric shock from a generator, beaten, kicked in the eye, tortured with a plastic bag over his head and handcuffed to a radiator.
   In February 1994, the Chicago Police Board ordered the dismissal of a former station commander and the suspension of two others for the "systematic" torture of suspects at the Area 2 station, in a predominantly black area of the city's South Side, from 1972 to 1984.

40) **Mack Charles Parker**
   28 years old
   April 24, 1959
   Picayune, Miss.

Parker was executed by police for allegedly raping a white woman. Parker was never tried for the crime he was accused of committing. Instead Sheriff J.P. Walker, then running for reelection, led a mob of thirty whites into Parker's jail cell, where they beat the prisoner senseless, bound him with rope, and dragged him down the stairs. Parker was driven to Bogalusa Bridge, spanning the Pearl River, where he was removed from the car and beaten further. Two shots from a .38 caliber revolver were fired into his chest at point blank range. The mob then weighted his body down with chains and dropped it into the river. Neither Walker nor the members of the mob he led were ever indicted for Parker's murder.

Where Are They Now?

CLYDE "THE MANIAC COP" MIMMS continues to be an employee of the Clairton Police Department, and continues to make the news. On Dec. 22, 1998 Mimms was involved in a car accident when his vehicle, moving at high speed, struck a stationary tractor trailer from behind. He was taken by helicopter to the University of Pittsburgh Medical Center Presbyterian Hospital, and discharged days later. The police department in McKeesport, where the accident occurred, reported they were investigating the incident.

JOHN RAHIS, at last report, was still working in the telecommunications industry as a cable installer.

EDWARD SANALAS has left the Clairton Police Department and now works for the Brownsville Police Department, also in Southwestern Pennsylvania.

BILL GUNN has retired from the FBI and now does private investigating and consulting work.

WILLIAM 'BUD' ABBET retired one year after the three motorists were assaulted and their civil rights were violated by Clairton police officers.

MAYOR LOU COSTELLO was reelected as mayor of Clairton.

RON JACKSON continues to work as a correctional officer for the Allegheny County Jail. Ron has recently been promoted to captain, and still lives in the Pittsburgh area.

PEEPER GREY is studying hard in school and practicing his basketball skills. Peeper wants to be an NBA basketball star one day.

DEVON GREY is now studying aircraft maintenance. He received a modest settlement from the Clairton Police Department's insurer.

LITTLE SONNY BROWN moved from the area upon receiving a

cash settlement from the City of Prayer (Clairton). Little Sonny is working for a chicken processing plant somewhere in the South.

DEREK GOODMAN has had problems with the law ever since the beating. He continues to face charges for alleged nonviolent crimes.

LEON 'BUSTER' GREY continues to work for the Port Authority of Allegheny County, and is a vocal figure promoting awareness of the scourge of police brutality.

What you should do if you believe you are a victim of police brutality:

1) Immediately hire a private investigator to document your claim of police brutality. If you can't afford a private investigator, do it yourself. Collect all the evidence you can from the crime scene. Photograph, tape record or take notes on every step of your investigation. Obtain the names, addresses and phone numbers of witnesses and urge them to write down or record their observations.

2) Get your story out. Contact media outlets, post flyers, and make guest appearances on radio talk shows.

3) Contact the Civil Rights Division of the FBI and file a complaint.

4) Hire an attorney who is not connected with the system. Johnny Cochran is my choice. File a civil law suit against the city and its police department.

5) Be strong. Don't depend on any civil rights group or other advocacy group to solve your problems. You must do it yourself.

What you shouldn't do if you believe you are a victim of police brutality:

1) Never cooperate with the local police. Their first priority is to cover up their crimes and tie up your case for years.

2) Don't waste your time marching and protesting.

3) Under no circumstances should you hire a local attorney to handle your civil case against the police. Most local attorneys are essentially bureaucrats who work for the system. Stay away from them.

4) Don't trust anyone. The system has many friends.

RICH LORD assisted in the writing of **No justice, No peace** (Voices of Protest). Mr. Lord 29, lives in Pittsburgh with his expecting wife, and works as an investigative reporter for the Pittsburgh City Paper.